D1617611

A Young Falconer's Walkabout

Hitchhiking through
Europe and Africa in the Sixties

by
Lawrence Crowley

hancock
house

ISBN 978-0-88839-666-2
Copyright © 2010 Lawrence Crowley

Cataloging in Publication Data

Crowley, Lawrence, 1936–
  A young falconer's walkabout : hitchhiking through Europe
  and Africa in the sixties / Lawrence Crowley.

  Includes index.
  Also available in PDF format.
  ISBN 978-0-88839-666-2

  1. Crowley, Lawrence, 1936– —Diaries. 2. Falconry—Europe.
3. Falconry—Africa. 4. Mavrogordato, Jack, 1905-1985.
5. Falconers—United States—Diaries. 6. Hitchhiking—Europe.
7. Hitchhiking—Africa. 8. Europe—Description and travel.
9. Africa—Description and travel. I. Title.

SK321.C76 2009   799.2'32092   C2009-904632-6

Printed in South Korea — PACOM

Editing: Theresa Laviolette
Production and cover design: Ingrid Luters

HANCOCK HOUSE PUBLISHERS LTD.
19313 Zero Avenue, Surrey, BC Canada V3S 9R9
(604) 538-1114 Fax (604) 538-2262

HANCOCK HOUSE PUBLISHERS
1431 Harrison Avenue, Blaine, WA, USA 98230-5005
(604) 538-1114 Fax (604) 538-2262

Website: **www.hancockhouse.com**
Email: **sales@hancockhouse.com**

CONTENTS

To my dear friends Dr. Wolfgang Kost, August Eutermoser,
Jack Mavrogordato and Captain Les Busch

ACKNOWLEDGEMENTS

In putting this together I called on some good friends for help and was rewarded with their encouragement, suggestions, help in proofing and editing and making this book a better, more readable product. Special thanks to Edward Stafford, Brent Warren, Rodger Ewy, Margaret Howe, and Janet Chu who waded in and really kept me on track. Belatedly, I would like to thank the many people whose kindness and friendship were extended to me back in the Sixties when I made this trip. Without those people, the experience would have been pointless and hollow.

To Burt
A friend + fellow
adventurer
7/2010
Larry Crowley

FOREWORD

When a magical moment presents itself, and when one recognizes the opportunity to take advantage of that moment, a life event happens that only a rare few get to experience.

Larry Crowley saw this quest for what it was worth and fully acted upon it. He documented his adventure and is now sharing it with us.

This journal is a snapshot of a time gone by. Following Larry's exploits is like opening and discovering the contents of a time capsule locked away in an old building cornerstone. The reader is transported back to the kinder, gentler world of early 1963. A simpler time with fewer worries and less fear. What is amazing is the changes the world would go through starting at the time this tour was in process. It was to be the death of innocence. What Larry got to do in 1963 and 1964 can not be done today. I think he sensed that such a journey would be unique and unrepeatable.

One can not say enough about the quality of the man that completed this trip and documented the journey. I've known Larry since shortly after he returned from this tour. I was ready to start falconry in the fall of 1964. Larry was available to make sure the start was a good one. When everyone else would start flying a hawk in falconry with a welder's glove, Larry saw to it that I got to meet Rose Northrop. She sold me a falconry glove exactly like the Air Force Academy was using and showed me how to cut my own jesses. In 1969 and 1974 I got to fly with Larry and his friends. Our life paths seem to cross and re-cross and, without fail, I always learn something of importance from him.

The world pictures painted in this journal are vibrant and alive, and put you there alongside Larry. Accompany him on his fulfilling falconer's walkabout and enjoy yourself just as I have!

C. Stephen Heying
Columbia, Missouri
April 25, 2008

PROLOGUE

March of 1963 was rife with portents. The cold war was beginning to heat up. Vietnam was about to become a familiar name. President Kennedy would shortly be assassinated. Naiveté would take some hits. I had already earned my B.A. in Zoology. I was consumed by a passion for falconry, having already trapped and trained hunting birds for half of my life. I was 26 years old and had just completed a tour of three years duty in the United States Army Artillery while stationed at Dolan Barracks in the 2000-year-old town of Schwäbisch Hall in Würtemburg, Germany. Each month I had sent home some part of my pay; the accumulated savings would pay for some months of travel. My Army buddy, Les Busch, who had also completed his tour of duty, and I purchased a red Volkswagen "bug" which we christened "Quimosabe." We both opted to receive our Army discharges in Europe, to travel, and then let the Army send us home at its expense at the end of a year. We each kept a journal of our travels. Of course, neither of us constrained ourselves to responsible journalism; so, sometimes we were industrious and at other times lax about keeping records. What follows are entries I wrote in my journal, supplemented by occasional information taken from letters written home to my mother, together with certain memories that returned when I reread these documents. We were two young men at the peak of our powers with no responsibilities or commitments, about to step into the unknown. We were ready to take on the world.

BOOK ONE:
DISCOVERING EUROPE

1 April • Schwäbisch Hall, Germany

Les and I spent the day preparing for our journey, partying, saying goodbye to Army buddies, to my long-time German girlfriend Margot and packing Quimosabe at the home of my best friend, Dr. Wolfgang "Pips" Kost. Pips' family has become my family throughout my stay here in Germany. He is a superb dermatologist and a master falconer. Although we had planned to drive to München today, we decided to overnight at Kosts.'

2 April • München, Germany

We departed at 12:30 P.M. for München, stopping en route at Dachau for a look at the concentration camp memorial. It was interesting and rather chilling to navigate the very pathways and chambers through which passed thousands of condemned Jews. That no one was gassed here surprised me. The victims were transported elsewhere for gassing, although many were shot and cremated here. Volumes of old documents, mostly indecipherable to me, were kept in the museum, and a most unforgettable notice posted in a variety of languages made starkly clear the tone of concentration camp life. It was a poster with an enormously enlarged flea, which stated concisely and coldly, *Ein Flog, Dein Tod.* One flea, your death. There were also hundreds of photographs. The visit was eerie and sobering. Les and I were very moved.

We pulled into München around 7:00 P.M., eventually managing to track down Les's friend Brigitte Schmitz, through the incomprehensible tangle of München's streets. Brigitte took us to a night place in Schwabing, the Käfig, which was one of the more swinging spots. We took her home at 12:30 then tried to find a place to sleep. Camping in the city was impossible, and finding a hotel was perhaps more

9

so. We attempted to doze in a seedy bar called St. Pauli. We were harassed until we left. By 4:00 A.M., after stumbling around in search of a cheap hotel, we were able to secure a DM 25 (25 Deutsche Marks) room till noon and gratefully closed our eyes.

3 April • Stanberg, Germany

After sleeping until noon, I checked out a Mercedes show room, drooling over a red, convertible Mercedes 300 SL, a car which elicited an almost sexual attraction from me. We chatted briefly with a female photographer who was posing a young model sporting new fashions in the street. That conversation went nowhere.

Nothing of interest was happening in München, so we headed to Starnberg to the Max Planck Institute for Behavioral Physiology for a visit with an American falconer friend, Dr. John Burchard. John was an excellent falconer, whom I had met and seen fly a wonderful tiercel goshawk at partridge at DFO (Deutscher Falkerorden, the German falconry club) meets. John had a Ph.D. and had been doing research here for five years. Some of his views were similar to mine, including that he was in no hurry to return to his golden homeland of America. We both enjoyed the novelty of being in a country that welcomed us and which had different ways of approaching life than the U.S.A. Unfortunately, John was tied up with a paper and didn't have much time for us. However, later he was able to show us around, and we conversed pleasantly over spaghetti and some salami sandwiches while John picked out Czech melodies on a guitar. He even introduced us to Joan Baez through one of his collection of record albums. I was enchanted by her voice. The evening was relaxing and enjoyable. We killed about four liters of wine, then Les and I sacked on the floor in a corner of John's room.

4 April • Rosenheim, Germany

This morning I enjoyed reading a bit from John's library. He gave us a more in-depth tour. We saw the famous Konrad Lorentz geese and even got in a rapid exchange of words with that great man, himself. Lorentz was cleaning out some aquaria and feeding a pet Moray eel which shyly peeped out from beneath the cover of several inches of sand in the bottom of the aquarium. Lorentz was perfectly unkempt: a great, ruddy-faced, powerful Bavarian clad in *lederhosen*. John pointed to some fish which resembled leaves. Lorentz related an anecdote about a previous aquarium cleaning session when a visiting fellow biologist was present. There were several brown leaves clustered in a bunch, floating in a corner of the aquarium. Lorentz stirred them with a finger and mentioned how well these fish had adapted protectively to the shape and color of old leaves; then he launched into a dissertation on protective coloration and camouflage. The man was completely taken in by the story of the remarkable fish, which in that case actually were leaves.

John showed us his old female goshawk, a lovely bird. We took her down to the lake to bathe. A duck, curious about the nature of this strange, new bird which was splashing gaily in the water, incautiously approached the gos. The gos, seemingly indifferent, bided its time, continuing to splash and bathe in the water. When the duck was within one leash length, in that instant, whoosh and splash! John pulled the old girl back in the nick of time, and the astonished duck fled to safety. We chatted while the gos dried herself on John's fist at lakeside. After thanking John for his being a much appreciated host we set out for Rosenheim and a visit with one of Germany's top falconers, August "Gustl" Eutermoser. We arrived about 4:30 P.M. Frau Eutermoser, Gustl's wife, received us at the family's wine store. Apparently the family Eutermoser had been wine merchants for many years. She introduced us to daughter Putzi, the cutest ten-year-old I ever saw, who with great charm conversed with us in high German, spurning for our sake, her Bavarian dialect. (Bavarian German is akin to a heavy southern dialect in America.) We dined and wined with the family Eutermoser, and Gustl showed us an assortment of color slides until it was sack time. We were generously treated to a fine double room and beds with enormous down comforters in the Eutermosers' hotel.

5 April • Rosenheim, Germany

I arose at 11:00 A.M., shaved, knocked out a few letters and read the first issue of the NAFA (North American Falconers' Association) Journal, which Gustl had loaned me. I found it to be quite an interesting magazine, especially an article on northern populations of falcons. We lunched at noon at the Eutermosers' on delicious *Pfankuchenstrudel*, a type of cake, and soup. Gustl drove us out to his summerhouse, where he had about 15–20 horses, including a lovely Lipizzaner, one goshawk in the moult, and a beautiful sakret, male saker falcon

(*Falco cherrug*), now in his second season. [This same bird would be given subsequently to Jack Mavrogordato, and I would fly him next spring in England, hawking a type of crow known as a rook]. We helped trim horse hooves with the stable hands, a novel experience which I do not care to repeat. The damned horses were shedding by the bushel, and I was absolutely covered with horsehair.

We spent the afternoon crow hawking. Gustl took us to his best hunting area. It was informative to watch him hunt with his bird. I say watch because he was totally self-sufficient. He drove one-handed, falcon hooded on his left fist scouring the countryside for crows. When they were sighted in a favorable open area Gustl proceeded to flip open the sunroof of his car and strike the traces — leather thongs which secured the falcon's hood — still driving one-handed, of course. Then, he suddenly charged full-throttle across the fields at the crows. The crows stopped feeding and remained on the ground, watching the approaching vehicle with increasing anxiety. Gustl began to make a chucking sound with his tongue to indicate to the falcon that flight was imminent. He said falcons learn this rapidly. At the last moment, just before the crows took flight, the hood was off and the falcon was out through the sunroof with a rush and the loud, clear ring of its bells. If the flight were unsuccessful, the falcon would return to Gustl's hand, which was extended up through the sunroof. The falcon would return even when the car was moving. Gustl explained he invented this technique as a result of a crippling auto accident, which has left his leg hindered and prohibits him from running about as he used to in his youth.

Our first flight found the sakret sharp, hungry and eager to hunt; he put in a fine stoop, chasing the crows to the cover of some trees. He circled up, then stooped into a group of houses in the distance. Gustl arrived just in time to retrieve his shrieking and indignant falcon from a man who had just plucked him from a chicken and was holding the truculent raptor by the wings. After paying for the chicken Gustl continued the hunt, throwing off his bird perhaps ten more times. Only once did the falcon put in a hard stoop, narrowly missing the crow and forcing it to the ground. However, it gave up on this flight and those subsequent, showing little inclination to hunt, probably a consequence of the warm weather and his unpleasant earlier capture.

We returned to Rosenheim, dined at the hotel, drank wine from grapes grown on the slopes of Holy Roman Emperor Frederick II's hunting castle, Castle del Monte, and enjoyed a fine evening of hawk talk, while Les prowled the town in search of feminine adventure. About midnight I took leave of Gustl and found Les in a nearby Gasthaus. I sold a carton of American cigarettes to a German to get some cash then hit the sack around 1:30 A.M.

6 April • Berchtesgaden, Germany

After lunch with the Eutermosers Les and I said goodbye and headed toward Innsbruck, Austria. Les took a wrong turn on the Autobahn, so we decided that we might as well continue on to Berchtesgaden and Salzburg. We spent the afternoon and evening wandering around with our five-liter beer stein in search of friendly faces. I sold two bottles of whiskey I brought to trade, to some GIs. God knows what I will do with the other eight bottles I had hoped to flog. We found a nice little opening in the woods just outside of town and camped for the night.

7 April • Berchtesgaden, Germany

It was a sunny, lovely spring morning. Les and I rearranged and straightened a mass of clutter in the car then drove to Obersalzburg to feast in the General Walker Hotel. We stocked up on supplies in the PX of an American post then went to a Gasthaus where I could bring this journal up to date over a beer. I phoned Ulrich Mugler, an old falconer friend who lived in Berchtesgaden. Ulrich gave us an overwhelming, friendly welcome, as did his sweet wife and friendly, 20-year-old son, Hubert. Their house is a beautiful chalet style piece of Bavarian architecture inside and out, built of wood and stone with hand painted, highly decorated closets and tile heaters in the rooms; it is literally a work of art. From its lofty position high above the town the view of the valley is superb. It is quiet and restful. Ulrich and his wife rent summer rooms to visitors and tourists. They have given us a lovely double room and asked us to stay awhile.

Tonight we all were driven to a small Gasthaus in Austria by Ulrich for a rather informal and delicious meal of schnitzel with mushrooms, accompanied by smooth, sweet, full-bodied dark beer. We returned to Ulrich's, cracked a bottle of Seagram's 7 and had more conversation.

8 April • Berchtesgaden, Germany

Another lovely day spent relaxing at Ulrichshöhe. Les, ever the artist, is sketching the house. Hubert is oiling up his little Fiat 500, which he just purchased. Ulrich has an eagle owl (*Bubo bubo*) and two peregrines (*Falco peregrinus*), a male and a female. He is keeping the falcons in a pen, clean and well made, in hope that they will breed. Both falcons seem to be imprinted on Ulrich and give greeting cries upon his appearance. I doubt that they will breed, since they should be imprinted upon each other, not on Ulrich. The owl is a lovely creature and also in somewhat of a breeding condition. He calls incessantly in the early evening. Unfortunately, Ulrich has no mate for him. We washed the car and will wax it tomorrow. Old Quimosabe is standing tall.

We had an excellent supper of scrambled eggs, diced red beets, fresh, soft, wonderful rye bread, cheeses and wurst. I was encouraged by all to try a huge slice of some most unsavory-looking wurst, which had been made by a young man, also at our table. Grimly, my suspicions were confirmed when I found myself crunching gristle in my mouth and learned to my horror it had been fabricated from some unfortunate animal's stomach, chopped into tiny pieces and set in a matrix of fat and gelatin. Summoning my best self-control, I praised the hell out of it then quickly snatched a huge chunk of cheese to avert subsequent food recommendations.

After supper we poured whiskeys and soda and got Ulrich pretty high. He and Frau Mugler rehashed old falconry experiences for us, and Les thumbed through an album of their photos. Ulrich related a couple of stories about Fritz Loges, Falkenmeister for Herman Göring (second in command of the Third Reich and Commander of the Luftwaffe, and who incidentally also was from Rosenheim) during the Second World War. Loges was noted for his contempt of authority, his ill manners, sharp tongue and a weakness for young girls, who, according to Ulrich, had a weakness for old Falkenmeisters. To friends who knew him well Loges was a splendid man, but to those who did not, he was a rather uncouth character. There is in German hunting circles a custom of wearing a *Bruch* or trophy taken from game in one's hat. Frau Göring made a point of letting it be known that she desired as a Bruch some tail feathers from Arabela, Loges' prized golden eagle. This Bruch consisted of the two best molted tail feathers — the central or deck feathers — which had much white on them. These feathers Loges reserved for himself and sent inferior ones to Frau Göring. Shortly thereafter, Göring, himself, made a visit to Loges, who snapped to attention in the presence of his superior. Frau Göring then appeared, sporting her hat, which bore the inferior Bruch. Loges immediately left the room, exchanged his hat for the one to which he had affixed his superior Bruch, returned and snapped back to attention. Apparently, he got away with the insult.

Ulrich also mentioned a time, years ago, when he and Dr. Breig, a fine falconer and friend of ours in Heilbronn, together with their wives, decided to take a young peregrine from a nest. After practicing lowering Frau Breig on a rope in the middle of Heidelberg from a tall building, much to the amusement of the locals, the time for taking a bird arrived, and the party traveled to the designated cliff. Frau Breig was lowered, and after swinging into the overhung nest she called, "Now, which falcon should I take?" "The one with the longest toes," replied Dr. Breig. She answered, "All are the same length." Dr. Breig shouted over the cliff, "Take any one, then. Whatever it is, it will be the wrong one."

Later this evening, Frau Mugler showed us around her home. It was nothing short of a museum. The rooms were all tastefully furnished with pieces of art and antiques of wondrous quality: lamps, clocks and handcarved Siamese statues, some centuries old and in beautiful condition. She and Ulrich have invested a veritable fortune in their home.

9 April • Berchtesgaden, Germany
We polished up Quimosabe, fed him five gallons of gas and after loading up some newlyweds, a honeymooning couple staying at the Muglers, headed for the Hintersee, a small lake near Berchtesgaden. Les and I climbed about three miles of trails. We watched three golden eagles in courtship flight high over us by the rocks above timberline. Upon our return to Berchtesgaden I bluffed my way into an Army PX to pick up a few sundries. Frau Mugler helped us wash our clothes in the afternoon. By suppertime we were back in Austria, in the town of Gartenau, at the same little Gasthaus, for some more fine cooking and delicious beer.

10 April • Schwaz, Austria
After thanking Ulrich and family and saying goodbye we set off for

Innsbruck. The weather was lousy with rain and wind. We had forgotten our coats; that cost us about 30 kilometers to retrieve them. We ended up in a horrid little town named Schwaz, where we got taken for 17.90 Austrian shillings, about 75¢, for two beers right off the bat. We found some cheaper beer eventually. Everywhere we looked, the town was dead. There was no action. People were indifferent or unfriendly. Disgusted, we went to bed.

11 April • Landeck, Austria

Innsbruck was another washout. I quote from an Innsbruck Chamber of Commerce propaganda leaflet: "With a magnetic force, the Old Town section attracts and enthralls every visitor by the sheer beauty of its walls. In this tranquil island of the middle ages, everyone feels… rejuvenated and experiences a deep joy…under the charm of these ancient buildings…unspoiled Old Town…one is joyously aware…" and some stuff about the beautiful university. Well, one word sums up my take on this inane babble, and that word is: bullshit! We rambled around the museum and through the hallowed halls of the university. There was no one about. We left for Landeck, taking a room at the Hotel Schwartzer Adler. After killing five liters of beer with Les, slurped from our monster traveling beer stein, we chatted briefly with four girls from Switzerland. It was nice to chat with the opposite sex.

12 April • Zürich, Switzerland

Through the rain we proceeded to Liechtenstein via the Arlberg and Feldkirch. We couldn't see much scenery, and Feldkirch presented us with more dour Austrian countenances to which we were now becoming accustomed. Liechtenstein pleased us much more. It was a beautiful little country, verdant, picturesque and welcoming. The people actually smiled at us once in a while. It was packed with friendly tourists. We left for Zürich toward 6:00 P.M. and arrived by 9:30 at Steve and Holly Baer's, old friends now also liberated from the Army and living in Switzerland, for a big celebration.

19 April • Zürich, Switzerland

A week in Zürich has already flown by in a succession of random-patterned days of sun and rain. From Laurel and Hardy movies, to a rendezvous with a saucy flirt across the street, to short runs with

Steve through Zürich streets and over Zürich bridges and past Zürich swans, to emptying our big stein in the old town, or *Altstadt*, it has been a fine week. I first noticed our resident coquette, Monica, the morning after we arrived. She adopted us immediately. Baer's apartment floats loftily 72 stair steps above Pfirsichstrasse. Monica's place is directly opposite us. With her warm, toothy smiles, scintillating undulations, and absolutely brassy gestures and glances as encouragement, we became friends at once. Immediately, I descended to the street, ostensibly to seek a book, and rummaged about in the bowels of Quimosabe. It was not long until Monica joined me; we stuck up a conversation, punctuated by her giggles, snickers and knowledgeable winks. A date was arranged for the following night. The interim was occupied by what now became the pastime of window flirting; window flirting included blown kisses, violent "twist" (dance) displays, incomplete striptease moves and lots more giggling.

Our date consisted of driving to the nearest patch of woods, no mean achievement considering my crass ignorance of the Zürich landscape, parking on a side road and necking enthusiastically. Our next encounter, disregarding the now commonplace episodes at the window, was last night. With a minimum of persuasion, via exaggerated window body language, Monica was induced to join us in Baer's apartment. She feigned a modest shyness, coyness and timidity until introduced to the gang. A young American aspiring writer, Charlie Webb, was also visiting the Baers, together with his young wife, Eve. Monica began the entertainment by telling a terribly filthy, wonderful joke. Holly was clamoring to hear it too, and with urging from Steve, Monica repeated it. The Webbs, who spoke no German, were rewarded by Holly's thoroughly adequate and hilarious translation.

Encouraged by our merriment, Monica rattled off another joke, then another, each dutifully translated by Holly. Monica declared that she knew thousands. "And where did you learn them?" I asked. "By my last boss," she replied. "She was a whore, and all of the men who came to see her told me jokes. I didn't know she was a whore, but lots of men came to see her, really!" Then, giggling, she attempted to bite me playfully on the neck, a hint of pleasures which she might discover to me later. Monica continued tales about her fat, fortyish, trollop boss performing stripteases for old men and providing them a night's diversion for only 50 francs. By 12:30 A.M. we were all done in, and I took Monica home where we parted with a classic Hollywood kiss.

25 April • Bern, Switzerland

I am in Bern at a camping area on the River Aare. It is a gray, cool, damp morning, but the birds are singing madly and copulating all over the lawn and in the trees. So, it really seems like spring. Looking across the river I see a fisherman, and farther, a stone and concrete wonder erected by man for sheep — the bighorn pen at the Tier Park. The sheep at least seem to understand the weather; they look appropriately dejected, strewn about on the rocks in various supine attitudes.

I want to get down our last days in Zürich. I saw less and less of Monica in the window, then finally nothing at all. I assumed she moved on. Her old boyfriend wouldn't come by anymore because of me, and she may even have seduced her new boss's 12-year-old son, no great feat for Monica. At any rate she was gone, and the street was a little poorer for it. I sprained my ankle trying to keep up with the neighborhood kids in playing ball in the street. I am still hobbling with a fair lurch.

Today I came upstairs, all 72 of them, with all the grace I could manage and found no one in the living room, bathroom or kitchen. The bedroom door was closed, so I deduced Steve and Holly were probably napping. I wanted to soak my foot and take a bath at the same time. Approaching the bedroom door in order to get my toilet kit, I knocked cautiously and said, "May I come in?" "No!" cried Steve; then a pause. "What do you want?" in an aggravated tone. "Nothing. Forget it," I said gleefully, hopping off on my one good foot. Half an hour later when they had finished their lovemaking, I had my bath.

One morning I walked in on Steve, who was having some difficulty trying to piss; he was just standing there. I told him to hurry up before I wet my pants, so he became even more flustered. Inspired, I pulled back my sleeve as if looking at a watch and began to count seconds aloud. Steve's neck reddened in the classic manner. "Get the fuck out of here!" he shouted good-naturedly. "When I reach a minute." I proffered. Feeling elated, I left him in peace.

We spent a wonderful last evening in Zürich. It started out with a Laurel and Hardy movie followed by bar hopping until we grew

18

hungry. It was a Fest day in Zürich. The various crafts' guilds had marched in extravagant costumes in a fine parade featuring multiple bands to celebrate the death of winter. Now the streets were filled with Arabs, Indians and medieval-costumed people. Drunken bands discordantly pulsated to the swaying masses in every alley and on every street corner.

Holly halted one partygoer to sponge a drink of wine from him, which she then slopped over herself and on the sidewalk. We encountered a hotdog stand, ordered four great, round wursts then proceeded down the street arm in arm. As we wandered along a tiny, winding street in the Altstadt, I noticed an open window above us and a young woman within who was washing dishes. I shouted up asking if she might have any mustard for us. She dropped us a piece of wax paper with a couple of ounces of delicious mustard. Thanking her profusely, we gobbled down our mustard-drowned sausages. A stumbling band passed by us. Irresistibly drawn by the festive beat, Steve, Les and I, in tight formation, marched in line along the gutter, left feet on the curb, right in the street, drunkenly, joyfully, each silently counting Army cadence, swaying awkwardly from side to side, arms swinging wildly, around corners, up side streets, following the band with Holly trailing after. We were all laughing, shouting cadence now, nobody giving a damn, for block after block.

Tiring of the march, we lurched along until we found a cool cellar with some hot jazz. It was packed with people, elbows and sweat. A black man from the U.S.A., a great black man, Champion Jack DuPree, who really turned it on with the piano, had impromptu joined the local musicians. Holly by now had a balloon tied to her earring. Some creep kept pulling it, clumsily attempting to make a pass. Everyone was up on chairs trying to see Champion Jack. The place went wild. The jazz was so loud it hammered us. Afterward, during a break we talked with Jack. He was great. He had drunk, seen and done everything; he told us he's got dozens of children and grandchildren, black or white, don't matter, a man is a man. Come visit him for some red beans and rice. Come to the Africana (night club) for an autographed picture. He was incredible! We pushed him back to the piano and cheered him on. "Come on, Jack!" He began alone. The rest of the band, to which he did not belong since he had just stopped in, was still on break. He sang *Big, Fat Momma*. The accordion player, eager to share the spotlight, attempted to upstage

Jack who cooled it with nobility while the upstart prattled in nonsense musical syllables. Jack picked it up and carried it. The rest of the band scrambled back, but Jack loned it. Finally, he finished. The people screamed. Jack left after I helped him on with his coat. The band continued, but it wasn't the same. The creep gave the balloon one final tug, and Steve dropped him with a right. As the creep slowly regained his feet he mumbled something about how this is Switzerland, not the U.S.A. Steve invited him to step outside. He replied, shouting and babbling more semi-incoherent syllables about Switzerland and America. I separated them, and we left, Les choosing to remain behind, to walk home. Holly was in her stocking feet when yet another creep made off with the balloon, which Steve in disgust had finally torn free.

We blew in around 4:30 A.M. Zürich normally closes up at midnight except on special occasions like this night, when everything stays open until everyone goes home. Les homed in at 7:00 in the morning, just as Steve was arising for his first day of school. I was dimly aware of an argument as Steve tried to shout Les off the toilet, where he had come to roost. Steve had the runs. Slow fade. Woke up at 9:30 A.M.

1 May • Firenze, Italy

Having procrastinated as usual, I have found it necessary to leave some pages in this journal blank in expectation of filling in at some later date [I never did] our adventures prior to arriving in Firenze. We arrived in Firenze early Sunday morning after a somewhat painful five hours sleep in the front seat of the VW parked on a creek bed. There were no parking areas on the old road between Milan and Firenze.

Faithfully guided by our antiquated copy of *Europe on $5 a Day,* we settled shortly on the Piazza San Maria Novella in the Hotel Nazionale. We have spent the last few days strolling among throngs of tourists, through museums, galleries, churches and the cathedral. It is a beautiful little city. There is so much to see. Due to my abysmal ignorance of art and art history I cannot comprehend everything I see, but the immense volume of art into which I have suddenly been plunged has printed some vivid images within me. Michelangelo is just wonderful. His *Four Prisoners, St. Matthew,* and two *Pietas* have impressed me the most, but all of his work is magnificent.

20

His art just cannot properly be appreciated through photographs but must actually be experienced. Observing his unfinished prisoners, I can readily believe the figures really are captured within the stone. As Michelangelo reputedly explained, he only had to chip away the stone to expose the figures within. I am eager to see his paintings in Roma.

While walking through the ancient streets today after spending the morning sitting in the Piazza Vecchio della Signoria writing letters and watching tourists, I stopped at a small restaurant behind the Uffizi Galleries to read the menu in the window. I heard a soft voice say, "Are you an American too?" I turned and replied, "Yes." A short, well-built, darkly handsome young man was smiling at me. I asked his nationality, thinking him Italian, and learned he was from Mexico City. He said he knew a cheaper restaurant around the corner; I asked if I might join him. Over a 65¢ meal I learned he had arrived from Roma last night with two suitcases, two trunks and a record player. He was staying no more than 50 meters from our hotel. He had been touring Europe alone by train. A very personable chap, José was quiet, soft spoken, polite and casual. I liked him immediately.

After lunch we wandered a bit. I asked José what he wanted to see. "Movies," he replied. "Movies?" "Yes, I love movies. I watch movies all the time. When I was in Mexico City, I worked with the movies. I went to the movies on lunch hour and at night after work, usually ten movies a week." "Then you should go to Zürich for the best in movies. You can even watch them in the morning," I advised. "But, here don't you want to see the art or the buildings?" "I have enough of that from Roma. When I was in Paris, I never saw anything of the Louvre. I was always in the movies. That's why I spent so much money there. The movies are expensive. In Mexico City they only cost 40¢, the best ones." "And, all you want to do is see movies?" I repeated. "Just movies."

We sat at a table in the Piazza della Republica. A second-rate band was playing second-rate tunes with second-rate singers. We each ordered a dish of sherbet and spent two and a half hours listening and conversing.

José was still a little hungry, so we ferreted out a greasy little kitchen, buried in a dark, tortuous alleyway where there were a few outside tables, all charmingly bedecked with moldy tablecloths, perfectly in keeping with the squalid, dingy neighborhood. The people in this tiny square were either young or old, no one in between, and all were poorly kempt. A phonograph blared out Russian music from an open window overhead. A giant electric sign proclaimed in blue and white, "Communist Party of Italy." People wandered in and out. Could it be a commie hoedown?

José told me he thought I should be a movie actor. He had connections in Mexico, and if I would come there with him, he was certain he could get me into the craft. I really should consider that, as I would be a natural. I thought the idea sounded pretty silly and wondered if it might be a pick-up line. The meal, spaghetti, chicken and wine, came to 400 lire or 65¢.

Now that his gastric cravings had been satisfied, José needed to take in a movie. After consulting the local paper for a complete listing, we ambled over the Ponte Vecchio, or Old Bridge, to a small, clean, modern theater and saw a rather interesting film. It was a French film entitled *The Story of My Life*. It dealt with 12 incidents in the life of a Paris prostitute. I could not understand the dubbed-in Italian, but José kept me informed, so most of it came through. It was quite a good film.

Having now satisfied his entertainment cravings, José was ready to head for home. We had a Coke in a stand-up bar then called it a day after we agreed to meet again.

3 May • Firenze, Italy

No sign of José today. Les found a couple of American girls whom he chatted up. We all had lunch together and decided to get together this evening. After lunch Les and I split up. I headed across the Ponte Vecchio, which spans the River Arno, and wandered the streets and back alleys. Since it was a hot day and I was thirsty, and as there was no water available, I bought a big bottle of cheap, white Chianti. By the time I got back to our hotel I was pretty much incapacitated and crashed on the bed. Les kept our date with both girls. According to him I had the better time.

9 May • Roma, Italy

Busy week. After leaving Firenze behind, having a quick pass at the Leaning Tower of Pisa and ending up one night together with José at a queer party, Les and I finally percolated into Roma. The past days have been spent strolling through boisterous Roman alleyways, skipping on my club foot, still sore from Zürich, among careening Alfa Romeos and Fiats, which sport disproportionately huge and obnoxious bleating horns and drivers, getting fleeced on all sides by fanatically coin-oriented street hawkers, wandering awestruck through ruins, and marveling at sculptures by Michelangelo and Bernini and paintings by Michelangelo, Carravagio, Coreggio, Del Sarto, Rafaelo and so many others. I wandered from the Borghese Galleries to the Piazza Venezia, to the Campadoglio, along Via Forri Imperiali to the Colloseum, back to the Pantheon, then on to St. Peter's and the Vatican, where Michelangelo's fabulous *Last Judgment* and *Genesis* are barricaded behind living walls of ubiquitous ticket sellers and postcard pushers. The Romans were friendly for the most part, although language barriers precluded any but the lightest of conversations. Of all the things I have seen here, Michelangelo's wondrous *Pieta* at the Vatican is what has impressed me the most. It is absolutely sublime.

Les and I are presently ensconced seventeen steps above street level on the Piazza di Spagna, a famous tourist destination in Roma. It is 9:35 P.M., and the good old five-liter beer stein, primed full with local brew, is nestled comfortably between Busch and me. People of unguessable nationalities eye us curiously as they stroll past; a few mutter encouragement or condemnation in Babylonian tongues. Tourists on parade, like pissants, gawking in all directions. Perverts lurk in the shadows, the bold ones flirting openly. Les has spotted a lovely Italian girl, whom he is about to ask to autograph his journal. Well, that's life! She just up and left attended by three hopeful Italian boys. Les loses again! Will he get an autograph? The air is pregnant with tension. No, it's too late. She's rounded a corner and vanished. Busch consoles himself with the mug, embracing it warmly, lovingly, pressing it to his lips. All is well again.

Our stein is half empty now, and there are no prospects for a refill. The locally available and abundant beer is Birra Peroni, which Les and I consider swill compared to German beer. It could be a long night. We had hoped to tie on a good one, but chances are fading now. The gays are moving in, playing little games on the steps. Two guards of dubious origin, resplendent in presumably nineteenth century costumes, shift from corner to corner idly watching tourists. Their function is unknown, perhaps unknowable, but the tourists revel in their presence and eagerly snap photos.

Busch in a flash of brilliance just scored an actual autograph of a lovely German girl. I owe him a nickel, damn it. I think the beer is getting in there. I don't feel it, but my logic is becoming hampered. Busch just ran off for a fast piss at the hotel.

The gays are restless. I may have to fend them off. Don't spill the beer! Busch returns, and the gays approach. One named Carlo requests a drink. Appeasement is granted. Hope the alcohol will kill off anything contagious. Emboldened by their leader, others quench their thirst from the mug and a two liter wine bottle Les has brought along. Carlo speaks English. "You are a gay? No? Well, I am not a gay cithcr. But that onc, shc is a gay." I agree, yes indeed, that one certainly appears to be a gay. Les explains in his semi-inebriated way how gays are OK in his book, as long as they leave him alone. Carlo is persistent, asserting that if Les is gay he'd like to make love to him. Les reaffirms his deficit of gayness and how queer is OK but leave him alone. "No, I am not a gay either," states Carlo again. Eventually the pack tires of the game and sidles off toward unknown delights of the night. Les kills the wine, I kill the beer, and we toddle off to our hotel.

11 May • Terracina, Italy

On the shore of the Mediterranean. We left Roma yesterday for Napoli, but as usual we got sidetracked. As we drove southward along the coast from Anzio, miles and miles of beautiful beach, sandy, clean, wild, with nary a person in sight, enticed us to the water. We left the car at roadside and changed in mid stride on the beach into our bathing suits while running to swim in the warm swells for over a half hour. It was Les's first experience swimming in an ocean. Afterward we lay on a blanket soaking up the old ultraviolet. I could not help recalling this beach must have been very different when the Allies stormed it in 1944. We ended up about 6:00 P.M. in a camping spot at Terracina, where we are now entrenched on the beach. Les has gone off to town for some coffee and groceries. I don't know or care how long we'll stay here. It's so relaxing after frantic Roma.

24 May • St Jean Cap Ferrat, France

After another long vacation from this journal, the burden of chronologically recording experiences becomes starkly immediate. After three wonderful days spent in Terracina, we pushed on to Napoli in high hopes of seeing a truly colorful city. Napoli was not what we expected. It was a sprawling, dirty giant with miles of shabby buildings sprinkled with occasional oases of modern apartments. Our decision was unanimous, forward to Sorento, or at least in that direction, to find a good camping area. However, ill fortune permeated the air. Storm clouds descended in a fury, pelting us with driving rain for the entire afternoon. Undaunted, we arrived in Sorento at the International Camping ground, a passable commercial camp, secured a well-drained square of land and settled in. Happily, we were surrounded by Germans who livened up the camp. Evening entertainment consisted of drinking beer and rotgut Chianti while engaging in raucous conversation with the Germans.

While Les went off on his own quest one cloudy day, I took in Capri, that fabled isle, and was unfavorably impressed by the grand array of tip-scrounging predators I discovered there. There was nothing of particular note to see except for the Blue Grotto. I was rowed out in a small punt with several other tourists in a choppy sea. The boat slipped through a low opening and there it was, a peaceful (except for all of the other tourist-filled boats), very iridescent deep blue in every way and place, cavern. It was very lovely. As usual, it rained.

The third day, after an entire night of rain with our tent sopping wet and more rain due any minute, we packed and left in disgust. We threaded our way through Napoli back to the sunny Roma Lido.

Here I note I have neglected to mention our side trip to Pompeii. Pompeii was actually the most interesting part of our southern meandering. First, however, it was necessary to get there. In the area of Napoli this was a real problem. The Italian government has gouged out a super highway — super for Italy — which connects the main points of interest to major cities. It is a fine highway and an expensive one, for in keeping with the customary tourist policy a fee is assessed by armed guards for use of this road. Well enough. To enable the traffic-weary traveler to find these timesaving arteries, giant signs proclaiming "Autostrada" are placed seemingly on every corner, pointing in every direction. It is safe to say, in Napoli all roads lead to the Autostrada. We normally prefer to snake our way through the legions of battle-hungry Fiats, with their incredible, five-tone, warbling horns, to take our chances with the belligerent Italian busses in dark alleyways, and to save a few hundred lire by so endangering our precious, young lives.

25

The Italian government, in an ingenious ploy, has removed almost all possibility of our becoming lost or injured anywhere but on the Autostrada. Purely to protect us, they have removed practically every sign, indicator and road marker, to Sorento, Vesuvius, Pompeii, Amalfi and other points of interest. Now it is amazingly simple to travel in Napoli without confusing and contradictory signs, indicators and road markers. All roads simply lead to the Autostrada. And the Autostrada, for a fee, will take you anywhere. Ah Italy! Everyone is so helpful, and polite and hungry for the tender tourist. But the master plan is in Napoli, where the helpless tourist is compelled to end up on the Autostrada or risk hours of blindly negotiating dark passages of hell, which are crammed with schools of the Italian piranha, The Fiat, which reputedly can strip a foreign car to the skeleton in seconds.

Pompeii. We ended up on the Autostrada, of course, after wandering through Napoli for more than an hour. The Autostrada led us directly there. After we parked in the lot before the gate near the amphitheater, a bribe had to be given to assure our car of immunity from robbers and bandits, who also can strip a car in seconds, miraculously avoiding detection by the ever-present attendants. One hundred lire and some magic words render the culprits visible, so the solicitous attendants can drive them off, albeit with difficulty I am sure. After crossing another palm with silver for a guidebook and yet another to enter, at last we were in Pompeii.

It quickly became evident that the guidebooks would not suffice. Pompeii is rather too large to see in a couple of hours. Crossing yet another palm purchased us the services of a guide. We proceeded to poke into the ruins and gaze at marvelously over-hyped graffiti and fertility statues. "Men only," was the rule with, of course, a requisite tip to each attendant. One brash young lady in a spasm of uncontrollable curiosity forced her way into the forbidden bathroom of the Brothers' House. Therein lurked a painting of one of the brothers, who was weighing his enormous penis on a balance, the other side of which was piled high with gold coins. The implied message was that his member was worth its weight in gold. No one except the attendant paid the lady much attention, and presumably her curiosity was satisfied. I do not recall seeing her tip the attendant.

Exploring the excavated streets of Pompeii was surprisingly revealing of the ancient life. There were Latin messages painted on building walls, rooms which still contained the ancient furniture, signs of everyday life in the now dead city. There were even preserved loaves of bread that had been baked centuries ago. Saturated with history, we moved on.

At the Roma Lido, a lovely stretch of beach whereon camped numerous tourists, we met two GI buddies we'd last seen in Sorento. The place was dead, except for a young couple who had a 23-month old-chimp. We really enjoyed playing with him. His owners were traveling with the Holiday on Ice Show and used him as a skater in the act. The swimming was bad; tar covered the beach and us too.

At the American Express in Roma we picked up our mail, had Les's tooth fixed by means of a root canal without anesthetic and set out for Viareggio, where we had heard there was a fabulous campsite. There wasn't.

We left for Genoa the following day and camped in an extremely basic and out of the way camp, located with difficulty in Pegli, near Genoa. We had to wait for our mail at the American Express office, since it was Saturday, and the office was closed.

No swimming was available at the camp, so we unlimbered our big mug and rode into town. That big fellow put down some sailors whom we met in the Texas Bar. Italian beer is not very good, and the establishment was pouring some real crud at twice the price of good German beer. The sailors didn't appear to know the difference. A glass filled with money was passed around the table. I inquired what that was about and was informed that it was for a "pussy pool." The winner would get to go upstairs with his choice of the ubiquitous bar whores. I won! Looking over these wondrous maidens left me weak and with a trace of nausea; so, thinking quickly, like a really generous fellow I used the money to buy beer for everybody, refilling the mug and feeling much safer in my investment. Fortunately, this pleased everybody, and no one questioned my turning down a chance of a lifetime to bed a Genoese whore.

We met a young American chiropractor who was working in England and hitchhiking about with one of his employees, a 19-year-old English girl. They were really enjoying hiking about and living in sin. It was delightful talking with them about their experiences.

Sick of Genoa and luckless with mail, we set out for Nice. After a tortuous and very uncomfortable drive we settled into a campsite at St. Jean Cap Ferrat, a high-priced, very classy residential area. The campsite was the most beautiful we had so far seen, with clear warm sea water, sun all day, a few trees and shrubs and lots of friendly people.

The first night we met three German boys who were on a short vacation; they informed us that a busload of girls, a church group from Wilhelmshafen, Germany, was encamped here. This was the best news we had had in many a day. An exploratory patrol consisting of Gustav and me, gave the girls a preliminary recon. That night Les and I moved in. To our horror we discovered competition: several other German boys had wangled their way into the church trip and were traveling with the girls. We joined the group and soon had a large cluster about us. As the evening wore on, the crowd thinned. Les and I each singled out a girl, and those remaining in our group headed for the bus where we twisted and danced in the aisle. Everyone was packed into the back of the bus. It was, for me, a novel experience to be kissing a girl while some German chap was simultaneously sitting on my lap, conversing with a neighbor across the aisle.

The next morning out of curiosity I attended the church group meeting. The first business of the day was a severe lecture concerning legal consequences which would befall the leaders should there be any trouble with the girls. The girls must be careful, remember their upbringing and be in bed early and alone. Next, the obese pastor stepped forward and delivered a scathing sermon, citing as an example of a particular occasion of sin, the hypothetical case of two Americans wandering into camp and causing young girls to become crazed. Eyeing me coolly, he continued in his sandpaper voice that the girls must indeed be in their own beds at an early hour and definitely not in someone else's tent until all hours. Now I noticed smirking and furtive eyes raised to mine. The old boy was hitting home. Winding up with one final tirade and a malevolent glare in my direction, he shifted the program to hymn time. Old Pastor would read a line, and then all would sing it. I found one particular line amusing; it was something about, "We must struggle against and drive out the devil, the Americans." The last two words were not repeated by the group but caused a round of chortles. Modestly, I smiled in acknowledgement.

I found myself somewhat alienated by the group. Undaunted, I pressed on to find Anita, who was not afraid of devils. She would not talk much, remaining mostly aloof for the benefit of her companions.

She fled from my presence upon the arrival of Old Pastor. Les and I rendezvoused that evening for a starlight walk with our girls. Away from Old Pastor they were wonderfully uninhibited.

Les and I bid the girls goodbye the next day with sincere regret as they headed out in their bus. We drove into Cannes. There we saw a wild film at the International Film Festival. The Cuban entry, it was entitled *El Otro Cristobal*. It was a fable based in Latin American and Cuban traditions, a sprinkle of Gulliver's travels and full of fantastic characters and situations. Afterward we ended up in Nice for a dandy meal of steak, green salad, soup and wine in a fine little restaurant.

Next night, after a day of swimming, we hit the Casino Municipal. I dropped three francs in the machines. Lost it all. We were barred entry to the gaming tables and wheels by an imperious sergeant type who indicated that ties were required. We drove back to a little restaurant along the way where racing Team Lotus was encamped prior to the Grand Prix. Les and I tried ordering food, but the language barrier made it difficult. Les wanted a ham sandwich. The waitress did not seem to understand. Since Les was a pretty fair artist, he drew a ham sandwich on a napkin and held it up. The waitress blushed and looked flustered. A helpful fellow waitress who did understand some English explained that our waitress thought it was a bed! Les got his ham sandwich. We got a good laugh. After lunch Les ran off with the Team Lotus mechanics.

25 May • St Jean Cap Ferrat, France

Les was not in when I got up. I spent the morning at the beach swimming and getting red. Les came in around 1:00 P.M., refused to talk to any of us and after a bit of sun went to bed.

I joined Jack Elmer, a sharp young American camped here with his wife, Eileen, and who is about to take some sort of exams in New York. We went for a spin in his Triumph TR4, a great little British sports car! In the evening another Englishman joined us, and we ran into town for the Formula Junior Grand Prix. Those cars really hum and whine; they are exciting to watch as they tear right through the city. I stopped by Team Lotus and watched the mechanics working over their three cars. God, what cars! Jim Clark, twice world champion, will drive number nine. He has put in the best laps in the time trials. We will go in to Monaco to see him tomorrow for the Formula One race.

I ate a giant cheese sandwich with a beer tonight in opposition to my getting-skinny campaign. Later I got a cheap bottle of sec, a dry white wine which was drinkable. I kicked Les out of the sack, and we ended up in a small café with Jack and Eileen Elmer and two English couples drinking rosé wine.

26 May • St Jean Cap Ferrat, France

Les and I took Jack and Eileen in Quimosabe and followed the two English couples to Monaco for the race. It was a hot, sunny day. We scrambled up a hillside, among the rocks, brambles and legions of spectators, above the hairpin turn in the track just below the palace. My first race! Those cars roared! What a sound! Sheer harmonic power! The course was laid out to include uphill and downhill runs, hairpin and "S" curves, and even a tunnel.

Jim Clark and Graham Hill, another world champion driver, took the lead, Clark passing Hill in about ten laps right under our noses. An exciting duel for third place developed between Ritchie Ginther and John Surtees. Surtees passed Ginther on our hairpin, driving beautifully. Bruce McClaren and James Ireland were in fifth and sixth places. Clark edged to a 14-second lead over Hill; then Surtees passed Hill momentarily in his Ferrari, but was taken by Hill a few moments later. Around the 80th lap, we watched Clark in his Lotus come screaming into the hairpin and vanish as usual behind some trees; but, he did not emerge. Everyone on our hill leapt up to see the Lotus frozen on the inside turn. Hill flew on past. To avoid a crash, race officials were trying to move the Lotus, whose gears had frozen. Not a chance. We watched Clark, his back soaked with perspiration, walk dejectedly away, being consoled by a few friends through an army of photographers. His Lotus just couldn't take the rough treatment. A helicopter followed the cars around the casino and over the tunnel, so it was easy to keep track of the lead cars' positions even while they were out of sight. Surtees dropped to third and the finish found only eight of the fifteen starters still running. Hill won, Ginther took second, McClaren third and Surtees fourth. I would never have believed two and a half hours on a rocky, uncomfortable slope in the hot sun could be so fascinating. What a sport!

29 May • St. Tropez, France

We arrived in St. Tropez after a nice, scenic drive along the coast yesterday, camped in a crowded little area and went into town. It was not much of a town. We drank beer, ate ham sandwiches and ogled our waitress who wore hip, low and tight pants. Later, we separated to each walk around on our own. I found four Californians, all quite grubby, in an old VW transporter they had bought from Telefunken, a German radio and television company. They had left the company name on it so they could park with immunity from the police. They were quite a bunch of characters.

An old bum, ragged and dirty, whom I had seen scrounging coins from sidewalk diners, approached us and halted. He tilted his head appealingly, eyes hound-dog sad, his weight all on one foot, hip jutting out and cap in hand. A giant, bearded Californian in greasy jeans and T-shirt, regarded him evilly. A younger, smaller Californian reached into his pocket and his hand emerged with a 20-groschen piece, of no value here, and placed it in the old boy's hat. The old fellow seized our youngster's hand and kissed it violently three times, then toddled off in search of new prospects. We all cracked up.

Ten minutes later back he came, paused, assumed the position, but this time facing down the street away from us, as if listening to some far off music. "Look, he's hopped up. He's on a fix." The giant took a sudden, menacing half step-half leap and loosed a horrifying shriek at the old man's back. The bum never flinched; he just stared off into space. He turned slowly, fuddled about in a pocket and produced a cigarette, which he obviously wanted us to light. He held it out to the giant. The giant, feigning incredible density, reached to take the cigarette, as if he thought it had been offered as a gift. The old man did not comprehend and continued to thrust the cigarette, until the giant, ever so gently, managed to secure it lightly between his thumb and forefinger for a fraction of a second. Sudden comprehension dawned on the bum's face, then shock followed by rage. He swept the cigarette back from the giant and stalked off, while the Californians howled with laughter.

I hitched a ride back to the camp with two German girls in a Sprite. Les and a German kid named Hans had picked up a couple of teenage girls from England and were making plans for great conquests the following night.

I grabbed a ride today with some German boys to Tahiti Beach, about ten minutes out of St. Tropez. Les wasn't functioning yet, having just arisen and not yet ingested his coffee, so we left him in a zombie-like coma.

"Tahiti Beach! You must go to Tahiti Beach! There are nudists there! Yesterday we saw some girls doing the Limbo there!" We had been well informed by our tourist friends, and I was quite curious to visit a nude beach. After a half-mile walk we found ourselves surrounded by a host of epidermal varieties: bulbous, elongated, pendulous, primarily male, but a goodly number of female. It seemed only natural to disrobe, which we did, and to have a quick swim in the beautiful, warm water.

We strolled around to see what kinds of people were nudists. Apparently, here they were German. We had traveled all the way to the fabled St. Tropez nude beach, and there was not a Frenchman nor Mademoiselle in sight. All Krauts! Some athletic ones were playing soccer. It was arresting to see lovely young girls and athletic young men, all quite unclothed, scampering over the beach after a ball. I had to go into the water.

Two gals, both with soft, deep-brown tans, maybe in their thirties and with wonderful, smooth bodies, appeared on the beach and disrobed. My German buddies made hasty tracks over to us, conspicuously gawking. I sat and talked with the girls, feeling no discomfort and surprisingly little desire here in the sun. It seemed very natural and comfortable. In the afternoon and without the German buddies, I went back for Les; we rejoined the girls at their camping spot down the beach for some wine. Naked and zipped securely in the tent, we sipped wine, ate cookies and spent a very pleasant afternoon.

The girls, Lilo and Regina, were on a four-week vacation with their former employer, Kurt, a man in his fifties. Kurt was short, pot-bellied, bald and incredibly funny. He kept us laughing all afternoon. At night we drove to St. Maxime, having worked up quite a hunger. Finding no suitable eating establishment, we returned to St. Tropez for wine and ham sandwiches. I left Les at home with some English girls. After a quiet and pleasant evening I took Lilo out on the beach, where we exercised vigorously behind a dune until one in the morning. Upon returning to their tent, I discovered my German buddies had deserted me. As I grimly prepared to negotiate afoot the few miles of road back to Les's and my camp, Kurt appeared and said I could sleep in their tent with Lilo. So there we slept, Kurt with Regina, I with Lilo, though truthfully it was not a very restful sleep.

30 May • Tahiti Beach, France

I awoke at 6:00 A.M. and went back with Kurt for Les. We brought some food back to Tahiti for breakfast. Then we sat around naked in the tent, as it was quite cloudy and not worth a trip to the beach. By 10:00 A.M. the weather had cleared, so we went back in the water. Lilo and I attempted to mate while swimming in the warm swells. Although altogether pleasant to try, we found it impossible in the deep water. After lunch we all retired, Les with Regina and I with Lilo, with Kurt stretched out in the middle of the tent between us. Later, we went to town for supper, then back to the tent. Kurt left us, and we continued where we left off that afternoon.

31 May • Tahiti Beach, France

Another day of sun, beach, water, bed and wine! Kurt found a farmer who sold him wine at one franc/liter. It was good stuff, and we slogged it down. We decided to have an informal party this evening in Kurt's tent. It started after supper. Kurt kept us laughing. He explained how the toreador in a bullfight must deftly flick his sword between the bull's hind legs to snip off its reproductive equipment. That is what makes the bulls so mean. We were all, of course, unclothed, and Kurt would every now and then reach out and give either or both of the girls a rude pinch or obscene tweak. They bore it good-naturedly. Kurt stuck the lid of a Dixie cup on Regina's breast. When she made a disgruntled face, Les removed it and licked her clean. So, Kurt extended his entire cup of ice cream and placed it over her nipple, giving it a final, dexterous twist. "Oh, Kurt," she said, feigning disgust. We were all in tears. The evening wore on well with lots of wine, good conversation and some ear nibbling. We were all sitting on sleeping bags around a small table in the center of the tent. Kurt suddenly extended his foot between Regina's legs and wiggled it, grinning wickedly. She protested mildly, so he wiggled it some more and made a comment in German, which I wish I had understood, because Regina and Lilo both broke into uncontrollable laughter. Later, Kurt left us to ourselves.

1 June • Tahiti Beach, France

I went over to Kurt's tent at 10:00 A.M. and hit the beach shortly thereafter. I sunned myself until 3:00 P.M., when my crotch and behind had become sunburned to a nice cherry red. I found it a painfully novel experience being burned in these regions. This was a first for me. We had bread, cheese and applesauce for lunch; then we cleaned up and drove with Lilo, Regina and Kurt in his Czechoslovakian Skoda to St. Maxime for supper. Once again we could find no suitable restaurant so returned to our little bistro in St. Tropez for steak, salad, peas, cheese and wine. Delicious! Afterwards, we regarded the yachts, schooners, yawls and other millionaires' toys in the harbor. We observed gangs of snug-fitting-slacks-wearing teenagers circulating, while we sipped drinks at a sidewalk café. I took Lilo to our tent and found Les asleep, so we dragged my sleeping bag out between the tent and the car and made love until the early morning. I very much regretted my sunburn.

3 June • Canet Plage, Spain

It had been a delightful respite, but Lilo and Regina had to head back to Germany, and Les and I were ready to move on, too. Having said good-byes to the girls and Kurt, Les and I packed up, noting an ant fight near the tent as we folded it up. We tried to get the ants to destroy a spider, but they were disinterested in arachnids. We departed for Barcelona around 9:00 A.M. via Toulon, Marseilles, Arles, Montpelier, Béziers, and Narbonne, finally coming to roost on Canet Plage by Perpignan. Presently, we are surrounded by many nationalities. I am told there are three lifers (career Army personnel) somewhere on the premises. I should go annoy them.

10 June • Barcelona, Spain

We have been camping at "La Balena Allegre" campground, about 12 kilometers south of Barcelona. The weather is fine, and swimming is pretty fair. We have surf, sun — the works. We met two girls from New Zealand: Gaile and Gay. Last night we took them to supper for our first paella, a traditional seafood and rice dish flavored with saffron. Delicious, especially the octopus tentacles!

We took in a bullfight last Thursday. Les, Gaile, Gay and I arrived late to the fight. It was already in progress. As we entered at the top of the stairs, in the ring opposite me I saw a group of costumed men fanning capes at the bull, turning him in circles, first toward one, then the next, round and round. He turned slowly. The band was playing loudly. After perhaps three minutes, the bull took three staggering steps. I remarked that he must be injured. He then fell to his knees, and I saw for the first time the hilt of a sword protruding from his thorax. Almost immediately, one of the men pounced on him, repeatedly plunging and twisting a dagger into the back of the bull's head until he lay still. I felt a bit uneasy in my stomach.

The next two bulls were killed with a lavish display of blood and not dispatched with particular grace. The fourth bull was fought by a handsome young matador; he worked the bull long and well and killed him quickly and neatly. He was awarded two ears. The fifth bull gored the matador, pitching him over his back, horn-hooked in the stomach; it then trampled him. Gay, who had earlier mentioned she would rather see the matador injured than the bull, had a change of mind. The man struggled to his feet, and waving assistance aside, after several bad thrusts, killed the bull. The matador was carried from the ring and did not return.

12 June • Barcelona, Spain

We have been enjoying the beach and the water, good food and wine and getting to know the girls. Les and Gay have paired off, while Gaile and I are finding each other pretty fun and interesting. After dark Gaile and I sat on the beach watching the waves roll in beneath the stars, holding hands and learning about each other. Two of Franco's Guardia Civil strolled by and acknowledged us with a *"Buenos noches."* We sat there a long time, losing ourselves in the magic of the place, the lovely, warm night, the crashing waves and each other. Eventually we wandered back to our tent.

13 June • Granada, Spain

Les and I took leave of Barcelona, packed Gay and Gaile in with us and headed for Valencia. We camped overnight then continued on to Alicante for another night. The scenery was beautiful and driving easy along the way. We pulled into Granada after a long day's drive, to camp at Sierra Nevada, just on the edge of town.

14 June • Granada, Spain

For the outlandish price of 400 pesetas apiece, we secured three tickets to the corridas. First we lunched in the open market, swam a bit in the pool and by 6:00 P.M. were seated in the Plaza de los Toros. I had wanted especially to see this fight because one of Spain's top matadors, El Cordobés, was to fight. The first matador was Pedres, who seemed nervous and lacked grace, making fast, choppy little steps and hops as the bull charged. The second was Mondeño, an elegant, gray-haired and graceful man who planted himself firmly and passed the bull close. I liked him very much. He seemed especially clever with the cape. Several times he placed himself between the muleta and the bull, then took short, quick steps, which brought a round of "*Olés!*" from the crowd. He was awarded both ears.

The third matador was the long-awaited El Cordobés. He reminded me of a movie star, long hair flying about, very theatrical in his movements. He moved fast and was very good. "Olé!" screamed the crowd over and over. A Spanish gentleman, who was sitting in front of us, very kindly explained the movements and passes. Cordobés finished off with a series of *manoletinas*, passes in which the muleta is held at the shoulder level behind the matador and extended out beneath one arm, the bull being passed under the arm. Very pretty and dangerous. El Cordobés missed with the sword and finished the bull with a special thrust at the back of the head. The final three bulls and fighters were unremarkable.

At 11:00 P.M., Gaile and Gay took me to a *cante jondo*, a flamenco singing festival in the Sacromonte, the gypsy section of Granada. The setting was breathtaking: a platform erected along the river, surrounded by white gypsy buildings, while above all towered the Alahambra palace, illuminated for the festival, awesome in its massive grandeur. We sat in wooden chairs and gave ourselves over to the singing and guitars. At 2:30 A.M., since the girls and I could scarcely remain awake, we reluctantly left.

16 June • Granada, Spain

Gaile and I visited the Alahambra today. It was a magnificent palace, superbly carved from translucent marble, and fairly glowed in the sunlight. We wandered leisurely through its chambers and courtyards, letting ourselves melt into its magic. The gardens were lavish in summer splendor. By the time we returned in late afternoon to the campground, we were hot, thirsty and covered in dust. At the tent I had left a bag of sweet cherries to which we both were looking forward as a little reward. Unfortunately, the cherries had baked in the sun and become a hot cherry mess. I don't recall which of us threw the first handful in the cherry war, but after an initial couple of volleys we rubbed them all over each other, laughing crazily, then headed for the showers.

17 June • Málaga, Spain
With the girls we drove to Málaga. The land between the Sierra Nevada and Granada along the road to Málaga is land the like of which I have dreamed: wild, open, rolling hills with cliffs, rocky outcrops and seemingly boundless. It appears to be more fertile and moist than most of the Spain we have seen.

18 June • Algeciras, Spain
On to Gibraltar! We stopped en route to visit one of the multitudinous gypsy caves which permeate the countryside. For 40 pesetas an old man brought out his wife, kids and in-laws for us to photograph; he showed us his home, offered to sell us almonds, cherries, sandals, and he spoke to us of his war wound from a Russian campaign.

The road from Málaga to Gibraltar was miserable, but the country was wild, rugged and barren. We saw several bee-eaters, absolutely gorgeous birds of the family Meropidae. They snap insects out of the air like our New World flycatchers. There were some Egyptian vultures (*Neophron percnopterus*) and a couple of kestrels along the way. We entered Gibraltar for a quick once-over then checked out the camping area; it was no more than a miserable parking lot. We also discovered that one cannot enter Gibraltar by auto and leave more than three times in three months. Spanish authorities, in an ongoing disagreement with the English, prohibit it. We drove to a nearby campsite in Algeciras for the night.

19 June • Algeciras, Spain
After a morning of sunning ourselves, I took Gaile into Gibraltar via the Algeciras ferry for some window-shopping. The Spanish government had no restrictions on the number of times one could visit Gibraltar by ferry. We walked up Main Street then to our left, up to the Old Moorish Castle which was rather a comedown from the Alahambra; still, it was interesting. Thence, we headed back down to the museum. We ate a fine dinner of fish and chips, lubricated by some Red Barrel Ale. We took the ferry back to Algeciras.

22 June • Algeciras, Spain

I took Gaile and Gay into Gibraltar and bought myself a wonderful tent for $23. Gaile and Gay informed us they were getting restless. Later that day they headed off on their own, hitchhiking toward Cádiz.

29 June • North of Córdoba, Spain

I talked with Dick Larsen who is from California. After having arrived by freighter he and his girl, Gigi, are planning to stay in Spain for a year to study flamenco guitar. He astonished us all in the Algeciras campsite with his guitar prowess; he claims he has been playing for only one year.

We are now driving toward Sevilla. We departed Algeciras around noon and just passed Cádiz. There are many white storks, a few kestrels and some cattle egrets. I note occasional little owls (*Athene noctua*) on fence posts.

We camped in the sticks about 100 kilometers on the Madrid side of Córdoba.

25 June • Madrid, Spain

Les and I entered Madrid and checked out Camping Madrid, a barren, deserted hillside, devoid of life and tenanted by a few of the hardiest campers. We ended up at Camping Osuna, not so bad. As we drove in I noticed a small, white tent and pointed it out to Les. By the gnashing of his teeth he confirmed my suspicions that Gay and Gaile were indeed here. Apparently, part of the reason the girls had left us in Algeciras was a falling out between Les and Gay. They now quickly made up, and by evening both of them were getting crocked on wine. It was good to see Gaile again, for both of us.

Gaile and I decided to head for the Zambra, a club which featured flamenco dancing.

26 June • Madrid, Spain

The Zambra was terrific! The flamenco show was divided into two parts: the first part, Flamenco Chico, the second, Flamenco Grande, also known as "Flamenco Jondo." The Flamenco Chico is the brighter dancing and singing, fast, stimulating and fun. Cante Jondo is deep, sad and emotionally heavy. We remained for the entire show and liked it so much, that we remained for the second performance, leaving only when the Zambra closed at 2:30 A.M. The bill for two rum and cokes and two whiskey sours was 600 pesetas ($10). Gaile and I returned to camp to discover our tent askew with its pole tilted at a drunken angle and with Les and Gay strewn inside. I retrieved my misappropriated sleeping bag, and we sacked out in Gaile's tent.

Today was spent in rest and recuperation. Rain being imminent in the evening, I had pitched my new, super-duper tent from Gibraltar to keep dry. The prospect of four people in Les's and my big and leaky tent was untenable. My new tent was authoritatively weather baptized by the most terrible wind and thunderstorm; it held its own. Gaile and I also baptized the new tent with one of the most incredible and intense lovemaking experiences of my short life while the wind, rain and lightning raged outside. Totally spent afterwards, we slept dry and deep. Les and Gay did not fare so well; since our old, leaky tent had been badly compromised, they spent a miserable, wet night. My new tent had already paid for itself!

28 June • Madrid, Spain
The girls packed up and left for Zaragosa and Barcelona. Les and I hit an AFEX, Air Force Exchange, ate in the snack bar and stocked up on beans in the delicatessen. Early to bed.

29 June • Madrid, Spain
My infernal colitis seems to have retreated. Nasty gut aches had plagued me continually until two days ago, when I got fed up and saw a doctor. He attempted to sterilize me with his god-damned fluoroscope; he plied me in Spanish with questions, and after deftly extracting 100 pesetas from my resources, prescribed a powdered culture of *Lactobacillis acidophilus* (98%) and *Streptococcus lacti*s (2%), plus a bottle of tablets of "Sulfintestin con Dihidroestreptomicina," some antibacterial agent plus some replacement bacteria for those beneficial species being incidentally killed off, all of which I apparently needed badly. He also forbade cold drinks, especially Coca Cola, other brands of soda pop, beer and fried foods and oils, all of which I had been drinking and eating voraciously. With proper diet and the medicine I seem to have recovered. It is good to be able to venture great distances from a toilet again.

Les and I visited the Prado Museum. I was especially impressed by Goya, El Greco, Velasquez and Ribera. Ribera seemed particularly strong on saints.

1 July • Madrid, Spain

We met a bunch of New Zealanders, one even from Wanganui, home of Gaile and Gay, traveling with two Irish friends in an old Morris ambulance to Iraq across North Africa. We had a wine party last night, to which we invited two Dutch girls, some Swedes and one Puerto Rican. Everyone got wiped out. Great party!

2 July • Santander, Spain

Les and I picked up two Berlin girls, Heidi and Uta, who were hitchhiking from the camp. We packed everybody into Quimosabe and headed for Santander. From a place called San Felice, about 125 kilometers south of Santander, there was some fabulous cliff country. The area had rolling hills covered with brush, like a sage in general appearance, great expanses of it, with many mesas and cliffs, very wild. Along the cliffs I saw half a dozen black vultures (*Aegypius monachus*), fabulous in flight but instantly ugly on the ground. We pulled into Camping Bellavista in the rain and slept four comfortably in our big tent.

3 July • Puente Viesgo, Spain

The Berlin girls left for San Sebastian this A.M. We had Quimosabe serviced and oiled. Then, we fed ourselves and took off carrying two young English chaps we had just met to Altamira, a fabulous cave located near the town of Santillana del Mar in Cantabria 30 km west of the city of Santander. We shared a beautiful drive through verdant, broad glacial valleys with charming villages and farmhouses dotting the landscape. The weather was cool and overcast.

Altamira! I was in awe once again. The Upper Paleolithic, late stone age (ca. 17,000–10,000 years old), paintings here were marvelous. They consist of drawings and multi-colored rock paintings of large mammals and human hands. Les, Ray, Derek and I spent several hours gazing from every angle in the Salon of Paintings, puzzling out various cryptic forms and savoring the skill with which the artists had utilized the natural projections and depressions of the cave walls and ceiling to give depth and shape to their paintings. One fine example was a bison with his head turned back toward his tail, the head being suggested by a triangular projection of limestone. Whole bison were fitted entirely onto bulges in the ceiling. Fantastic! A series of guides paraded groups of onlookers in and out, driving us out at the end of each performance. But, we lagged behind to attach to each new group, and returned to gaze again, until we had seen every corner and painting.

Les and I visited the tiny museum, where I bought a nice bison print. Still insatiable, we decided to check out La Cueva de los Aguas in nearby Novales. An hour of driving and frequent inquiries as to directions brought us to a zinc mine at the end of a dirt road in some rather desolate countryside. Two very helpful Spaniards from the mine led us on a good half-hour bushwhack through a tree-and-brush-filled canyon to the prehistoric caves. We'd never have found them by ourselves. The first cave had two entrances which then converged and led about 60 feet back into the hillside. All was filled to about three feet of depth with water. I waded in checking all over, but could locate no paintings. Further passage through the tunnel was prevented by water, but the cave seemed to continue beyond the area where I could walk. The next cave was located on a river, which erupted from its mouth. As there had been much rain lately, the river roared impressively as it emerged. We traced it back about 200 feet until our light gave out when I dropped it into the river. It was beautiful, and we thoroughly enjoyed wading around, exploring. We offered our Spanish friends some money for their trouble, but they wouldn't have it.

After finding a campsite, we unleashed the "big fellow," our big beer stein, and celebrated with a beer blast and steak sandwiches provided by a local shop.

4 July • Puente Viesgo, Spain

We are at El Castillo cave, near Puente Viesgo, awaiting someone to open it up. The weather is still overcast. The country up here is really pretty. I can look out over miles of rolling hills and valleys. It is pleasant to imagine our ancient predecessors hunting elephant, bison, deer, horse and even lions here.

Later. This afternoon was exceedingly worthwhile. A fine, old gentleman of a guide took us through four of the Puente Viesgo caves. The first was Las Monedas, so named for some coins which were found by early explorers within it. Las Monedas contains the

41

most ancient art, 35,000 years or more old, consisting of Inferior Aurignacian horses, bison and deer sketched in charcoal on the walls. In the flame of the carbide lamp it was eerie entering these remote recesses which were likely used by ancient men for their religious rites. Surrounded by glowing stalactites and stalagmites, fans, tortuous, twisted stone shapes, I admired the courage of the first people exploring here and sense the awe they must have experienced from the rites which were performed here. For their new initiates it must have been terrifying.

The second cave we visited was La Pasiega, entry to which requires special authorization, which we managed to extract from our friendly guide. The paintings in La Pasiega were from Upper or Superior Aurignacian, 35,000 to 22,000 years ago, red and black. Superior Aurignacian culture is associated with early *Homo sapiens* and is characterized by artifacts such as figures of stone and bone, graphic artwork, the use of dress and adornment, and a type of stone tool culture. Again, there were horses, deer and cryptic glyphs painted in a narrow passageway. There were also some engravings. The paintings were clearer and had broader painted lines than those in Las Monedas.

Our third cave was the gorgeous Las Chimeneas. A staircase provided access; it spiraled a good 25 meters down a spectacular "chimney" through a profusion of multicolored cave formations: gigantic, flowing forms, which mushroomed up and outward, flowing down and over each other in glorious array. And there were the paintings deep in the profound recesses of the cave, wondrous paintings of deer sketched in black 15,000 years ago.

The final cave was El Castillo, an immense cave which contained art from the most ancient to the more recent Magdalenean; it was illuminated by dim electric lamps, which subtly revealed the cave and its art. The earliest paintings by men were here: hand prints. People placed their hands against the wall then blew paint around them from their mouths. Interestingly, there was a predominance of left-hand prints that would hint at a preponderance of right-handedness in the people. We encountered the usual bison, horses and deer, and there was even one elephant, one of the two known in Spain. Engravings of the Superior Aurignacean or possibly Solutrean, 22,000 to 17,000 years ago, which included not only a beautiful stone technology but also the first significant development of cave painting, were here, too. Once again we observed cryptic red signs and symbols. We were shown a Magdalenean bison, between 17,000 and 10,000 years old, which utilized the contour of the rock and reminded us of those we saw at Altamira. Magdalenean art was the apogee of Paleolithic art, the finest and most complex of the prehistoric works. Two and a half hours after our tour began, we had covered four caves and perhaps 20,000 years of art history.

8 July • Pamplona, Spain

After three wild days. Les and I arrived here on July 5th and established ourselves at the local campsite. A wealth of nationalities was present, but the great majority of people consisted of scroungy Americans, mostly from California. About 50 of them had blocked off a corner of the campground, above which someone had raised an American flag. An array of sleeping bags and blankets were strewn about the American quarter, and few tents were in evidence. Most of the kids were drunk and passing time with migrant English-speaking folks from New Zealand, Australia, South Africa and England who had camped on the border of the American sector. People were pouring in all day and night. Bugles, guitars, banjos and wild shrieks punctuated the air. We went into town with Hank Lindenmeyer from Pittsburgh and pronounced it dead by 10:30 P.M. We returned to camp and sacked.

On the 6th I tried to get some tickets for the Sunday corridas but had no luck. I sunned all afternoon. Les and I paired up with a couple of American girls, Sue and Penny. We all took in a terrific film, *The Comedy World of Harold Lloyd* then walked all over town until Sue, Les's girl, pooped out and wanted to sleep. We waded through drunks dancing to flutes and tenor saxes in the streets, chains of snake dancers, wild laughter, botas squirting wine everywhere. We returned to camp and found two Americans, Marvin and Charlie who hailed from Colorado, singing folk songs and playing guitar and banjo. Great guys! They played and sang bawdy songs all night.

At 6:00 A.M. I headed into Pamplona for the running of the bulls. Thousands of people were already packed into the narrow streets. Mobs surged now in one direction, then in another. People pushed and clawed to get to places where there was no more space. They were animals heeding only their own instincts. Some people perched on walls, some in windows, on car tops, in trees, on shoulders, ladders, fences, sign posts, on every conceivable vantage point. Mob, shove, trample, drink some wine, dance and get with the Festival of San Fermín! Rockets went off, the bulls chased festive people, and I saw only the backs of thousands of heads. But, no bulls, for a barricade of bodies 60 feet wide separated me from any view of the proceedings. After the bulls had run, Penny and I forced our way into the Plaza del Toros amid scores of shoving celebrants. Cops beat back the surplus of bodies trying to surge past forbidden points or through forbidden doors. Amid flying clothing and with people scrambling under and over us, we finally glimpsed the Capea de Vacillas, an event in which cows are turned into the crowd in the arena, and would-be toreadors can play big time. I saw the crowd part, and someone being dragged on the tail of a cow flashed past, before the mob closed again. Salvaging what clothing of ours had not been torn off, Penny and I escaped back to camp.

I spent all afternoon attempting to sleep; then, in the evening I started drinking Scotch, wine and beer and joined the guitar and banjo for one of the finest song sessions I have ever attended. Even girls joined right in. The party lasted until about 2:00 A.M., reaching a magnificent climax with the old limericks song, authoritatively concluded by Marv and Chuck, with the most, obscene and sacrilegious, hence best, verse of all time. "There once was an Angel named Kerry..."

Today, Les showed up about 9:00 A.M., telling a wondrous tale of being run down by a cow in the Capea de Vacillas. Les persisted in embellishing his tale to being gored by a bull, which was turned into the crowd and ran rampant. He was bumped by a cow! We broke camp as the police began moving in and arresting people who were rallying around the American flagpole, where someone had hoisted a bra beneath the flag. I did not understand why the police decided to attack the raucous but mainly peaceful crowd, but decided a quick exit was in order. In the melee people were being pushed and beaten by the police; one person near me had his camera seized and smashed by them. This was Franco's fascism close up. We fled and pointed Quimosabe toward Saint Girons, France.

9 July • Montesquieu-Avantés, France

Les and I drove to Mas d'Azil, France to visit more caves. We approached the caves via a roadway through a shallow, wooded and pastured valley, quite verdant and picturesque. The main cave was immense, and this became particularly evident as we discovered that the road did not turn aside but continued directly through a magnificent 500-meter natural tunnel in the limestone. It was spectacular to wind through this enormous cavern in our little VW. We left Quimosabe and paid 1.50 francs to enter a side cave and to view the art located there. This cave was also quite large and spectacular, but much of the area was closed to the public, the key being in possession of a local pharmacist who was on vacation. Azilian art and culture apparently was the most recent period of the Upper Paleolithic, roughly 10.000 to 9,000 years ago, and was characterized by an overall decline from the splendid art and technology of the Magdalenean. Painted stream pebbles were found here in abundance and characterize this cave. Abundant water, shelter and game must have made Mas d'Azil a fine place to reside.

We continued on to Montesquieu-Avantés to seek Count Bégouen, the owner of some very special caves: Tuc d'Audoubert and Trois-Fréres. He was ill and hospitalized, but the women of the household kindly showed us his small but excellent museum of objects excavated from his caves and reproductions of the art. They gave us the name and address of Monsieur Boullion in nearby Moulis, who might take us through the caves. We located Monsieur Boullion at the National Center of Scientific Research, a biological research station of high caliber. He introduced us to a young bacteriologist, Miss Williams who, being English, translated for us. She agreed to accompany us the next day. Monsieur Boullion, a very friendly chap, gave us the address of another cave at Pas du Portel and the name of Monsieur Verzian who would guide us through that cave. Monsieur Verzian happily did accompany us through this very fine cave. Pas du Portel had several salons of painting and engraving. Here Aurignacean art was considered by noted French prehistorian Abbe Henri Breuil to consist of the red paintings and the black to be Magdalenean. One exception was a black Aurignacean bison, which, according to Monsieur Verzian, was Aurignacean because of the horns, which were not pictured in profile but head on.

The cave had patterns of red spot, horses, goats, bison and reindeer, both painted and engraved versions. One particular salon was breathtaking. After a descent of 200 or 300 feet we entered it. To our right was a fan of limestone which descended about 20 feet rather steeply, flanked by lovely stalactites and stalagmites. At the top, a small hole led into a fantastically twisted and marvelous passageway which wound through, over and beneath weirdly shaped forms then plunged back deeper into the earth until finally, toward the end of the passage there were beautiful horses and bison, each about two feet long, executed in charcoal; they appeared very fresh and impressive. There was an engraving of a fish about a foot long, very stylized but definitely a fish. And, finally in this cave were two paintings of a man himself. The artist? A shaman? Both were rather unclear but recognizable as human. One image even bore genitalia. Monsieur Verzian led us back into every corner and indicated where cave bears had slept and clawed the rock. He showed us excavated layers from Aurignacean and Magdelanean time. After one-and-a-half hours we ascended to the surface, thanked Monsieur Verzian profusely, crossed his palm with silver and returned to camp.

10 July • Montesquieu-Avantès, France

A great, red-letter day! With Monsieur Boullion, Ann Williams and Les, I visited the fabled Trois Fréres cave. It was an exceedingly beautiful cave filled with carrot stalactites and stalagmites, glacial clay and flows of calcite, moonmilk and a rich collection of art. As usual, there were some Aurignacean handprints. Two lovely barn owls were depicted life-size over one hollowed out area. There were two lions in profile but with their heads turned toward the observer; their abdomens were pierced by arrows, and blood ran from the wounds. Paintings of bison were profuse, and there was a particularly large and marvelous painting of one. Engravings of horses were sprinkled throughout, and at the end of one particularly long, thin passageway I discovered a cubicle with very fine horses engraved in great detail; notably, one group included a colt. Caribou were abundant and detailed with fine attention paid to their hooves. There were engravings of three bears and two donkeys. Again, we found long rows of black dots with occasional red ones nearby as well as indecipherable scrawls tucked into remote recesses. Here almost all Magdalenean art was in black. The early Magdalenean bison were in profile, excepting horns, which were turned toward the observer. Little detail was given to the animals' extremities. Later Magdalenean art showed the entire animal in profile, horns and all, with great detail applied to the extremities.

Trois Fréres was also very rich in fossil bison and bear which were buried in the glacial clay that was forced into the cave by the weight of the glacial ice. Bones protruded throughout the cave. Perhaps the most notable picture was a painting located high overhead on rocks, of the sorcerer clad in an animal skins and crouched in a position suggesting dancing. When the three brothers Bégouen discovered this cave in 1914, they ran about exploring with no thought there might be signs of prehistoric man. Therefore, many of those signs were destroyed. There was one amazing exception. A shallow depression in the mud in the cave floor, filled with about three inches of water, contained the marks of a man's hand, where he scraped with his fingers, mud from the bottom. The marks of the individual fingers were as clear and fresh as they day they were made. Beside the small puddle lay the scraped pile of the clay rolled into a log shape and glazed by an ancient layer of calcite. I felt wonder to experience this mark of man, so fresh and new in appearance, produced long before he began to conquer the world. In his early explorations of the cave Monsieur Boullion found traces of elbow and footprints in remote passageways of an ancient human who was apparently quite small.

This afternoon promised a visit to an even more fabulous cave, Tuc d'Audoubert. Monsieur Max Bégouen, the Count himself, now 70 years old and one of the original discoverers, was to take us through! Tuc d'Audoubert was discovered in 1910, and fortunately, the signs of early man were better preserved here by the Bégouen family than in Trois Fréres. Almost no one was permitted access to this cave. Only under very special circumstances would the Count permit anyone entry, and then only under the strictest surveillance. Les and I had been asked by the researchers at the CNRS in Moulis if we would agree to a little conceit to get us all into the cave. They explained to the Count that Les and I were cave "experts" who had come all the way from America just to see these caves. Count Bégouen had acquiesced, undoubtedly eager himself to re-experience this cave. It was our understanding that no one has been permitted in Tuc d'Audoubert since the end of World War II. It was very special.

We entered the cave in a rubber rowboat, rowing up a subterranean stream. Via a passage which led off to a chimney, we easily ascended by means of two ladders. At the top of the chimney a small, locked, steel door excluded unwanted visitors. We passed through the door into a long passage, where there was a small engraving of

47

a mouse. In Tuc d'Audoubert there were beautiful stalactite and stalagmite formations, forest like. Our group of explorers climbed and crawled through a maze of them on our bellies, twisting along many feet, while noting throughout the passage Aurignacean scratches on the ceiling. Engravings of bison abounded. Then we passed through a long, clay-filled corridor with areas of special interest taped off: bear skeletons, the canine teeth of whose skulls had invariably been removed. And, then the footprints! There were footprints crusted over with calcite, human footprints thousands of years old! And there were even two tiny footprints of a child, every toe plain and clear, where an adult carefully had placed its feet then lifted it away. There were places where some curious ancient poked his finger into the mud.

We continued by crawling around a fairly large pit, again on our bellies, until we came to a low-ceilinged, broad passage, where Count Bégouen halted us. He told us that he and his brother had been searching here for paintings and engravings October 10, 1910. Despairing that this region of the cave was devoid of art, he saw in his lamp what we were about to see. With this introduction we continued into a low-ceilinged chamber, about 50 feet long, 30 feet deep and five to six feet high. It was domed in the center, beneath which stood, sculpted from glacial clay, a group of two bison and a mound of clay suggesting a third. Count Bégouen explained that there had been a third bison, a baby, which had been stolen. The male bison was above and behind the female, apparently copulating. A third bison was engraved in the cave floor. Originally, there were many human heel prints encircling the group, but early cave enthusiasts, shortly after the cave's discovery, obliterated them. However, in another chamber several feet lower and behind the bison, there remained other heel prints where prehistoric people danced. There were also three pieces of clay, which had been gouged out of the mud and rolled into cylindrical shape between the hands and laid on the cave floor. We were humbled by the antiquity and considerably moved by the magic of this place. Count Bégouen led us back to the water, where we exited by means of the small boat. We returned to the research station after a round of heartfelt thanks.

10 August • Rosenheim, Germany

I am catching up my journal. We spent one more day in France traveling past some beautiful cliffs north of Grenoble, which looked suitable for falcons. We drove through Geneva to Bern, where I called Toni Lutz, a falconer friend. Toni was engaged in moving, but he and his wife, Heidi, invited us out to supper anyway. His new Swiss falconry club is not yet off the ground. They are still trying to get their constitution worked out. Toni has an eyass (taken as a nestling) female peregrine, which he wants to fly at pheasants and crows. Next day we drove to Zürich to see Steve and Holly Baer, but they were not at home. We hit a movie, Alec Guinness in *The Detective*. It was amusing. After the movie we returned to Steve's. We learned that the Baers were away for the weekend, so Les and I pushed on to Schwäbisch Hall in time for Saturday night beer formation at Berger's Gasthaus. We were tired but glad to be back. Kasper, Baca, Frenchie and other Army comrades welcomed us. We had a fine party.

I spent three weeks in Hall, eating mostly on post and sleeping at Kosts' in a little room they kindly provided me.

Les was very low on cash. He wanted to head north to Scandinavia. I preferred to remain in Germany, so we decided to split up and try to sell our trusty VW; we found no takers. Les and I parted, he living on post while working for room and board as an artist and draftsman, and I choosing indolence, remaining at Kosts.'

Gaile and Gay, our New Zealand friends from Spain, stopped by Hall for three days. I pitched my tent with theirs, temporarily abandoning Kosts' for reasons easily imagined. It was mighty good to be with Gaile again. However, I had to keep a wary eye to avoid my old flame, Margot. I did not want any unpleasant encounters. Later I led a leisurely life at Hall, swimming, partying, talking with old friends and enjoying the Kosts' hospitality.

I bought Quimosabe. Les is now on his way north to Sweden. And, here I am in Rosenheim, staying again with Gustl Eutermoser. His entire family is living at "Gutl," the family's summer home; it is very relaxed and enjoyable here. Uwe Beyerbach, a young falconer friend and veterinary student, is also here. Uwe has two very fine sparrow hawks (*Accipiter nisus*). He is also working with a haggard (trapped as an adult) female lanner falcon (*Falco biarmicus*), trying to get her to hunt crows. Gustl has quite an array of birds: three eyass lanner tiercels, one eyass prairie falcon (*Falco mexicanus*), one eyass prairie tiercel, two haggard female lanners, one haggard tiercel lanner, one eyass saker tiercel and a five-year-old female goshawk.

He wants to keep the gos, female prairie and saker and make crow hawks of them.

There is hawking every day. Uwe has been taking starlings and sparrows with his spar and musket, falconers' terms for female and male sparrow hawks. I inherited a foundling musket which yesterday killed a young sparrow for me. Gustl and Uwe fly their prairie and lanner falcons every evening and should be taking crows shortly.

Yesterday, I met a Dr. von de Wahl from Max Planck Institute for Behavioral Physiology Seewiesen, Starnberg, who wants to drive to Finland to meet a man named Rajala, who is associated with a Finish wildlife research station. He would like a companion, and I think I may take him up on it.

16 August • Rosenheim, Germany

Uwe left today. Ana Eutermoser, Gustl's older daughter, and I are suffering from the *Schwartzermagen Krankheit*, roughly translated as black stomach disease. In short, we each have a very bad set of intestines. The doctor was of little help; he told me to eat zwieback and porridge and to wear long underwear. He also shared his opinions about Russia, the U.S.A., Germany and what a sharp president Kennedy is. Now, I am eating nasty little carbon pills and trying to figure out what else I can safely ingest.

Uwe and I have been hawking every day. He chalked up a real triumph with his spar the other day: four starlings and three sparrows. Not bad! My little musket killed a sparrow and made me very happy. I went hunting alone yesterday with my musket and had one good flight in the rain, but we caught nothing. I like to hunt from an old bicycle, hawk on fist as we cruise down country lanes.

20 August • Rosenheim, Germany

I went out with Gustl yesterday evening to hawk crows in the Inn Valley at the Austrian border. It is absolutely beautiful country with rocky outcrops on the mossy, forested mountain slopes and fertile, green fields in the lowlands. We had three flights. Gustl explained that he would continue to cast off his eyass prairie, Pawnee, at crows until she finally took it on her own to hunt them. Meanwhile, although she ignored them, she would get some flight practice and training in catching a dead crow, which Gustl would throw up instead of a lure, to call her back. He explained that in late August and early

September prairies have an aggressive period during which they begin to hunt. When that time comes, then the bird will take crows but probably not before.

It happened today! In the first flight Pawnee, Gustl's prairie falcon, attacked and struck a crow which had remained on the ground when she was loosed. Lacking experience, Pawnee dropped to the ground; the crow took off, easily leaving her behind while he gained cover. The second flight was poor, since all of the crows had too good a lead. The third flight found one crow, which chose to remain afoot while his friends flew off at the falcon's approach. Pawnee struck him, pitched up and stooped again. The crow was evidently sick or injured, and it hopped feebly trying to dodge the falcon, refusing to take to the air. Pawnee hit him again then dropped and bound to him. She had a good neck and shoulders grip when I ran in; she was very excited. I helped her hold and kill it. The crow had one bad eye, which explained its reluctance to fly. In a local Gasthaus, Gustl and I properly drank to the dead crow that evening, and Pawnee gorged on our black friend.

I took my musket out this morning and caught our seventh sparrow. I kind of cheated a bit. I got tired of seeing sparrows disappear into grass and shrubs and fishing out my hawk which always crashes in after them. He flaps about, trying to catch them on foot, and eventually scares them all out, leaving no further chance to catch one. This time when I uncovered him in the grass I saw the sparrow hiding about six inches beneath him. I carefully reached in, killed it, pocketed it then picked up my hawk. I really shouldn't count it. The other six sparrows have been fair, though. He hunts as if his life depends on it, which it certainly would in the wild. He sees sparrows over 100 meters away and tenses up, eyes bulging. The closer we get, the more horizontal his body becomes, until at last he is crouched in an almost prone attitude. Usually he cannot contain himself and bates or leaps from the fist, either too soon or too late, frightening everything off. If he hasn't caught the bird in the first 30 feet, he quits. Until the last three days he would come down from his perch very well. But, lately that is getting worse. It took three quarters of an hour to retrieve him after his last flight today. I had to use a dead sparrow to call him down. I felt lucky to get him back. He also now shows an unreasonable aggression toward hands, and he manifests it by flicking his wings at and even footing my hand when I present it.

His bad behavior has culminated in the nasty habit of his carrying off his prey, but I am pretty sure I can break him of that with patience. [In retrospect, these were all symptoms of flying him at too high a weight, a problem typically experienced by tyro falconers.]

Uwe called me to Gustl's backyard this afternoon. There was a flock of starlings feeding about 30 meters out in the grass. Carefully, Uwe brought up his Spar and let her go. She flew low, surprising the starlings at close range. They erupted into the air as she plunged, apparently seizing one on the ground. We ran in to assist her and found her standing several inches deep in a fresh and very wet cow pie. A good bath remedied the little hawk's mistake.

4 September • Rosenheim, Germany

I am still in Rosenheim. Much has occurred since my last entry. First, news of my musket. He never killed another bird. Two days after taking his seventh sparrow, he was eaten by Cassipoeia, Gustl's haggard lanner. I returned one evening, and Gustl insisted that I immediately check on my hawk in the weathering area. He said it was very urgent and that I should hurry. I found a spray of feathers and bodily fragments between the lanner and sparrow hawk perches and one brimfull lanner, peering out of her shelter at me. I hung my head in shame as I realized I had tied my little bird too long. I hated to own up to my mistake, but the fact was incontrovertible. That was capital blunder number one. Number two followed about a week later. I decided to fly the two eyass tiercel lanners in a cast (together), then later Gustl could try crow hawking with them. One, being shy and reticent, I reserved for intensive work. The other, tame, eager, and familiar with the lure, I decided to fly loose. Alas! Away he went in great circles, soaring in the wind until lost to sight, never giving me as much as a backward glance. Capital blunder number two, flying a falcon without bells or identification or proper training, a very stupid mistake. I thoroughly deserved to feel guilty.

I carried on with Lady Sunshine, another haggard lanner female weighing 590–615 grams depending on the weather, and had her doing 40–50 good stoops or flying passes at the lure morning and evening. I even got the reticent tiercel lanner in the air. Then, my hand went bad. Pawnee, having punctured my hand as I was helping her dispatch her crow some days back, had planted an insidious seed within it. By August 31 the first fruits blossomed: a painful and swollen infected hand accompanied by headache and fever. My falconry instantly ceased, being replaced by bed, megacillan and a team of doctors. Here I lie, perhaps incapable of making capital blunder number three, a victim of my sport.

In any case, I am now awaiting Gustl's decision, probably negative, on a trip to Labrador. He got a letter from Webby, Harold Webster, a Denver falconer, who has a ten-year gyrfalcon study almost ready to hatch. Webby recommends the George River system near Ft. Chino, Canada. He says the best dates are probably September 10–25. Also, some data from Disko Bay, Greenland, indicates birds should be there in October, but there will be very little daylight available. Freeze-up comes in mid October. Cost for the plane from München and back is about $1000. Pretty high. I'd love to go, but now it is very chancy. We wouldn't have much time to catch birds, but what an opportunity!

9 September • Schwäbisch Hall, Germany
I drove to the Kosts' from Rosenheim today. I saw former girlfriend Margot, who was still friendly but distant, and had a good reunion with family Kost. Gustl had to cancel the Labrador trip because of my hand. He called it off Friday, when the surgeon made a new cut in my hand because my infection had turned to blood poisoning, and by the time it healed, it would be too late to trap gyrfalcons. I am both relieved and disappointed. Maybe we can do it next year.

10 September • Schwäbisch Hall, Germany
Mom sent me a check for my upcoming birthday! My hand is better now, healing fast but still pretty stiff. "Pips," the family's nickname for Dr. Kost, assured me ten minutes ago that all will be well, and the bad part has passed. My immediate plans are: Schwäbisch Hall until the hand heals, then Rosenheim from about 25 September on. Then, I want to go with Gustl to Austria in October for a big international falconry meet.

8 October • Heidelberg, Germany
I sold Quimosabe in Hall for $340. That is, for a half year's use it cost me about $85. Not bad, eh? Now I will have to hitchhike.

From Hall, after celebrating my twenty-seventh birthday quietly, I went to Rosenheim for two or three days. I mailed home some falconry art prints by Swiss artist Willi Baer, which I bought from Gustl.

Oktoberfest in München! I tented for three days in the meadows with a group of Australians, New Zealanders and other British colonials while waiting to meet up with friend Gaile and make some concrete connections for a later visit to London. I learned that I am no drinking match for the Aussies. One evening after over-imbibing and being carried back to my tent, I spent a miserable night. Morning arrived accompanied by a colossal hangover. I went to check on my Aussie buddies who had long outlasted me in the beer tents. Upon awaking, they immediately popped the tops of some beers and continued drinking. I was clearly out of my league!

I returned to Rosenheim for a day then on to Kärnten, Austria, with Gustl for a very interesting meeting of the Austrian falconry club, the Osterreichischer Falknerbund. It was notable from the perspective of making personal acquaintances but not for hunting, which was poor. And, the weather was lousy. I met Colonel R.L. Meredith, sometimes called the Father of American falconry because he was one of the first American falconers and founded the Falconry Club of America, and Steve Gatti from the U.S.A. Even 12 Hungarians came over for the meet. Col. Meredith had a radio controlled bow net, an ingenious device for trapping falcons, which he enjoyed showing off. It was a pleasure to finally meet this legend of American falconry. He said he has plans to resurrect the Falconry Club of America, and that it has just been "hibernating." He was not happy about the formation of the North American Falconers' Association, promoted by his long-time rival, Harold Webster. NAFA was a club competing with his own, and in forming it, Webby had challenged him for leadership of the American falconry community.

Falconry Meet headquarters was a wonderful old castle, Burg Hochosterwitz, atop a hill overlooking a verdant valley. A gentleman named Kahn brought a hobby (*Falco subbuteo*), an elegant little falcon, and a golden eagle. He took pleasure in letting his eagle soar picturesquely above the castle to the delight of us all. It was also a treat to see a hobby again. They are such beautiful little flying machines. One evening we had a sumptuous banquet in the castle, a meal which let us feel as if we had stepped back into the middle ages. It was great fun involving late hours and little sleep, frequently due to early outings to find lost hawks.

My hand is now usable and almost normal, but I still have a swollen knuckle which is not yet perfect. Anyhow, I'm in no way handicapped. I'm still afoot with an old, Spanish Army pack and some U.S. Army equipment to see me through the winter. Les is in Sweden after a stint in Denmark, washing dishes for a living and loving it.

I am currently in Heidelberg, Germany, sitting in a Gasthaus, with a goshawk on my fist. I have been traveling from Austria to England in a small Morris auto with two Welch falconers, John Buckner and Ken Banergee, the world-famous Lorant D'Bastyai, a Hungarian refugee and master falconer, a lovely Hungarian eyass female goshawk and a prairie falcon. Presently the men are all off seeking lodging somewhere, and I am tenting on a little island in the river below the castle: one, to save money and, two, because it would be prohibited to keep this beautiful monster in a room. I will sleep later right next to her to keep her safe and out of mischief. She's tame as a kitten and very playful for all her ferocious size and appearance. And, she is a demon at catching pheasants. Wish I could keep her!

11 October • Oostenede, Belgium
After Heidelberg we visited Dr. Beckers, a falconer in Köln, and killed a pheasant with the gos. Dr. Beckers' bird, a tiercel peregrine, knocked down two pheasants but couldn't hold them on the ground. The Spanish peregrine tiercels which are used here in Germany, though courageous, are just too small to succeed with pheasants. We drove to Oostende, Belgium, where I spotted Gaile and Gay around 11:00 P.M. as they were walking down the street. I yelped to get John to stop, jumped out, ran up and gave Gaile a big hug. She was astonished to see me. They were headed to England too. I will meet them later in London.

12 October • London, England
I reached England this morning by means of a ferry from Oostenede then hitchhiked from Dover to Earle's Court in London, arriving by 8:00 A.M. By 9:00 A.M. I found Gaile, living with Gay and Gay's sister Tricia, at 75 Philbeach Gardens. We had a big celebration.

20 October • London, England
I stayed awhile at Philbeach Gardens sleeping on the floors of various

rooms and judiciously avoiding the landlady. Les Stroud, an Aussie friend, let me stay awhile with him. Gaile and I explored London. We moved to the Walkabout Club on Fulham Road with me still sleeping surreptitiously, now with the girls, to avoid paying rent.

31 October • London, England

I'm temporarily back in London, staying with Gaile, Gay and Tricia in a room at the Walkabout Club, crowded but friendly. I'm going off to Africa. Just thought I'd toddle on down. The girls having determined that London winters are miserable, opted to go to Southern Rhodesia to work for the duration of the cold season. Having no better plans, I decided to go along. We leave for Cape Town on 28 November via the *Empress of England* on the Union Castle Line. Cost is a mere $235, a lot of money to me, but what the hell?

It is necessary when entering many African countries to convince authorities that one is sufficiently solvent to support oneself during one's sojourn in their land. To avoid "embarrassment" to the country, should he be a deadbeat and go broke, proof of sufficient funds may be required. If it is determined I possess "insufficient funds," a country might demand a large deposit as a guarantee and safeguard, which I would have to leave with them until I depart their borders, and which they could use to deport me to the U.S.A. should I go broke. To circumvent this deposit, I must have one of the following: a return ticket (out of the question since I'm hitchhiking back through Africa), or a ticket forward (again, out of the question for the same reason), or "sufficient funds" or proof thereof. Hence, I need a nice, official document, preferably half a dozen copies, with which I can prove that I can pay my way home and am not going to become a liability to any of the various governments. [In the end, I simply asked Mom to send me a cashier's check for $500.]

I want to hitchhike through South Africa, Southern Rhodesia [now Zimbabwe], Northern Rhodesia [Zambia], Tanganyika [Tanzania], Uganda, Sudan, Egypt, Jordan and Israel, Syria, Turkey and Greece; thence back to Germany. I will try to do it by March. Wish I could see more of Africa, but I can't likely see it all in one lifetime.

I'm getting a bit of an idea of the life and layout of London, now. I took a week off and went on a mini-adventure with Gaile last week to see a bit more of England. We rented an Austin Minor and headed for Devon and Cornwall. First, we visited Cyril and Jan

Morley, falconer friends, in Sevenoaks, Kent. Cyril took us hedge-hawking blackbirds (*Turdus merula*) with his Spar. Let me mention that hawking blackbirds, the European counterpart of our American robins, is a long-standing tradition in England. Blackbirds cling to the cover provided by the hedges while the hawking party attempts to evict them with shouts and beating the bushes with sticks. The hawk makes repeated attempts to ambush the blackbird as it dashes for the next section of safety. Eventually the quarry is caught or the hawk and hawkers tire and go home. We left the blackbird to sing another day.

Then Gail and I drove west to Clovelly, a charming and photo-perfect little fishing village. We ambled through its cobble-stone streets and among its charming cottages and strolled on its gravelly beach, fantasizing about how it would feel to live in such a lovely place. Probably boring.

Finally, we worked our way out towards Land's End and visited the ruins of Tintagel Castle, thought by some to have been King Arthur's castle. Picking through its crumbled remains evoked a deep impression of history and myth. With the gray, misty setting high above the crashing waves on the rocks below it was a mystical place.

On the way back to London we stopped at sundown at Stonehenge. Gail and I had it all to ourselves, and we walked among the ancient monoliths, trying to conjure up Druid times. Being alone in this prehistoric setting and with the sun setting, casting long shadows, colors brilliant, was literally a once-in-a-lifetime experience for us.

The weather was superb, and we camped all along the way. Funny, England has had miserable weather until I arrived; then it became fine. A bit of Colorado must have come along with me. What gorgeous country!

In the morning I leave for Wales, to the town of Newport, for a meeting of the Welsh Hawking Club. I will be gone one to two weeks, visiting falconers, then come back and get my visas and other last minute details in order. I am really looking forward to the trip.

12 November • London, England

The Welch Hawking Club meet was great fun. The Welsh were fine hawkers, hospitable and enthusiastic. Most of the hawking was with short-wings and done in the rain. Game was scarce and slips were even scarcer. Only one flight was of note: a fine Hungarian goshawk chased a pheasant for about 300 yards and crashed into cover, only to miss. Lorant D'Bastyai lost his prairie falcon, Mimi, but after several hours of searching on our part, she found us at the pub warming ourselves with copious libations of local spirits. Someone heard her bell about 100 yards from the pub and five miles from where she had been lost. She came right in to Lorant's lure. Now, that was some seriously good luck!

Afterwards, I stayed briefly with Lorant, who was just elected president of the Welch Hawking Club, and his lovely wife, Nancy. He regaled me with tales of hawking in the Hungarian wetlands. He was a very colorful character, opinionated on everything, and had a heart of gold.

I visited several falconer friends, including Jack Mavrogordato, for a few days. [I refer the friendly reader to a brief impression of Jack Mavro in the Postscript: Loose Ends portion of this treatise.] He showed me his hawking area on the Wiltshire Downs. The countryside is ideal for falconry: wide open, gently rolling hills and valleys, mostly grass-covered, with widely scattered stands of hardwood trees in which nest and roost large numbers of rooks. Most of the land is agricultural, but some belongs to the military and is used for tank and artillery practice. Jack has permission to hunt on most of it.

Jack enchanted me with stories of falconry in Pakistan and falcon trapping in Sudan. He introduced me to Eustace and Dulcie Brown, his next-door neighbors; Mr. Brown, a quintessential English gentleman, was formerly a falconer and lives in Gilbert Blaine's old house. Blaine was a famous Wiltshire falconer in the early twentieth century. Jack lives in a charming cottage, South Manor, that also was part of Blaine's estate.

While I was in Tilshead, a television company was doing a short show on falconry, and they incorporated me into it. My big debut on British telly will happen December 11!

In Evershot, Dorset, I visited Michael and June Woodford for a weekend. June is the secretary of the British Falconers' Club. We had a wonderful time drinking in the Tiger's Head Pub, telling stories, laughing a lot. Then I hitched back to London where I've been trying to get visas and paperwork straightened out.

18 November • London, England

Jack Mavro called to say he was coming to London and to ask me to meet him at Victoria Station for a quick conference. At Victoria, he seemed genuinely pleased to see me. I was quite moved that he valued my friendship. He invited me to meet him in the Sudan and to trap falcons to use hawking rooks next spring. The plan is: I will hitchhike up to Khartoum from Cape Town, and Jack will sail to Port Sudan. We will meet in Khartoum to trap some big falcons; then Jack will take them back to Wiltshire. I will hitchhike back to England, and we will train and fly the new birds at rooks, a type of crow that is traditional quarry for British falcons. Jack brought me three lovely pencil sketches of accipiters by George Lodge, renowned British painter of raptors. These were preliminary sketches for Jack's book, *A Hawk for the Bush*. He also gave me some old Indian falcon bells and a Mollen (famous Dutch falcon trapper and hood maker) hood that had belonged to A. Newall of the Old Hawking Club back in the nineteen twenties. Apparently, after Mr. Newall died his daughter discovered a trunk full of falconry equipment in the attic and passed it on to Jack. These gifts are particularly special.

21 November • London, England

One week to sailing time! Here is a brief and revised outline of my Africa plans. In Cape Town, I want to contact a friendly falconer or two then zoom up to Johannesburg to visit yet another. Then, I would like to go to Kruger National Park and on north into Southern Rhodesia, arriving by 21–25 December. I will go to Salisbury, Southern Rhodesia for New Year's with the girls who will be working there. Then, I'll head on through Northern Rhodesia to Tanganyika, up to the Mt. Kilimanjaro area, thence around Lake Victoria to Uganda to Murchison Falls National Park, where I will meet with another falconer. From there, I'll travel north to Khartoum in Sudan, where about the first week of February I will meet Jack Mavrogordato to trap falcons for a couple of weeks. Plans from there are indefinite. Probably I'll hitch on up to Alexandria, Egypt, take a steamer over to Greece or Italy and hitch overland on back to England. I want to be in Tilshead, near Salisbury, England, by 15 March 1964. Jack Mavro has even invited me to take a falcon back from the Sudan. Since Jack is probably the greatest practicing rook hawker in the world, I can't see passing that up. Then, along about May rook season being finished, I'll probably head to Scandinavia to see that part of Europe I've missed, aiming to get home next autumn. Of course much may happen to alter plans, including an Arctic trip in the fall. We'll see. I think I'm going to have a bit of trouble eventually settling down again somewhere.

28 November • En route to Liverpool, England

Gaile, Gay, Tricia and I are on the train to Liverpool to board ship. Lovely day. Somehow, I feel it should be cold, wet and miserable so we could properly rejoice in leaving, but it's beautiful.

Gustl Eutermoser came through London last week on his way to the American falconers field meet in South Dakota. I spent about an hour with him. He was very glad to speak a little German again. He seemed a bit confused and dazed, but as he is traveling with June Woodford, I'm sure he'll be OK. They may go down to Denver to visit Webby to plan a gyrfalcon trapping expedition for next year.

The British people and I are still shocked and in a state of disbelief at the murder of President Kennedy. Incredible! People who know that I am an American have given me their condolences. Even the man from whom we bought our beer and cider in London was in tears. Jack Mavro sent me a nice telegram expressing his sadness. How do I deal with this event?

BOOK TWO: AFRICA

5 December • South of Senegal on the Atlantic Ocean
Our ship left Dakar, Senegal, this morning after a day in port. I am aboard the Empress of England, Canadian Pacific Line, en route to Cape Town, South Africa with Gaile, Gay and Patricia. Presently I am lying on "A" deck absorbing sunlight while sipping a lemon squash. Dakar was only a quick stop, but passengers were allowed to debark and look around. I wandered in the open market. It was noisy and very colorful, but since the people here speak French and I do not, communication was minimal. I did take some photos. I felt a little uncomfortable and apprehensive immersed in the peculiarity of the place: no white faces, incomprehensible tongues and peculiar smells of a (to me) new continent. I did not linger.

13 December • Cape Town, South Africa
We arrived at Cape Town! The girls and I glued ourselves to the rail as the ship approached land. What a splendid view! The welcoming city and the towering Table Mountain, a flat-topped mountain over-looking it, were so inviting! The weather was clear and warm, just perfect.

The trip down here was one huge party. There were lots of young Australians aboard. In retrospect I cannot recall anyone older than forty. Australians always seem to liven up any happening. Chief among them was Blaze, a lean, tan character with traditional leather hat and a take-charge attitude. He was the center of the party. He took an immediate fancy to Gay. Gaile, Gay and Tricia shared a cabin. I shared my cabin with a pleasant Aussie who seldom slept there. So, Gaile and I alternated sleeping in her bed or mine, depending on which was more private at the time. One never knew exactly who would roll out of a neighboring bunk in the morning; however, I got used to saying "G'day mate!" to Blaze, over in Gay's bed when I woke up.

One afternoon, Gaile and I found our cabin steward passed out in a chair and surrounded with a liberal quantity of barf in my cabin.

We did not report him and as a result received wonderful service for the rest of the trip.

Meals were served three times a day with snacks in between. We could order any of several appetizers, entrées, and desserts. Most of us guys would order everything on the menu, all of the appetizers, each of the entrées, and every dessert. If there was something that we did not like, we ordered two of something else. What luxury! With a big road trip coming up, laying in all the food possible seemed like a good idea.

There were a couple of guys on board who sported "Beatle" haircuts. They were the center of attention for some of the girls. I had only recently heard of the Beatles; I regarded them as shabby imitations of good, old American rockers. Elvis ruled! Aside from their haircuts, these look-alikes on the ship seemed to me to lack any talent for anything. It was amazing to me what mimicry could accomplish with women!

We were shown newsreels of the Kennedy assassination. This was the first time I had seen photos, and I found the event horrifying and difficult to assimilate. I watched them over and over.

15 December • Mossel Bay, South Africa

The past two days we spent in Cape Town with young falconer Ray Black and his girl, Susan. I had briefly corresponded with Ray who was also a member of the British Falconers' Club. Ray had met us at the ship. We talked hawks the entire evening. Ray is a wildlife illustrator, just starting out and very talented. He says there are only about eight members of the South African falconry club. H. von Michaelis is the president, largely due to his personal prestige as an artist, although he no longer trains falcons. His 18-year-old son reputedly has an old peregrine in a cage.

Ray gave me a blitz course on South African raptors, much of which I was unable to absorb. I tried my first biltong (jerky) and first South African Castle brand beer. We stocked up on supplies. I made a deal with Ray for my wonderful tent. He will paint me a black sparrow hawk in exchange for it. I am trying to reduce pack weight and will take a cheap, plastic, lightweight tent along instead of my nice but heavy one, hoping for mostly good weather.

Gordon Spence, a friend of Ray's, drove us up Signal Hill for a splendid night view of Cape Town. Looking out to sea over the lights of Cape Town was breathtaking. Later, I found our approach to sleeping arrangements rather amusing. Ray and Sue, not yet married, did not know what to do with Gaile and me. At first they offered to have the girls sleep together, but after a good laugh we decided instead to alternate each night in the double bed.

Gaile originally had planned to hitchhike north from Cape Town with Tricia and Gay to Southern Rhodesia, but at the last minute the sisters chickened out and took a train. Gaile and I decided to hitchhike, save about $30 and have an adventure together.

I am now on the road east from Cape Town with Gaile, Ray Black, Ray's girl Susan and a lady named Di, a friend of Susan's, plus five colored people compressed inside a VW bus. I think I should clarify what is implied here by "colored." Colored refers to people of mixed African and European or Asian decent. Neither the Africans nor the whites fully accept them in this country. They are relegated to a purgatory of second-class citizenship. Ray is pointing out all of the birds of prey, and I'm trying to assimilate lots of new names and to associate them with the proper birds. The country is gently rolling grassland with low, treeless mountains to the north. Laughing doves (*Streptopelia senegalensis*) are calling in a small valley forest. Steppe buzzards (*Buteo buteo*) soar overhead. We have seen greater kestrels (*Falco rupicoloides*), rock kestrels (*Falco tinnunculus*), black-shouldered kites (*Elanus axillaries*), and one yellow-billed kite (*Milvus migrans*) so far.

Our VW bus threw a rod, and the engine blew up. It died with a bang and a bleed out of a lot of oil. I was driving, as the bus owners with whom we were hitchhiking were not comfortable driving it themselves. Alas! I flagged down a big, black Cadillac, driven by a couple of old Afrikaners and asked them to please take one of our colored people to the next town for help. They looked at me as if I was crazy. I had momentarily forgotten that Apartheid rules here. Apparently, even associating with colored people is an imprisonable offense. However, they did take our friend. We held out our thumbs and soon found another ride.

Later today on the road to Mossel Bay we saw a hammerhead stork (*Scopus umbretta*) fly up along the road, and also what Ray called Naumann's kestrels (lesser kestrels, *Falco naumanni*). We camped in Mossel Bay after stocking up on ostrich biltong from the ostrich farms just to the north.

16 December • Humansdorp, South Africa

After leaving Ray and his entourage at Mossel Bay, Gaile and I hitched east to Humansdorp, making a brief stop in George to visit Rudi De Witt, one of the original South African falconers. Rudi had a lovely, one-and-a-half-year-old martial eagle (*Polemaetus bellicosus*) named Grace. He showed me a fine snare trap for kites, kestrels, and similar raptors. Along the way we saw a few birds: cape raven (*Corvus albicollis*), black crow (*Corvus apensis*), white-rumped swift (*Apus caffer*), European swallow (*Hirundo rustica*), red-winged starling (*Onychognathus morio*), and pied starling (*Spreo bicolor*).

In Humansdorp I met John Blignaut, another B.F.C. member I had contacted by mail. He was raising two eyass, female red-breasted sparrow hawks (*Accipiter rufiventris*) which were just at the brancher stage, the age when they would be hopping from their nest to nearby branches. I photographed them. They appeared to be warrantable (a Mavro term signifying their worthiness as falconry birds) little hawks. John showed me the nest, where there was supposed to be one remaining youngster. There was no sign of it when I climbed to the nest, located in a eucalyptus tree about 30 feet up. It was in a wooded strip between plowed fields. John said adult birds weigh between seven and eight ounces, roughly the similar in size to our sharp-shinned hawks. We shot a Cape turtledove (*Streptopelia capicola*) and three goldfinches for his eyasses. We saw a bok-makierie shrike (*Telophorus zeylonus*). John says they are terrific quarry for a spar. We also saw an African hoopoe (*Upupa africana*), crowned plover (*Vanellus coronatus*), Cape turtledove, a fork-tailed drongo (*Dicrurus adsimilis*), and paradise flycatcher (*Terpsiphone viridis*).

I talked with John about the South African Falconers Club. He is the secretary. He says they cannot get legal recognition for falconry in the Transvaal, the center of falconry here. It is illegal to take a hawk without a permit and also illegal to hunt with one. Authorities are unhelpful. John spoke of a Natal Falconry Club, whose secretary is E.B. Woods in Durban and showed me their lengthy constitution.

John is a hardworking young rancher who raises mohair goats and sheep on a 4000-acre ranch. He is quiet, straightforward and serious; he prefers eyasses, and will only keep accipiters due to time constraints. John believes the South African club will fold if von Michaelis can't get legal recognition of the sport. So, although South African falconry may never be legal, falconers will fly birds anyway with or without a club.

We stayed the night. Gaile and I were given separate rooms.

17 December • Middleburg, South Africa

From Humansdorp we hitched through Port Elizabeth along the lovely coast east toward Grahamstown. Then, we cut inland to Cookhouse over the Little Karroo. It was very hot, dry, brushy hill country, reminiscent of western Wyoming. We saw a few buzzards, On the road from Cradock to Middleburg we counted 180 Naumann's kestrels. The place was alive with them! We also saw six pied crows (*Corvus albus*), a flock of about 50 storks, species unknown, and three black-shouldered kites. The land is vast, flat, surrounded by arid, low mountains and punctuated with occasional buttes.

Gaile and I arrived on the outskirts of Middleburg about sunset to find thousands of Naumann's kestrels circling about and coming in from all directions to roost. They have been coming in for an hour and are thick. Unending streams of them are flying by. I just counted 60 in one group in less than 30 seconds. Beneath the roost trees lie thousands of feathers and mutes (excrement), matting down the vegetation for an area of at least an acre in size. They are everywhere there are trees in this part of town. Now, thousands more are streaming in, circling like swarms of insects. The tree branches are absolutely packed with kestrels; each kestrel seems to try to defend its perch to about six inches on each side, as far as it can reach without moving. They look like bunches of fruit packed into the trees. Every time a local steam engine backs up or pulls forward they explode into the air, wheel around and land again, like a living tornado, squabbling a bit, but amazingly quiet.

18 December • Warmbad, South Africa

The kestrels awoke us at 5:00 A.M. as they erupted from their roosting trees to fly to their feeding grounds. There is a group of 300–400 still here, hunting large grasshoppers from wires and fences. Minimum distance between birds is roughly 18 inches. They are remarkably free of hostility toward one another.

Gaile and I spent last night in a roadside ditch, serenaded by the sound of distant drums and wild shrieks echoing from the town where the locals were partying. It is now 6:30 A.M., and we are on the road trying for a lift to Johannesburg.

Traveling through the Orange Free State, headed toward Bloemfontein, about halfway to Johannesburg and pretty much the middle of South Africa, we are finding abundant buzzards and Naumann's kestrels. The landscape is flat, with occasional low hillocks and grassland, brush being confined to the rises. It is very hot and dry.

About 50 miles north of Blomfontein we saw two yellow-billed kites, more buzzards and kestrels. The landscape consisted of flat grassland with occasional small clumps of trees, very open and with almost no brush. I saw a small, blackish bird with a long, black tail. We passed swallows, the occasional Abdim's Stork (*Ciconia abdimii*), and cattle egrets (*Bubulcus ibis*). We crossed the Vaal River, where I saw about 30 sparrow-sized bright red birds with dark wings in the bushes by the river (Red bishop birds, *Euplectes orix*).

Approaching Johannesburg I saw another black, long-tailed fellow with definite scarlet wrist patches (Long-tailed widow bird, *Euplectes progne*).

20 December • Johannesburg, South Africa

We camped in Warmbad north of Pretoria. Yesterday Gaile and I hitched to Witwatersrand University Medical School in Johannesburg to see if we could find Raymond Dart, the man who pioneered much research on *Australopithecus*, a genus of extinct, bipedal apes which may have been ancestral to humans. We met instead a very fine chap, Professor P.T. Tobias, who opened up a wonderful collection of Australopithecine material and patiently allowed me to snap photos and ask many questions. He even let me hold the famous Taung's child skull! It was exhilarating to physically hold the actual skull that began the controversy about whether humans had evolved in Africa or elsewhere. This little skull of a small, man-like ape was the first strong evidence that humans evolved from a creature with the body of a human and the brain of an ape, rather than vice versa.

Dr. Tobias also let us in on a big news scoop. Dr. Louis Leakey, another famous researcher into the origin of humans, has found a new creature, which appears to be midway between *Australopithecus africanus* and *Homo erectus*, that is, between apes and humans. It was found in Bed 1 at Olduvai Gorge, Tanganyika, about 18 inches below a previous contender for human ancestry, *Zinjanthropus* [now known as *Australopithecus boisei* and considered a dead end side branch not ancestral to humans]. Professor Tobias feels the new fossil is true Homo or human, and the maker of the pebble tools associated with and formerly attributed to Zinj. He also believes the new creature, which he calls *Australopithecanthropus* [now known as *Homo habilis*], killed Zinj. Dr. Tobias has parts of the braincase and some very human-looking teeth and jaws. [*A. africanus* was only found in South Africa. *A. boisei* was found in South Africa and Tanganyika. So, in Olduvai, lived *A. boisei*, the new mid-man, and a very heavy-browed *Homo erectus*. Zinj was argon dated at 1,750,000 years. So, mid-man is at least Zinj's contemporary.]

Gaile and I left the museum and went to visit local falconer Paul Venter and his wife Barbara. Paul showed me a dark phase black sparrow hawk (*Accipiter melanoleucus*), very rare he says. He also showed us an eyass bird in juvenile plumage but molting. It was about the size of our American goshawk tiercels, but it had longer legs and a different head, quite lovely. I also was shown a pair of lanners, both adult and both snow-white breasted, almost unmarked except for a bit of flecking on the sides beneath the wings. Otherwise they appear the same as the more heavily breast-marked North African birds. The white-breasted phase is common here.

We met Collin Williams, an interested beginner, who was the owner of the lanners. He showed us a fine African goshawk (*Accipiter tachiro*), a three-year-old eyass, named Diana, who was similar in size to our Cooper's. She had beautiful, large feet, and according to Collin, was a real killer. Falconers here hold African goshawks in high regard. They likewise consider all yellow-eyed eagles excellent, claiming them to be the most rapacious of eagles. The red-breasted sparrow hawk (*Accipiter rufiventris*), Ovampo sparrow hawk (*Accipiter ovampensis*) and little sparrow hawk (*Accipiter minullus*) are all highly valued; the shikra (*Accipiter badius*) not so much. Both African hawk eagles (*Aquila spilogaster*) and Ayres' hawk eagles (*Hieraaetus dubius*) are reported to be good birds.

Paul wanted me to go trap a lanner with him, one of a hunting pair 27 miles from town the following morning. He uses a dho gazza, a net trap, and says lanners are easy to catch. Paul also told me he has given up on trying to promote a falconry club, and he wants no part in organizing one due to the sport's illegality in the Transvaal. He believes the government officials are quite narrow-minded on the subject of falconry, and should his name be connected with the sport, he could lose his permits to keep birds for scientific purposes, the only way he can legally keep birds now. He has little hope for recognition and legalization of falconry, since the government has a record of surveillance and blacklisting of anyone they believe is practicing the sport. Thus, Paul believes no group effort for legislated legalization is to be expected. Personally, he prefers to spend his time hawking rather than promoting falconry. As a result South Africans are with few exceptions mostly beginners with little expert advice available to them. Because of all of the above problems they chiefly aspire to keep their birds in good health and flying, actual hunting being too difficult for them to achieve.

21 December • Potgietersrus, South Africa

We are in the northernmost province of South Africa. I just saw a jackal buzzard (*Buteo rufofuscus*, also known as an augur buzzard). Additionally I spotted about 30 Abdim's storks (*Ciconia abdimii*). The weather is getting warm and cloudy and we may have thunderstorms tonight. Last night we camped and stayed dry. We just caught a ride that will take us to Ft. Victoria, so we should be in Mashaba tonight. The country here is hilly and mostly covered with brush and grass, with abundant scattered small trees.

North of Pietersburg I saw many yellow-billed kites and more flocks of Abdim's storks. The land is flatter now, arid with widely spaced trees and bushes over red grassland. Round, thatch-roofed huts, clustered in small groups, dot the plains. There are yellow-billed kites everywhere. It should be great for hawking, were it not so hot.

Forty miles north of Louis Trichardt, almost to the border of Southern Rhodesia [Zimbabwe], I spotted a probable drongo (a small black bird) and what looked to be a hawk eagle in the top of a tree. The landscape was dry and brushy with red, sandy soil, little underbrush and few clearings. We just crossed the border into Rhodesia. It is hot and dry with miles of brush land on the ubiquitous red soil. We are seeing few birds because the brush limits visibility.

About 50 miles south of Ft. Victoria [Masvingo], Southern Rhodesia we are into beautiful, forested hills. There are lots of native huts.

About one hundred miles south of Salisbury [Harare], Southern

Rhodesia, we now are seeing lovely open grassland, bush and abundant trees. I think this would be called savannah country. I noticed two dark partridges, possibly Francolin's, quite large and apparently unmarked, plus one jackal.

22 December • Salisbury, Southern Rhodesia

Gaile and I are encamped in town. I just met Allan Savory. He and his wife, Shirley, live on the outskirts of town in a comfortable but simple, unfinished house. Allan is a rugged "iron man" whose pastimes include falconry and parachuting. He is a wildlife director and in the course of his work has killed thousands of game animals in order to thin overpopulated herds. He does this by running each animal down on foot then shooting it at point-blank range. He says it is fairer to the animals, is sporting, and it keeps him fit. Allan is very lean, fit indeed and a survival expert.

Allan keeps no hawks at present; he has vowed never to keep tame hawks if he cannot fly or hunt with them. Since his job is very demanding, he presently does not have time to keep a hawk. He is hoping to change from a public job to a private employee shortly and then will be able to fly short-wings, true hawks as opposed to long-winged falcons; short-wings are more suitable to the enclosed nature of the country. He told me he learned falconry from Major Eustace Poles, who now lives in England, and who is also a British Falconers' Club member.

Allan and Shirley invited us to overnight. Gaile and I were quartered together in a guest cottage, no questions asked.

24 December • Mashaba, Southern Rhodesia

Gaile and I left Salisbury yesterday. Allan drove us out to our road, and after about a three-hour wait we got a ride to Fort Victoria with a young cop. About 40 miles north of Fort Victoria I saw four all-black crows, one secretary bird (*Sagittarius serpentarius*), and several bee eaters which looked the same as those we saw in Spain. We spent an hour in drizzle and wind waiting for a ride to Mashaba [Mashava], a small mining town, finally arriving by 4:30 P.M. We are staying with the parents of Gordon McKenzie, a friend of Tricia and Gay. The two sisters are here too, so a Christmas party is definitely in order. I estimate Gaile and I have hitchhiked 2100 miles in Africa.

25 December • Mashaba, Southern Rhodesia

I celebrated Christmas in Mashaba with the McKenzie family and the New Zealand girls. We had a terrific turkey dinner, tried our hands at lawn bowling, and I ended up talking politics with "Mac," Mr. McKenzie. There were even a few presents for me: two handkerchiefs, one book, one bush hat and a half-pint of Scotch from Gaile and a contribution from my Mom to my traveling fund. I spent a final evening with Gaile, since I am leaving in the morning. There were several weaver birds building nests in Mashaba.

26 December • Livingstone, Northern Rhodesia

Gaile and I parted today. I am a bit unsettled about how to handle our separation. We have shared so much.

On the way to Bulawayo I saw three secretary birds near Gwelo, a town in the center of Southern Rhodesia. About 30 miles from Bulawayo, still in Southern Rhodesia, I passed four ostriches by the road, improbable looking birds. I made Livingstone this evening as planned, after being picked up by a family, the Gabby Bassons, who have taken me to their home here and established me in a trailer in their back yard; they even fed me supper and provided me with a bath! What fine people! They have a house full of pets, including one monkey, three dogs, two cats, untold chickens and pigeons, one daughter and two sons. They will show me Victoria Falls tomorrow. We passed it when we came in tonight. It was sublime in the moonlight.

27 December • Livingstone, Northern Rhodesia

The Basson family took me to Victoria Falls and turned me loose for the day. I walked from David's Cataract to Eastern Cataract through the rain forest that is formed from the spray. I got soaked, but it was well worth it. The falls are stupendous, over a mile across I am told, generating so much spray that it is impossible to see the entire falls from any one point. I had to view it from many points to construct the entire picture. As yet it is unspoiled by lights, tourist shops and warning barricades. I encountered no other people and walked unchallenged a few hundred feet out onto the falls itself by carefully hopping from one rock to another.

The Zambezi River crawls along like a fat snake then suddenly plunges down these magnificent cataracts into a series of tremendous gorges, zigzagging along to the great Kariba Dam. I searched for Taita falcons (*Falco fasciinucha*), which are reputed to nest in the area but to no avail. An all-black swift (*Apus barbatus*) abounds in the gorges. I found perhaps a dozen hornbills very conspicuously frolicking in the surrounding forests. They appeared to be trumpeter hornbills (*Ceratogymna bucinator*), black and white with the black extending ventrally along the neck and enclosing the panel, breast and belly being white. They were very impressive. A fish eagle (*Haliaeetus vocifer*) circled high above the Zambezi, and I found there a sacred ibis (*Threskiornis aethiopicus*). I spent the entire morning photographing the falls and drinking in the scenery.

Around noon I returned to Livingstone to visit the museum. It was a fine little museum with excellent exhibits on different tribes, the evolution of man and archeology in Africa. I met the director, Mr. Clay, who showed me the research facilities, library and natural history collections, the latter being poor in number, since the museum's emphasis on collecting is only recent. When I enquired about the Taita falcon, Mr. Clay informed me that the museum tech, C. Holiday, has one as a pet. Mr. Holiday was on vacation in Tanganyika, but his brother said the bird was still here, and I might see and photograph it. Overflowing with expectation, I followed Mr. Clay to the Holiday home only to learn that the falcon had accompanied Mr. Holiday to Tanganyika. Thoroughly disappointed, I returned to the museum to spend a half hour in its library trying to identify birds I've seen.

I hitched a ride back to the Falls Restaurant and watched and photographed the tame monkeys there while I awaited the Basson family. There was a flock of tiny, brown birds with pink heads at the Victoria Falls Hotel. The Bassons took me to visit the "Big Tree," a monster baobab. Then, we took a scenic drive through the bush to experience various gorges along the Zambezi below the falls. We saw several more hornbills as we had a lovely drive through the game park along the upper Zambezi to look for hippos and other large mammals.

The Bassons took me again about 11 P.M. to see the lunar rainbow, a phenomenon which is locally famous; it is formed by the spray of the falls when there is a high, bright moon. The experience was transcendent. I do not suppose I shall see its like again. I observed some nightjars, species unknown, sitting on the road and several baboons. We headed back to Bassons' and to bed.

28 December • Livingstone, Northern Rhodesia

8:00 A.M. Supplied with a bag of mangos from the Bassons I am on the road north at the edge of Livingstone. I am unsure just why they were so kind to me. Perhaps they enjoyed sharing this wonderful part of their world with an eager stranger. Maybe they found me interesting, too. For whatever reasons they were good Samaritans, I am grateful.

I have been waiting an hour for a ride. There is nary a sign of one. I suspect it will get tougher to find rides from here on. I just saw a tiny accipiter fly by. From its size I would guess it to be a little sparrow hawk (*Accipiter minullus*). I also just noticed a chameleon crossing the road; it walks very deliberately, alternating diagonally positioned feet to a four count for each step. Step one, pick up right front foot and left rear foot; step two, move them forward; step three, put them down; step four, rock body forward. It takes about two seconds to complete one four-count step. When I photographed him, he hissed and erected a "collar" behind his head. The weather is sunny and hot.

Finally, I caught a ride and am on the way. I saw a small hawk with a dark, slate-gray back and around four thin, highly contrasting white stripes on its tail. It was about the size of a large, European sparrow hawk, looked accipitrine, and I think it had red feet.

Just north of Kalomo, Northern Rhodesia [Zambia], about 100 miles north east of Livingstone, I spotted two black-shouldered kites and a Bateleur eagle (*Terathopius ecaudatus*). About ten miles further I passed a medium sized, brown eagle with a slightly wedge-shaped tail. A little later, I saw another Bateleur fly up. It had a beautiful red-orange back and tail against a black body and wings. Of course, my drivers are consistently disinterested in what wondrous birds and mammals we pass. It is my little secret.

6:00 P.M. and I am in Broken Hill [Kabwe], roughly 50 miles north of Lusaka. It looks like rain. I saw a few yellow-billed kites, Bateleurs, and another large, brown eagle, not as wedge-tailed as the earlier bird. I am feeling a bit lonely, but paradoxically I want to be alone. I wish there were a good campsite, but there is only dense brush full of insects. I hate fighting off mosquitoes.

9:00 P.M. at Kapiri Mposhi, Northern Rhodesia, about 100 miles north of Lusaka. I was eating in the Café Reno at Broken Hill when a young chap offered me a lift this far. He bought me a beer and left me at a little hotel/filling station/bar. The manager has offered to allow me to sleep on the veranda. There is not much happening here. That makes 439 miles today, for a total of 3000 miles in Africa!

30 December Mpika, Northern Rhodesia

Well, here I sit in Mpika on the Great North Highway about 225 miles north east of Kapiri Mposhi. It is 7:45 A.M. at the Hotel Crested Crane. It is raining. Prospects for a lift are slim. I got a ride from Kapiri Mposhi yesterday to Serenje, hardly more than a dot on the map. The road was just dust all the way. I waited from 1:00 P.M. to 6:00 P.M. for a lift out of Serenje, but only one car passed, and it was full. I met Hans Norton of Cape Town, who is also hitchhiking to Egypt, but he is headed first to Dar es Salaam. I can't say it distresses me to travel with him, as it is actually nice to have company. However, I feel my chances are better alone, since there is so little traffic. He is a nice chap, though. We have been waiting here for ten hours for a car to pass. We sit quietly by the roadside, trying to look harmless, maybe even interesting. If anyone does pass, we try to appear eager and hope for pity.

Hans and I finally got a lift yesterday with an ex-Pakistani fish merchant who runs fish from Abercorn to Salisbury in Northern Rhodesia. He brought us to Mpika, where stands the only hotel since Kapiri Mposhi. We slept on the veranda after a meal of Pakistani curried pancakes. I saved £1.5 by not taking a room. This morning, I awoke with Mexican heartburn from the curry. Presently I am sitting in the rain, rather dismal, protected by the hotel veranda roof. By the way, when I say hotel that means a mud-walled, one story small building with actual wooden floors and not much else. It is not what we would call a hotel back home.

11:00 A.M. I am entrenched at the general store, still here at Mpika. Barefoot native kids sporting well-worn clothing are out and about. One little girl is weaving some sort of two-dimensional animal out of grass. Cute little kids, always friendly. They don't beg but just hover in my proximity and mumble a shy thanks, sometimes in English, if I give them a cookie or a penny. The police from the Mpika station, about 500 yards from here, drift by on bicycles as does the rest of the population. Some people talk to Hans and me a bit in English. "Where you going, boss? Where you from? Egypt? Mmm." They always have a big smile, are polite, friendly people, like pretty much all of the native people I have encountered on the trip. Here they live simply in thatched huts in the bush, working sometimes, eating their corn, saving for a bicycle, hitchhiking from their village to the general store, sometimes a hundred miles away I am told. Now the kids are showing off their western influence, by performing the twist dance for us with a mixture of shyness and exhibitionism which seems natural to all small children.

A couple of Indians run the store. It is typical that they do, for most of the brush businesses are run by Indians. Many Indians came to Africa in the nineteenth and early twentieth centuries to do contract work and build railroads. They remained and cornered most of the mercantile market. The whites with whom I have talked here in Northern Rhodesia are resigned to the coming independence from Great Britain. The white proprietress of the hotel in Kapiri Mposhi expressed the common opinion when she said, "What else can we do but stay? Our lives are here. We can't leave. I only fear for my little ones, not for myself." There is forced optimism here. The whites hope that the new government has learned from Kenya and the Congo that violence and anti-Europeanism have no reward, save poverty. However, there is unrest. I wonder if anybody has learned.

Hans and I just baptized my bush hat with the remainder of my Zambezi water from Livingstone. It is now, as far as I can interpret local custom, a bona fide Rhodesian bush hat, even if it was made in England.

5:30 P.M. I am stuck. A car pulled in for gas, but the driver steadfastly maintained he had no space, even in the face of our most pitiable entreaties. I can think of many better ways to spend a day than watching the locals pass through Mpika. We are hoping some car stops at the hotel tonight, so we can scrounge a ride north.

We're in the rainy season now, and when it rains, it rains like hell, and it rains two or three times a day. But, there's food and Coca Cola, and life could be worse. I just hate wasting time here.

Fortunately, I have time. I don't have to be anywhere until the rendezvous with Jack Mavrogordato in Sudan.

31 December • Mpika, Northern Rhodesia

Hans and I slept in the police station, but in style on benches, not on the floor. The police customarily provide free haven for travelers in the desolate country of Northern Rhodesia. We tried to hitch a ride north this morning with a police convoy. No luck. So here we are, back in front of the Mpika general store, waiting. Two cars came by headed for Tunduma but treated us with icy indifference as they vanished into the dust.

At noon, a bus loaded with Indian students and teachers pulled in. After a bit of haggling, their leader agreed to take us to the border. They are a friendly bunch; we've been singing songs, eating curried whatnots and discussing the three topics, religion, sex and politics, about which one is warned never to converse. We arrived at 6:30 P.M., too late for customs.

1 January • Tunduma, Tanganyika

Happy New Year! We slept last night beneath the roof of the customs shed at Tunduma, right on the border of Tanganyika through 12 midnight, twice. East African time is one hour ahead of Rhodesian, so we had the opportunity to party through two new years events. Earlier we had tried to find an actual party with the customs officers. No luck. Next we tried the hotel bar; no people. We tried the African bar; wrong people. So, Hans and I cracked the Scotch then went to bed, missing the moment.

This morning there was a rush for the one toilet and its accompanying sink at the customs house. We were serenaded by 53 people, I counted them, hacking and snorting water through their nasal passages as they practiced their morning ablutions; it was an improbable chorus and definitely worth experiencing. Apparently it is an Indian ritual to cleanse one's nasal and esophageal passages in this manner every morning. Drawing a piece of string through these conduits is also frequently employed to get things really clean. By 9:30 A.M. the air had cleared enough for me to enter and wash up.

I was the first man out of Northern Rhodesia today and the first into Tanganyika! Presently, customs is dismantling the bus, seeking booty for duty. The weather is sunny and bright. We should make Mbeya by noon. Unintelligible languages abound. The local chickens are picking through treasures discarded from the bus.

In Mbeya at 2:15 P.M. it is clouding up. We expect rain shortly. Hans and I had an easy trip over the "Great North Road," a miserable dirt track filled with ruts and dust winding through the beautiful Rift Valley. We amused ourselves by arm wrestling and endless narratives of Indian jokes with our Indian friends. On the bus there was an unforgettable girl, about 15 years old, with beautiful, fresh, young features, large, dark eyes and a full-lipped, sweet smile, glistening, white teeth and soft, brown skin. But, she had polio-deformed legs, so she could barely progress unaided by her braces and crutches. She was a lovely little girl.

Mbeya is a beautifully situated town with verdant hills, conifer forests and grassy slopes; it almost looks alpine. The natives pass in slacks and open-necked sport shirts. Almost all of them stop to greet us with a hearty *Jambo*! Hello! in Swahili. Then a short demonstration of sign language with bilingual vocal accompaniment ensues wherein we indicate our mode and direction of travel.

We were just passed by a parade of locals in their Sunday best, including some wearing shoes, going off to bury Sir Roy Welensky, the former head of the now-dissolved Federation of Rhodesia and Nyasaland. The parade was preceded by a host of children; then came four arm-swinging, khaki-covered cops and two drummers. There followed a group carrying flags and a coffin, adorned with a photo of Sir Roy atop, to symbolize the end of the Welensky rule. There was wailing and chanting, beautifully harmonious. I asked a Sikh, one of the ubiquitous African-Indian population, if it were permissible to photograph the people; he said yes. I merely lifted the camera and found myself surrounded by kids, pushing, shoving and scrambling to be in the photo. I had to keep backing off to get any shots, as they continued to step ahead of one another advancing upon me, each hoping to have his or her picture taken. It was cloudy, but I hope the photos may turn out. It was a joyous celebration.

10:00 P.M. It has rained like crazy on and off since 7:15 P.M. I walked about two miles out of town trying to find the guesthouse that Hans had located earlier while I was at supper. I ended up with wet feet here, where I have been allocated an open vegetable shed with a long, dirty table. I tried my best to wangle a free bed at the guesthouse, but the owner said he ran a business; he was tired of people touring the world at his expense. I can't really blame him, but it is a miserable night, and he might have done better for me. The rain has abated now, so I will go try to sneak in and bunk with Hans, who actually paid for a room, and maybe take a bath, too. I'll probably get bounced out, but what the hell? The owner is waiting on the porch. He spotted me right away, since this place is spotlighted. I'll just bed down here in the vegetable shack.

2 January • Mbeya, Tanganyika

We have been waiting on the road at Mbeya for two hours now, without much traffic. I saw six yellow-billed kites, a buzzard, plus many Cape ravens and pied crows. There were about 20 of the little brown, pink-headed birds feeding in the fields.

Finally we are on the road to Iringa. We just were dropped off at a little village called Makumbako. An English farmer in a Land Rover running on three cylinders gave us a lift from Mbeya. As we climbed from below 4000 feet to above 6000 feet, the going was slow. He compounded the delay by filling his overheated radiator while we stopped briefly at a pretty waterfall on the Kumani River. Along the way we picked up two rival hitchhikers who have been dogging us a while. They are presently drinking beer and fraternizing with the natives at the local huts which serve as stores. We are not really pleased to have their competition, but they pose us no real threat, since the farmer will probably take us all to Iringa, and we can leave them there.

Tanganyika was a beautiful sight as we rode along the "Great North Road" from Mbeya to Makumbako. Entering from high up into the Rift Valley, the panorama was marvelous with great mountains rising up from the vast, flat plain. We first passed through open country, then brush, but the scenery was always striking with views of miles and miles of wild, open land. The native huts were different here in Tanganyika from the thatched, round huts of Rhodesia. These were square and rectangular with thatched and even some sod roofs; the walls were of bricks and mud rather than of wood and mud. There were no chimneys. Signs on otherwise indistinguishable huts proclaimed them to be hotels or stores selling beans, corn, onions and warm Tusker brand beer.

Our friend told us on the way up that Tanganyika is getting increasing foreign aid as it slips inevitably backward into darkness and becomes less civilized. It has resources but little money to exploit them nor railroads to transport them. With the decline of the European, there are few native organizers with the skills to develop them. I saw a large group of people working in the fields. We were told by our English farmer-driver that this was a cooperative plan in which everybody helps with the work, be it farming or road building, all share. Our friend claimed that it will be a short-lived concept. It certainly appears like something akin to communism. Perhaps it is more like what our American pioneers had to resort to.

Along the way I saw a widow bird (*Euplectes macrourus*) with yellow-white shoulder patches. Bateleurs were common. The wires were adorned with rollers, birds of an unknown species. About 50 miles north of Mbeya I saw what I took to be a lanner falcon on a pole. In the same area a basically gray bird with black and white patches and a long, decurved red bill, maybe a sickle-billed hoopoe, flew across the road. I saw a brownish-gray harrier with white rump patch and barred tail.

It is now clouding up, and rain is imminent. I wish a bus would show up. To date I calculate I have covered 3700 miles.

3 January • Makumbako, Tanganyika

7:45 A.M. No bus ever arrived. I camped in my tent next to the village and enjoyed light rain and wind most of the night. It is cool and very overcast at the moment. I am waiting on the veranda of a shop.

At 9:30 A.M. the bus arrived and departed, full-up with mendicant blacks staring out from the interior. There is supposed to be another bus later.

The second bus arrived, only half full this time. For ten East African shillings apiece Hans and I were transported to Iringa. Our bus rapidly filled up. Sandwiched between assorted people, with chickens running between our feet and strange and familiar odors assailing our nostrils, we proceeded to Iringa. When the bus became so full that we couldn't expect to force another louse in, we'd stop, and without benefit of grease two or three more people would slide in bearing hands full of chickens, gourds, pangas (large knives) and assorted other luggage. Tiny, chocolate children were firmly affixed to their mothers' swollen breasts. Periodically with the bus running full out, the conductor would climb out of the window, scramble up the side and pull himself onto the roof to inspect the baggage. Then he would reappear feet first through the same window. No one seemed to consider these proceedings extraordinary.

The man sitting next to me had his wife, two children and a sister with him. He spoke and read English and had a portfolio crammed with political books from both Russia and the U.S.A.: Marks, Lenin, Khrushchev, some of each. I put in a plug for capitalism. He was a teacher of handicrafts. He represented one of a handful of new-thinking people in black Africa. He agreed that Africans must become educated and "given freedom" only when they are ready. I liked him.

We arrived in Iringa after frequent stops at widely scattered villages. Usually in each village were one or two shops selling cloth, baking soda, cans of margarine, beans, flour and candy. Normally an Indian owned the biggest store. Sometimes I found a butcher in a hut, flies covering already-turned, non-refrigerated meat. Frequently, there was a hotel, another basic mud hut with a dirt floor and little else. And, of course, there would be a bar, another hut exactly like the others but with two or three rows of beer bottles on shelves and a wooden counter of sorts separating the bottles from the door.

Hans is off to a movie, *All Fall Down*. I am staying at the Iringa police station, having secured a cozy corner of the floor in a room bearing the sign "Investigation." Presently, I am surrounded by three women, one nursing a child, all sitting on the floor. I do not know their status, but they are friendly as are almost all of these people, and they smile back. My Swahili is fantastic. I can say hello, thanks, how are you and fine. For food I bought some red-hued bananas and some triangular meat pies, spiced with onions. Not bad. I have to live on Indian food, as there is not much else that I trust to eat.

There are no buses to Arusha on Sunday, so I will attempt to hitch all day in that direction. If I fail to achieve Arusha, I'll hop the bus on Monday. I think I'll take care of a few personal necessities, wash and hit the hay. It is raining.

4 January • Arusha, Tanganyika

Last night as Hans and I were about to go to bed, two English chaps, a young British lieutenant, Gavin Peebles, and his friend, Charlie Parcell, turned up at the police station seeking shelter. As luck would have it, they were also headed for Arusha. They offered to take me along for 10 shillings gas money. We left at 9:20 A.M. after I cashed $20 worth of Amexco travelers' checks. I figured out that it cost me 3.18% to use travelers checks. This confirms my thoughts that they are not a good value.

Apparently, one of Gavin's fellow officers had had to leave this car in Rhodesia when his unit pulled out for Nairobi some months ago. Gavin accepted a wager that he could find and retrieve the car, hence his and Charlie's trip. Gavin has no interest in replacing the car's windshield in his quest to win his wager. That being the case, today we had a great drive along the Great North Road in the old, three cylinder DKW, sans windshield. The road from Iringa provided a beautiful panorama of the Rift Valley. The landscape varied from open plains to scrubby, Rhodesian-like brush on the flats, to quite dense forests in the mountains.

I saw quite a few large, rather pale buzzards, with unmarked tails which are very square when spread. About ten miles north of Iringa, there was a medium-sized, all-brown eagle, the shape and color of a golden but with no white on wings or tail. In the same area I saw another giant bird, either an eagle or perhaps a vulture. It was entirely dark except for a clearly demarked white belly. Approaching Dodoma, about 20 miles out we startled a four-foot-long, sleek, glossy black cobra which spread its hood as its head rose up in the classic manner. I photographed it from the car, being too fearful to exit and face the serpent afoot. After a brief staring contest with me, it fled to cover.

In an area called Salanka, between Dodoma and Arusha, we saw a guinea fowl and three southern ground horn-bills (*Bucorvus leadbetteri*). These last were large, black turkey-like birds with stork-like beaks and prominent red wattles. This country was the most remote I have yet experienced. There were no wire pole lines. The only road was the rough dirt road on which we were traveling, and it was mostly washed out. I noticed mountains, flats, forests, plains, giant baobab trees, banana plantations, and tiny mud villages. We observed several very impressive, highly decorated people bearing bows, arrows and spears in the bush. They were near the roadside. One hurled a rock at the car, the first unfriendly gesture I had seen from a native. Gavin told me they are of a tribe closely akin to the Masai, very proud hunters and quite arrogant. I could see from their dignified demeanor and bearing that they were something different from the usual people we have been seeing. We saw more of these people all along the road from Dodoma to Arusha, but this first group stood apart from the rest.

I have been working to convince Gavin and Charlie that they need to make a digression from their trip back to Kenya, to Olduvai Gorge on the Serengeti. So far they are resistant. I think they need to go.

We arrived at 10 P.M. in Arusha. Due to darkness we did not get to see the surrounding area or Kilimanjaro. That is for tomorrow. Total trip mileage 4256.

5 January • Arusha, Tanganyika

We slept at the police station. Hans went off to Zanzibar. I wonder if our paths will cross again. I posted some letters to friends and family this morning then treated myself to a couple of "American" hamburgers and a double-thick malt at the Cha Cha bar. Gavin drove us to Moshi to try to see Kilimanjaro, it being totally obscured from Arusha by clouds.

About 12 miles from Arusha we stopped to visit Dr. A. von Nagy, a friend of Lorant D'Bastyai, my Hungarian falconer chum back in England. Dr. Nagy is a "white hunter" who has a lovely home with cottages for his clients in a lush setting beneath Mt. Meru and Mt. Kilimanjaro. Dr. Nagy maintains a few large birds and antelope in a park-like surrounding of grass, trees and a pond, all tastefully constructed and aesthetic. He wants Lorant to come here to direct the Africans who are the workers who take care of the animals and to assist in building Tanganyika's first and only zoo. Lorant, in exchange, would get a trip here, a home, food, an allowance, a free hand to practice falconry and the directorship of any zoo that evolves. It sounds like a fair deal to me. Dr. Nagy insists we spend the night after our afternoon adventures.

We drove on to Moshi. Kilimanjaro remained clouded over, not a glimpse to be seen. On the way back 15 miles from Moshi we saw a herd of at least 50 zebra by the road. Then, 22 miles from Moshi I saw two chanting goshawks (probably *Melierax poliopterus*) and two jackal buzzards together; one was light colored and the other melanistic. These are the common birds here. About one mile farther I spotted a long-crested eagle (*Lophäetus occipitalis*) on a phone pole.

While birding we encountered two young shepherds. Gavin thought them to be Masai. Both were around 12–13 years old; they wore only dusty robes. Each carried a stick and a spear. One had the upper rear portion of his ear pierced and plugged with wood. I gave one of them a six pence to pose for a photograph. Gavin also gave them bananas, which they ate readily.

The landscape from Arusha to Moshi changes from brush to green forest, which then thins gradually into open plains and grassland. It is beautiful here. Dr. Nagy informs me that Francolin partridge and hare both abound. It looks fabulous for falconry. There are even yellow-billed kites.

81

Kilimanjaro finally poked its head out, and I photographed it gratefully. It is very majestic soaring above the landscape.

Upon Dr. Nagy's return from errands we dined luxuriously upon roast beef, drank freely of beer and talked about Lorant and his tentative position. I will advise Lorant to come.

6 January • Arusha, Tanganyika

Dr. Nagy gave me a tour of his grounds. There were several trees full of weaver birds. One type has a chestnut-red breast, a black head, and a yellow back. The other birds were yellow-breasted with red caps and yellow faces with a pinkish tinge.

I had a bad morning. There was a mail mix-up in Arusha. The imbecile postmistress sent my incoming mail off to the Lake Manyara Hotel, 83 miles away. Fortunately, we are passing by there anyway, but her arrogant attitude put me off. Mail is an important connection to the outside world, and I have come to depend upon it.

We are currently under way to Ngorongoro Crater and Serengeti Park. My campaign to persuade Gavin and Charlie finally paid off. Now Gavin, Charlie and I are all excited about our detour to Olduvai. Jackal buzzards abound on these beautiful, rolling plains.

Twenty-four miles from Arusha, still in grassy plains, there was a flock of Abdim's storks circling with white-headed vultures (*Trigonoceps occipitalis*). Nine miles from the Ngorongoro Crater turnoff, we passed a flock of fan-tailed widow birds (*Euplectes axillaris*) and many rollers.

At 12 miles, we saw two bush buck, tan with a forward curved tip to the horn, and four ostrich. There is a great, tree-covered escarpment which overlooks the plain that runs to Lake Manyara. While climbing the escarpment above Manyara, we observed a baboon troop in the forest.

We stopped at the Manyara Hotel to pick up my mail then had a swim in the hotel pool in our clothes. Inspecting the restaurant menu, I was alarmed to see "Monkey Gland Steak" listed. A staff member explained that it was really only ground beef. Good joke!

Looking out over the lush, green crater floor from the east rim of Ngorongoro Crater, an enormous volcanic caldera and local landmark, was a breathtaking sight; through my field glasses I discovered four rhinos. We watched a rainstorm across the crater on the north rim, miles away.

7 January • Ngorongoro Crater, Tanganyika

Last night we camped out on the grounds of the Ngorongoro Crater Lodge. We are presently awaiting a ride down into the crater in a lodge-owned Land Rover for the paltry sum of 30 shillings per head.

In the center of Ngorongoro Crater, we encountered tremendous numbers of wildebeest, Thompson's and Grant's gazelles, several eland and buffalo, one waterbuck and a female rhino with a baby. A perfectly lush, green, grassy plain covered the crater floor. Jackals and hyenas were everywhere. There were numerous crested cranes (*Balearica regulorum*), Abdim's storks, European storks (*Ciconia ciconia*), some lovely gray, black and white plovers (probably blacksmith plovers, *Vanellus armatus*), fan-tailed widow birds and a harrier. We found an additional flock of five superb starlings (*Lamprotornis superbus*), another eland and two more rhinos. The crater was a wildlife oasis.

In the bush I saw a small, very long-tailed black bird, like a widow bird but with a scarlet head and black beak (Red-collared widowbird, *Euplectes ardens*), a yellow bishop bird (*Euplectes capensis*), and many Kori bustards (*Ardeotis kori*). A dozen ostrich, some with half grown young, and five saddle-billed storks (*Ephippiorhynchus senegalensis*) were feeding in the grass. Around 100 Egyptian geese (*Alopochen aegyptiacus*) were along the crater floor near its edge. A medium-sized eagle, very pale tan, allowed us to approach within 50 feet as it stood on the ground. Quite a few birds built like starlings with black and white patches in their primaries (probably anteater chats *Myrmecocichla aethiops*), a Frankolin partridge (*Francolinus* sp.), some helmeted guinea fowl (*Numida meleagris*), one black-shouldered kite and perhaps six black crows plus a few Cape ravens were added to my list. Yellow-billed kites were common. On the way back, I saw several small, dashing falcons, which I could not identify as they were silhouetted against the sky. They might have been hobbies or even red-headed falcons (*Falco chicquera*), but I could not tell. From the lodge, looking down into the forest which lay between us and the lake, I saw four elephants standing in a small clearing. I noticed a secretary bird and four more superb starlings as well as more blacksmith plovers. Several black-faced monkeys lurked in the trees.

8 January • Ngorongoro Crater Lodge, Tanganyika

I identified what I believe to be a fiscal shrike (*Lanius collaris*). We set out for Olduvai Gorge. Ten miles out we were seeing many ant-eater chats and white storks along the roadside. Coming down onto Serengeti Plain we found ourselves surrounded by lush, green, short grass and rolling hills.

Twenty miles from the lodge on the edge of Serengeti Plain there was a Maribou stork (*Leptoptilos crumeniferus*), together with six Masai children and adults, working over a cow on the ground. Masai giraffes, recognizable by their "cornflake" shaped spots, were present in small groups among the trees that dotted the countryside.

We are passing numerous zebra, wildebeest, Thompson's and Grant's gazelles. A superb Kori bustard struts with its neck puffed out, exposing an enormous white "flag" on its throat; its tail is cocked so far up over its back, that it touches against the bird's neck. He deflates and stalks off upon our approach. Lilac-breasted rollers (*Coracias caudate*) are abundant. Approaching Olduvai through the brush we surprise a dark chanting goshawk (*Melierax metabates*), which is attempting to drive off an offending jackal buzzard from the dry creek bed it calls home by means of stoops and vocal epithets. An ordinary African hoopoe peers out from the bush.

We drove into the Olduvai Gorge excavation camp. A native worker showed us where *Zinjanthropus*, a 1.75 million-year-old ape which was once believed possibly ancestral to humans, resided until his timely resurrection by Dr. Mary Leakey. He showed us sites where a fossil human child and a foot were found and lots of bones from long-dead mammals. He led us to a pile of stones which was found in association with many stone tools and a heap of bones, many of which had been cracked open to extract the marrow. The stone pile was roughly circular; it might even have been a dwelling. If so, then it would be the first known, human constructed edifice. Our friend gave us a mimeographed history of Olduvai.

I inquired if Dr. Louis Leakey might be in the camp area. No, he was in Nairobi. I had hoped to meet him. I thought we had received special treatment, so I inquired as to why we had been given such a terrific tour. The answer was very pragmatic. Anyone who came all the way out here might just have significant money to donate to the project.

Charlie, Gavin and I spotted a kerosene-driven refrigerator in the camp and noticed some beer and soda pop cases nearby. Although we hinted broadly that we would be very happy to buy some beer or soda, our entreaties went for naught. I rebaptized my bush hat in the puddles of the dry season remnant of the Olduvai River.

Now back on the Serengeti we are passing Masai giraffes, which are cloistered among the trees, and ubiquitous zebra which kick up clouds of dust as they run ahead of our car. I am in the back seat. With our windshield missing we are collecting lots of that dust together with an accompanying rain of insects. Our car scoops up quite a collection of grasshoppers, beetles and flies, some of which miss Charlie and Gavin and come at me at high speed. The space behind the back seat is filling up nicely with those insects which get past me. Crowned plovers (*Vanellus coronatus*) are very common, and flocks of yellow-necked partridge (*Francolinus leucoscepus*) by the hundreds cover the plain. A troop of seven baboons tenant a wooded, dry creek bed. I note ten ostrich and a gray harrier with no rump patch but sporting black wing tips.

At the Lake Manyara Hotel we stopped for a couple of beers; then we headed back to Arusha, the Cha Cha snack bar, and finally the police station to sleep.

9 January • Arusha, Tanganyika

9:30 A.M. Gavin, Charlie and I just left Arusha, headed for Nairobi. The countryside is wooded, sprinkled with occasional banana estates. It is a beautiful drive to the Kenya border on a well-kept road, the best one I have seen in many a mile. We are passing through open grassland, which spreads over hillocks and flat plains; then the brush gradually encroaches. Igneous mounds and buttes dot the land, while Mt. Kilimanjaro dominates the scene, its head still lost in the clouds. Huge vultures circle everywhere.

I identified a tawny eagle (*Aquila rapax*) in the road approximately twenty miles into Kenya. Superb starlings abound.

After miles of brush-land we finally entered a game-rich open plain. Jackal buzzards were common. We located a youth hostel about seven miles west of Nairobi where we had security for about two bob a night. I bid Gavin thank you and goodbye as he left with the DKW to return to his outfit. Then I settled in.

10 January • Nairobi, Kenya

I inquired about Dr. Leakey but was told he had returned to Olduvai. Charlie and I, after a day's shopping around Nairobi, ended up in a brick-walled hut with a sheet metal roof, which stood behind the youth hostel. It was an African establishment, the manager being a rather untidy, hulking woman. We had a big conversation about *uhuru*. The word signifies independence and self-determination for the Kenyan people, and *harambee*, Swahili for coming together as one, with the locals. Kenya having become only recently independent, these topics were ripe for discussion. There has been no trouble here since Uhuru. The people are just beginning to become disillusioned about freedom. They're finding out it does not arrive on a golden platter; they must work for it. They are very pro U.S.A. in East Africa, due in part to lots of American aid and the influx of many American teachers.

A rather hefty African girl appeared and took a fancy to Charlie. One of our new friends, a 17-year-old boy named George, told Charlie that he would arrange for a rendezvous later in the evening. We all left the hut. I was curious to discover what might follow. The girl quite brazenly squatted in the path and produced a most astonishing amount of urine, giggling as she splashed away. Having finished, she sprung her trap. Although she wanted Charlie, she did have two kids to support, and well, you know, business is business, so for only ten shillings… Charlie bargained gamely through our young Swahili interpreter, and he got the young lady grudgingly down to five shillings; this negotiation indicated her sincere interest in Charlie. But Charlie was adamant about paying no money. Finally, Charlie and his beloved disappeared briefly behind a hedge only to re-emerge sans fulfillment due to a last minute demand for the fiver. No agreement could be reached. I consoled Charlie all the way back to the hostel.

11 January • Nairobi, Kenya

Charlie got word, via George, the interpreter, that his love awaited him, and tonight it would really be for free. But Charlie was in no mood for international relations and refused to budge from the hostel.

I went to a movie: Kirk Douglas in *Lonely are the Brave*. It was not a bad film.

12 January • Nairobi, Kenya

8:15 A.M. I am trying to hitch out of Nairobi to Kampala, Uganda. Since it is Sunday I am not confident of my chances.

Did it! The ride today to Kampala went smoothly. I had around eight lifts. It was all beautiful plains and grassland to Nakuru. I tarried at Lake Nakuru to see its legendary flocks of flamingos. Indeed, they were an impressive sea of pink.

Beyond Nakuru the land rose steadily until I passed Molo; here the land became increasingly hilly, and the first evergreen forests appeared. I took a photo of a sign that proclaimed I was now standing on the equator. I thought about the phenomenon of not having a shadow if one stood on the equator but quickly realized that would happen only at noon on an equinox. Hence, I had a nice shadow on the equator. As I headed north from the equator, the landscape was mostly evergreen forest with patches of open fields. Shrikes, jackal buzzards and yellow-billed kites were quite common.

From Eldoret there was open bush country. It was arid and windy today. There was a descent to Tororo into Uganda and ever downward to Kampala, whose altitude was about 4000 feet. Upon entering Uganda, the vegetation became lush, luxuriant and profuse. Forests lined the road; trees strove up for light, and were strangled from below by mats of vines and shrubs. Open fields were few but filled with vegetation. There were banana trees everywhere. Then came sugar cane, coffee, tea, and rubber trees. It was all very impressive to this newcomer. Oh yes, at Jinja I visited the source of the river I shall surely come to know well, the Nile.

I am again in jail. This time it is a super jail, Kampala's finest, with a comfortable cell, barred windows and a locked door between me and the outside world. The police even included a sink, toilet and a bed, all at no cost. Everyone is friendly. One cop, a Kenyan, borrowed my soap to wash his hands. These dry, free jail "hotels" are a wonderful way to go. [Of course, genocidal dictator Idi Amin would later use this jail for more sinister purposes, imprisoning, torturing and killing political dissidents.]

I met several Kikuyus but no Mau Maus. The Mau Mau were Kenyan rebels against the British from 1952–1960 and were reported to be very terrifying. One chap informed me for the real inside information on the Mau Mau I should procure a book, *Mau Mau Oathing*, preferably the police copy. It reputedly contains detailed data on initiation rites, examples of which do not belong in this narrative.

Traveled distance is up to 5300 miles. I need to write some letters now.

14 January • Kampala, Uganda

I have spent the last two nights in jail and have not yet decided whether to stay again tonight. I may just sleep in the park. I am still trapped in Kampala, a town that rates right in there with Lawton, Oklahoma, in my book. (Lawton was a seedy place with lots of bars and shady people. I spent eight weeks of Army training there) Well, actually it is really not that bad, but it lacks a bit as a capitol city. The post office is the most impressive I have seen in Africa, two stories tall and a block long. It ranks with the Johannesburg train station, another imposing stone and brick edifice replete with columns. Banks seem to thrive in the tropical sun, and they spring up here in splendor. The Parliament Building is perhaps the most imposing structure of all, a rose among many squalid, dingy, greasy little Indian shops. There are occasional temples and a mosque that stand at respectful distances from one another, looking like delicious, white wedding cakes.

By and large people here are friendly and come in all colors. There are the most pitiable beggars as there were in Nairobi: stumps and claws, twisted and mutilated, hunching along the sidewalk in unnatural gaits. Actually, I'm getting pretty sick of rags and dirt. I feel somewhat depressed and hemmed in by Asians and blacks, seeing only the occasional white face.

Presently I am sitting in the Spike Hotel, clean, modern, quite nice, writing to relieve my boredom and restlessness. The last two days were spent tracking down a ride to Juba, Sudan. Apparently, only smugglers travel to Juba, so I have been working the local bars to locate them. If I am to get to Sudan at all, it must be with smugglers. I have now located three rather grubby Sudanese who claim to be going north; they have promised to take me along for £5. I am hurting for cash, having £17.75 Sudanese and $5.00 American plus a few East African bob. It's going to be tight getting to Khartoum. I just hope these procrastinating Sudanese get off their collective asses tomorrow, and we go to Juba. I have pretty well exhausted any other chances to get there by sailing time.

It turns out that my Sudanese drivers are indeed smugglers; they have their own reasons for the daily delays. Smugglers do not advertise their travel schedules. Only one ship per week leaves down the Nile, so unless I want to wait another week, I have to be in Juba by Sunday.

I am a bit lonely tonight. I tried reading J. Wyndham's *The Day of the Triffids* and Machiavelli's *The Prince*. I even took in a Donald O'Connor film about Aladdin, but nothing helped. Waiting all day for the Sudanese to leave has not helped either. Sometimes I really feel the need for someone, and tonight is one of those times. But she is thousands of miles from me, and I'll not likely see her again. I suppose these feelings go with being a stranger in a strange land.

I met a hell of a nice chap, 17 years old who works at the Jaffries Hotel. We shot the bull; he even bought me some fish and chips after hearing my sad story. The worst part was I had not really expected that and had eaten previously. I got the food down and was grateful.

15 January • Kampala, Uganda
I'm still in Kampala at 3:30 A.M. I loaded all of my junk on an ancient Mercedes truck, ready to beat a path to Juba.

We did not get past the first petrol station, though, for a gas stop, when there was a problem. I had to pay my transport fee with £4 Sudanese. No one else had East African currency, so my smugglers panicked. None of us was happy about my little surprise of Sudanese currency; the smugglers ran off to exchange it. Sudanese money is apparently not worth scat here. I reckon it cost them a good 16 bob in the transaction. Too bad for this greedy bunch! I may suffer now because of it, but it is a good gamble, and seeing their panicked faces makes it almost worthwhile.

Vengeance and the Sudanese have wreaked their wrath upon me. After losing an hour due to the money changing not to mention losing some change in the deal, my hosts have transferred me from my luxurious seat in the cab to a loftier one atop the cargo on the back. Oh well, it is a nice day for motoring.

About one-and-a-half hours out of Kampala, we blew a tire. The Sudanese smugglers stopped to fix it, and we were on the road again by 6:00 P.M. We proceeded to a small village, where the tires were worked over until all hours. Eventually, we continued on to Gulu, about halfway between Kampala and Juba, while I froze my butt in my sleeping bag, clinging atop the truck. Arriving in Gulu in the wee hours, we got about four hours of sleep.

16 January • South of Juba, Sudan
This morning we picked up Hans Norton, who had just arrived in Gulu, and Doug, an expatriate Englishman who is ex-officio of the

now defunct Federation of the Rhodesias. We also picked up a friendly young American, Ken, who had just had an unsettling adventure. He had hitched to the Congo to meet Dr. Albert Schweitzer. In that he was successful. Ken confirmed that he was able to personally meet Dr. Schweitzer, and Ken had been very impressed by him. He really did not speak further about the meeting. On Ken's way back to the Congo border, as he was passing through a small town someone mistook him for a Portuguese. The Portuguese are roundly hated by many black Africans as a colonial power. A crowd soon gathered and began to shout at Ken. Then they began to stone him. The police rescued him from the crowd but threw him in the jail. After a few days, an anonymous white lady arrived to visit him in his cell. She did not identify herself but did ask him a lot of questions. Apparently satisfied that he was indeed American and not a threat, she commanded that he be taken to the border and advised him not to return. Ken concurs that was good advice.

Hans also had had a big adventure since I last saw him. During the time I traveled to the Serengeti, he had hitchhiked to Zanzibar. While he was in Zanzibar a revolutionary coup occurred. The new dictator immediately cracked down, closing the ports and installing some drastic reforms. Hans said that when the new leader drove past, any people who did not prostrate themselves beside the road would be shot. Being a South African (as popular as the Portuguese in the rest of Africa), even though he carried an English passport, Hans was apprehensive. After some difficulties he managed to bribe a ship's captain to sneak him to the mainland concealed with the cargo in the hold of the ship.

Now, as we all proceed into southern Sudan, who knows what awaits us? Southern Sudan is officially closed to outsiders. The Arab North, which has been exterminating the Christian and animist people of the South, does not like witnesses. Since my only way back to Europe is through Sudan, Jack Mavrogordato was able to help me obtain a visa. Hans, Doug and Ken will take their chances about being allowed entry.

It's been hot, damned hot. It's hot enough to sweat in the wind atop the moving truck. We have protected ourselves as best we can with ponchos, rags and coats. My old bush hat has had a workout; it is acquiring a classy patina. I have been wearing it since Christmas, when Gaile gave it to me.

I have been seeing many yellow-billed kites and a few jackal buzzards, one fish eagle, and many eagles of the tawny eagle size. We pass occasional small hornbills, and I even saw two of the great ground hornbills.

We just landed in a ditch. About 45 miles out of Juba the clutch gave it up on a hill; our truck backed down into a ditch, dumping us hitchhikers into the brush. It is now 6:30 P.M. The sun is about four fingers above the horizon. Our "mechanics" have anticipated the problem and are vigorously roughing the surface of the clutch plate with a file in hope of getting us out. Well, perhaps Allah will smile upon this venture, but I have my doubts. Meanwhile we are sipping tea, thoughtfully provided by our smugglers, which though heavily sugared, tastes mighty fine.

We are waiting halfway up a long hill in typical bush country; we have been here all day, since the truck is still immobile. It is dry and the land has been burned over by the natives; it teems with insects. A flock of about 15 small, blackbird-sized parrots just flew by. There are birds singing and chirping all around. It is still warm but cooling fast.

It looks like we might still make the steamship on time, but it will be close. This Sudanese crew has little apparent concern for time. They just laugh and say, "In a little while." They seem to never be in a hurry or to worry.

As we bedded down in the middle of the road, since the bush is so thick, a short, wiry man stepped out of the brush. He wore only a loincloth and carried a bow and quiver of arrows. He circled, studying us intently, then he melted back into the bush. I slept somewhat uneasily after that, knowing nothing of his intentions or those of his possible companions.

17 January • Juba, Sudan

A small Mercedes search bus found us around noon. It had come out from Juba with comrades of our Sudanese lorry crew. After removing the entire gearbox and associated parts from the truck, our crew decided the differential must be broken, so they yanked it, too. We left the lorry and proceeded to Juba without further incident. Our hosts ejected us half a mile from the Nile ferry which takes people across the Nile to Juba. Evidently they did not want to have to explain us to any officials with whom they had business with their contraband.

91

Hans and I assisted Doug with his luggage, which was substantial, until we reached a village of Barias or fishermen people: tall, stark naked Nilotics, very impressive.

The village lay across from Juba on the east side of the Nile. The men rose to greet us, not a one of them being less than six feet tall, wearing only an occasional earring, bracelet or beaded belt for decoration. Fabulous people! Doug negotiated to have his gear ported for five bob. Then came the local girls, running, laughing, shaking our hands, all of them naked from the waist up. They giggled and stared closely into my blue eyes. I felt a little uncomfortable, being especially nervous about offending one of the massive men. The entire group of perhaps 20 people accompanied us to the ferry landing, where I amused them by sharing my binoculars to pass time. While crossing the Nile I wondered what I was getting into and what new challenges awaited.

We found lodging in Juba in a "rest house" for five bob apiece. The rest house was a long, rectangular wood building with bedrooms all in a row, each with a window opening onto a communal, screened porch. I had my own room and had thrown my backpack and clothing onto a chair between the bed and the window before retiring. In the middle of the night I awoke to see, framed in the window, a man in a hat crouching over my backpack. Instantly, both anger and fear erupted inside me. Someone had come through my window to rob me! Without thinking, I emitted a primal shriek and leaped from the bed to seize the miscreant by his neck, hoping to surprise him, wrestle him to the floor and arouse help from the neighboring rooms. My hands closed upon the backpack beneath my hat, which I had placed atop it when I had earlier removed it. There was no man. The pack and hat had produced a perfect illusion. I felt very embarrassed and stupid. By the time the lights came on and people were running to my room, I had barely a moment to think up a plausible, less foolish excuse. I had experienced a bad dream, I said. I thanked the people, and apologized for having awakened them so rudely. Then everybody tried to go back to sleep.

18 January • Juba, Sudan

We stocked up on supplies today and fought for third class bunks on the steamer. Everyone seemed to have forgotten last night's "dream" incident, or at least was kind enough not to mention it.

19 January • Juba, Sudan

I am aboard an historical Nile steamer. It certainly appears old enough to be historical. I just had a most unpleasant experience. I was talking with a Sudanese soldier when a violent old black man appeared, his harsh voice grating in English an incoherent jumble of phrases. "You must not! Blacks do not talk to whites! You are an American!"

Rather irked, but trying to be civil, I affirmed, "I am an American." Then, still shaking his fists in the air, he continued with some more black-white rot. "I do not like! Fuckin' white!" and so on. My soldier friend advised me to discretely vanish, which I did. As I turned away the old man shouted, "Go!" and thrust his fist, index finger extended dramatically upwards, and launched forth again. By now the soldiers were all awake and shouting at him to shut up. My soldier friend returned a short time later and said simply, "He is a madman." Then he left. I felt a bit shaken for a moment. I am always careful to avoid nasty situations. There is a good European contingent aboard and a number of soldiers, so there is probably little real danger from such a simpleton. But it is still unsettling. I have become accustomed to most Africans treating me in a good-natured way or with indifference.

It is 12:15 A.M. The steamer is comprised of several barges, lashed with steel cables to the paddlewheel driven unit. The compartment in which I am located has screened windows all around. A few lights still burn, and packs and clothing hang from hooks along the footway casting shadows of extraordinary shapes. The shadow of my pack resembles a tremendous, fat spider hanging in its web. There are 60 beds in my compartment, steel frames with 1.5 inch steel bands interwoven about eight inches apart forming a stiff latticework for support. People are arranged three deep in bunks, head to foot, each bank of bunks intersecting at right angles. A boy, perhaps 11 years old, sleeps on a straw mat beneath me on the floor. He wears baggy shorts and a large Army shirt. I think he may be the son of the man sleeping directly beneath me, as I am in the middle bunk. Hans is above me. Three Africans are at my feet, one beside me and three Europeans toward my head. All of us are comfy even with no mattresses. The smells of stale sweat and unwashed bodies are beginning to be noticeable. The night air has finally grown a bit cool. It is quiet except for a few voices murmuring in the background. Occasionally an Arab passes. The violent old man has subsided behind his stairway partition. Everybody appears to be equal here in third class. We sail at 6:00 A.M.

1:00 P.M. The Arabs have sacrificed three goats and at least one chicken. They stand on the victim's wings or legs and ceremoniously saw through the throat with a knife while twisting the animal's head back. The blood is very red and fairly jets from the severed arteries. However, it soon settles down to a steady flow as the animal quivers, kicks and dies. I believe the Koran requires them to kill animals in this ritual way. Animals which are not killed in this manner are considered unclean and inedible.

We stopped at three villages this morning. The process is always the same. The steamer approaches, blasts the whistle and drifts around 180° to face upstream. Then, as it collides with the bank, Arabs and Africans leap to the shore, while dozens of Nilotic villagers hurry down to the ship with bowls of milk, mysterious-looking gruel, goats, chickens, guinea fowl, chunks of firewood, peanuts, mangos etc., which they hope to sell. They are tall, well-built, very black people. Some have bows and steel-tipped arrows. Others carry spears. All have some sort of walking or throwing stick. Some men and women are covered with a white powder, probably clay, which gives them a ghostly appearance. Others have used red earth mixed with fat to color their hair. There are rings in ears and noses and tribal scars. The women are covered with a cloth, at least from the waist down. Some of the men are similarly clothed, but many wear only a belt or an anklet. I surreptitiously snap a couple of photos from the hip, as photography of these people is forbidden, and I do not want to lose my camera. They crowd up to the ship. If they come too close, police beat them back with rhinoceros hide whips and sticks. I step off the ship and walk among them. They appear healthy and strong and dirty. Here, dirt does not seem to matter. An Arab spits through his teeth. So does an African beside him. People spit everywhere without a thought.

The ship's whistle screeches, and the last of the village people scramble from the bank into the water, thrusting logs of firewood out toward the people aboard ship. One man has placed one of his logs on the ship but retains his grip with his right hand. Now an Arab takes hold of the other end of the log on the ship also using one hand. A tug of war ensues, while the African extends his free hand for some money. The Arab has some piasters in his free hand. Their hands come together gingerly as both try to hold the money. Then the African releases his grip on the log and claws the proffered money from the Arab's hand. The transaction has been successfully completed. This scene is repeated a dozen times. As the boat pushes off, one man in a final effort runs out holding a goat over his head. The goat is dragged aboard by a rope around its neck, and the money is tossed to the African in the water. Then the ship rotates about in a slow 180° turn and resumes its meanders back down the river.

Several fish eagles, darters (*Anhinga rufus*), and an occasional heron adorned the trees. Two hippos, looking very improbable, bobbed to the surface of the Nile then submerged again to feed on the bottom. One small crocodile swam past, about four feet long, rather punier than what I picture as the fierce Nile crocodile.

20 January • Nile River north of Juba, Sudan

The ship is progressing right along. Occasionally we crash into a bank or a floating island of papyrus on a turn, and sometimes the ship may even do a complete 360° cartwheel, before it continues down the Nile. By and large the journey is peaceful. Sometimes at night I am jarred awake in my steel bed by these minor navigational mishaps.

We wind through seemingly endless miles of papyrus swamps. Fish eagles are common; some have nests with young. Goliath herons (*Ardea goliath*) flush as we startle them on the banks. I saw another crock, a good six-footer, sunning himself on the bank. Hans, Doug and Ken have set up a crock watch so as to miss nothing big. So far no goats have been immolated today, probably because we have not taken more aboard. It should begin again at the next village.

There were about 15 pelicans in a tree. Although I am not certain, I believe them to be white pelicans (*Pelecanus onocrotalus*)

I read to pass time and have even learned a few rudiments of bridge. I am a miserable player, but my friends need a fourth person. I think the appropriate term is a "dummy."

21 January • Nile River north of Juba, Sudan

We just made a stop at another village. The usual assortment of merchants came out into the water. I purchased a nice grass mat to protect my tender body from the steel bed. I have just installed it and am happily reaping the rewards.

Last night I made an unsettling discovery: the ship navigates blindly at night. It is no surprise then, to discover our bodies suddenly slammed against the sides or feet of our beds at odd intervals as the ship collides with the bank. Why worry? The boat makes this trip every week.

22 January • Nile River nearing Malakal, Sudan

We are approaching Malakal now. We should arrive momentarily. The countryside has changed from high papyrus swamps to relatively short reeds swamp with increasing numbers of trees. Darters are exceedingly common as are Goliath herons, gray pelicans (*Pelecanus rufescens*) and yellow-billed kites. I saw a medium sized falcon, perhaps a lanner, but I could not be sure. There are also a vast number of small herons with a uniform creamy mantle and head, a few streaks on the throat and upper breast, white belly and a conspicuous white along the leading edge of the folded wings. I suspect them of being Squacco herons (*Ardeola ralliodes*). I saw a black-headed heron (*Ardea melanocephala*), several white egrets (*Casmerodius alba*), and 15 plovers; my best guess is they are white-shouldered plovers (*Hemiparra crassirostris*).

10:30 P.M. We are under way again after a brief stop in Malakal. It is a dingy, squalid little town with an array of dirty little shops side by side, each apparently selling the same basics as its neighbor. I tried to find a cold bottled drink. On the ship we whites only drink the warm, bottled soda or warm beer. In Malakal there were empty Pepsi bottles everywhere, but I could find no Pepsi for sale. I finally found a greasy little cave with tables, whose proprietor disappeared to run down "something" for us. He returned with U.S.-made Pepsi Cola bottles filled with lemonade. We drank it, hoping for the best, and are still experiencing some unpleasant side effects. Apparently the Pepsi bottles here are used only for bottling locally brewed fruit drinks, none of the original product being available.

Oh yes, I forgot to mention there are a number of Sudanese Catholic seminary aspiring priests aboard. They've been very friendly to me. They are gentle people, warm and guileless. Yesterday they gave me a large, cold, cooked potato as I lay in my bunk munching on a supper of fig bars, canned spaghetti and corned beef. I have been living on canned food, which I brought along to save money, so I accepted the potato as a generous and friendly offering and recipro-

Larry Crowley, Ulrich Mugler and Les Busch
in Berchtesgaden, Germany.

Campsite at St. Jean Cap Ferrat, France

Marble columns
in the Alahambra,
Granada, Spain.

View of Granada from the
Alahambra, Spain.

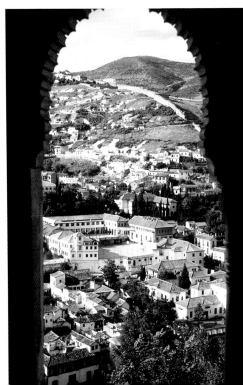

Gay and Gaile with Quimosabe, Malaga, Spain.

Gustl Eutermoser and the Woodfords, Rosenheim, Germany

Lorant D'Bastyai, Wales, England

Arriving at Cape Town, South Africa.

Susan, Ray Black and Gaile, Cape Town, South Africa.

The engine-blown VW, east of Cape Town, South Africa.

Rudi De Witt with martial eagle,
George, South Africa.

John Blignaut with a young
red-breasted sparrow hawk,
Humansdorp, South Africa.

Young red-breasted sparrow hawk, Humansdorp, South Africa.

Larry Crowley heading north, Mashaba, Southern Rhodesia

Victoria Falls, Livingstone, Northern Rhodesia.

The "Big Tree," a monster baobab, Livingstone, Northern Rhodesia.

Hans Norton and Larry Crowley stuck on the "Great North Highway," Mpika, Northern Rhodesia.

The general store, Mpika, Northern Rhodesia.

Young Masai, east of Arusha, Tanganyika.

Distant Kilimanjaro from downtown
Arusha, Tanganyika.

Kilimanjaro from Moshi, Tanganyika.

Ngorongoro Crater from the
east rim, Tanganyika.

Across the Serengeti Plain, Tanganyika.

The Equator, near Molo, Kenya.

The broken down truck with smugglers and Doug south of
Juba, Sudan.

Nile paddlewheel steamer north of Juba, Sudan.

A Nile Village north of Juba, Sudan.

Our paddlewheel steamer at dawn, Rabak, Sudan.

Trapping a pole line near Khartoum, Sudan.

Gasim Rizgala with female lanner Johara, Larry Crowley with tiercel saker Sindibad and Jack Mavrogordato with female peregrine Selema at Khartoum, Sudan.

A greedy, little haggard Barbary tiercel just trapped near Khartoum, Sudan

Jack Mavrogordato with fresh caught lanner falcon, Johara near Khartoum, Sudan.

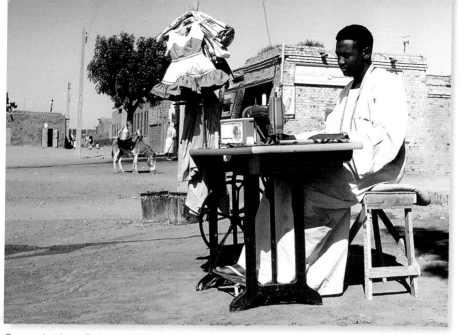

Our neighbor, Rahem Tulla, in the village square of Burri el Mahas, Khartoum, Sudan.

Water tower on which Jack used to see peregrines, but now has lanners and Barbaries, Khartoum, Sudan.

From left to right: Haggard female lanner, Johara; haggard female Barbary, Saidna; haggard tiercel saker, Sindibad; haggard tiercel lanner; passage tiercel lanner, Scruffy; passage tiercel Barbary; passage female peregrine, Selema.

Construction of the Sadd-el-Ali or high dam at Shellal, Egypt.

Temple of Horus at Edfu, Egypt.

Temple of Deir el Bahari, the mortuary temple of Queen Hatshepsut, Luxor, Egypt.

Hypostyle Hall at the Ramaseum, Luxor, Egypt.

Temple of Luxor, Luxor, Egypt.

Valley of the Kings,
Luxor, Egypt.

Painting of Horus in
the tomb of a noble,
Luxor, Egypt.

Unpleasant urchins in
Thebes, Luxor, Egypt.

Temple of Karnak, Luxor, Egypt.

118

King Djoser's Step Pyramid, Cairo, Egypt.

The Great Pyramid of King Khufu, Giza, Egypt.

The Massalia,
Alexandria, Egypt.

View from the Acropolis,
Athens, Greece.

Derek Moore and Jack Mavrogordato, together with Tessa, the Clumber spaniel, in the weathering yard at South Manor, Tilshead, England.

Leonard Potter with Venus on a rook kill, Salisbury Plain, England.

Leonard Potter, Gasim Rizgala and Derek Moore readying for a slip, Salisbury Plain, England.

Germany on a rook kill, Salisbury Plain, England.

Gasim with Dhib on a rook kill, Salisbury Plain, England.

Venus, intermewed passage peregrine falcon.

Pearl, haggard female
lanner falcon.

Shiva, haggard female
saker falcon.

Dhib, haggard
female saker falcon.

Germany, eyass
tiercel saker falcon.

Germany, eyass tiercel saker falcon.

Sindibad, haggard tiercel saker falcon.

Madam Butterfly, eyass female eagle owl.

Willi Meyer and Kurt Koller, Akureyri, Iceland.

Larry Crowley at the cave with the hot springs, Námaskard, Iceland.

Eyass gyrfalcons in nest, Dimmuborgir, Iceland.

cated with half a box of fig bars. Later, I received a beautiful green mango. Today, before I could even stir from bed I was presented a sheet of newspaper in which lay six small fish, freshly netted and still gasping, which they had purchased from a Shilluk, the tribe of the local people here, in a village where the boat had last stopped. Naturally, I had to clean, cook and eat the fish. But, fortunately I was able to enlist some friends to help me orally dispose of the tasteless little creatures. This afternoon the final gift arrived, a cold, very greasy chicken wing, fortunately cooked, which I ate as best I could. These boys have been so nice asking about America and my trip. I showed them Denver on a map and gave them a history book to read. Tonight, they are about to leave the ship at the next village and have been saying their good-byes. I shall miss them, even though I have scarcely spoken with them, and even though they look alike to me: tall, black, thick lipped, toothy, warm, smiling faces with a row of knotted, tribal scars from temple to temple across their foreheads, their gentle voices saying, "We will pray for God to watch over your journey, Lawrence." I think with some sadness of the difficulties these men will face here in Arab Moslem Sudan, a country that wants to eliminate Christianity. A fleeing missionary told me about entire villages that had been killed off by northern soldiers.

23 January • Nile River somewhere north of Malakal, Sudan
It is another beautiful day, cool and sunny with a nice breeze and a slight haze which keeps the heat down. Since we left Juba the weather has become steadily cooler and more pleasant. The breeze helps remove or at least ameliorate the sour odor of cooking goat which permeates the atmosphere. It is a rather sickening stench which does little to promote my appetite. Of 19 goats brought aboard two days ago, 14 remain, the other five having died gushing blood from gashed throats as have dozens of chickens and doves. The deck runs red with blood, but the washing of clothing and pots in the same spots soon clears it away.

Insects have been pleasantly absent during the voyage except for a few mosquitoes in the evening. Perhaps the grimmest areas aboard are the toilets, of which there are several: the crew's, first class, second class, and third class (our class). They each consist of a flat, porcelain plate perforated by a hole, upon which one stands and squats. They are covered in filth. I delay a trip there as long as possible, until biological demands must be addressed. I once found myself urinating while standing on one foot just to avoid the slime.

25 January • Kosti, Sudan

1:00 P.M. I am aboard the train to Khartoum, just pulling out of Kosti. The steamship arrived last night, but a turntable bridge which spans the Nile obstructed the river and prevented our landing. This morning I left the ship at Rabak to catch the express bus to Kosti. I learned that the bus left for neighboring Kosti at 6:00 A.M., not 7:00 A.M., as it was supposed to. Three Sudanese in a van picked me up and took me to Kosti. One of them, Mustafa, took me to his home, a modest structure of brick, roofed with tin and with a dirt floor. Being very hospitable, he spread a tremendous breakfast of delicious fresh bread, sardines, fried eggs, tomatoes, fresh-fried beef liver and heart and tea. I ate, unable to refuse his generosity. He would not permit me to stop until I had convinced him I was entirely full. We spoke about his family, of how the Sudanese people wept for President Kennedy, about Egypt and Sudan and of my home. It is my understanding that the religion of Islam requires treating strangers with kindness and generosity. But, I think this good man was not only adhering to the dictates of the Koran; he was genuinely interested in exchanging ideas and time with me.

When I had finished eating, he led me outside to a water tap, where I washed up. Then we took a bus, for which he also paid, into the main market place and to his office. The office consisted of a tiny, open cell, one of many in a block-long clay building. Then he made me comfortable and fed me up on bananas, peanuts, dates and raisins. He called his family, with whom I spoke on the phone, the first I have seen in Sudan. Then, his brother and father came down to the shop to personally meet me. Again, there was small talk and pleasantries. Mustafa set a watch up the street for my companions, Hans, Ken and Doug, from the boat; they arrived at 11:00 A.M. After another round of bananas, we were off to shop for supplies and train tickets.

We are crossing the desert now. It is absolutely flat with remnants of short grass, burned brown in the powdery, tan, sandy dust. There are occasional shrubs and trees. Now and then a donkey laden with sticks and a rider jogs past. It is hot, and dust rolls into the car through the permanently open windows. There are some Sudanese soldiers on board. They seem friendly enough and carry small, automatic weapons which appear to be in poor repair. I wonder if any of them have participated in the genocide in the South, about which the Arab North permits no one to speak. Since we are white strangers just passing through, I am guessing that our presence on the train is of little consequence to these men. The only birds I've seen are jackal buzzards, one chanting goshawk (*M.metabates*), one European roller (*Coracias garrulous*) and one Abyssinian roller (*Coracias abyssinica*).

26 January • Khartoum, Sudan

I arrived in Khartoum at 3:15 A.M. after a long ride from Kosti, which was made more pleasant by playing cutthroat bridge with my three colleagues and by reading a James Bond novel, *Moonraker*, which was lousy. After farewells to Doug, Ken and Hans, all of whom are heading north, I learned that Jack Mavrogordato is not yet here to receive me. So, I returned to my traveling companions; we spent the rest of the chill morning clandestinely sleeping aboard some first class coaches in the railroad yard. I awoke with a start to discover our train moving. After the initial shock and having jumped out of my sleeping bag, I found there was no problem; the train was just getting cars hooked up for a trip to Wadi Halfa. We left the railroad yard at 6:00 A.M. to wander the waking city. We watched the markets setting up, then having bid my comrades another farewell, I set out to find Jack.

I finally encountered him at the Sudan Club, a traditional haven for British expatriates. He explained that due to ship delays from a dock strike in Port Sudan, he had only just arrived two days prior in Khartoum; therefore, nothing was as yet prepared. Jack and I spent the rest of the day looking for a house to rent. For supper Jack treated me to a meal in the garden at the Sudan Club. We dined on pigeons from the local *suk* (market), fending off feral cats, which had to be physically knocked off our table.

Perhaps a word is in order about Jack's connection to Sudan. Jack had been a career diplomat who spent many years in colonial Sudan. He had learned Arabic and trapped and studied falcons here throughout those years. At the time when Sudan gained its independence from British rule in 1956, Jack was the Attorney General for the Sudan. He actually drafted the provisional constitution for the new country. Of course, the new independent parliamentary government was quickly overthrown by a coup d'état, so Jack's constitution was short-lived. He has important history here.

27 January • Khartoum, Sudan

2:45 P.M. Jack and I just finished a fine roast beef meal at the Sudan Club. Jack was upset. He had been to see President Abboud to try to get some presidential assistance in liberating his Land Rover, still aboard ship at Port Sudan. A palace guard, who had no knowledge of or interest in Jack nor of his history in Sudan, physically threw Jack down the palace steps. Jack was justifiably incensed by this treatment. He did prevail, met with the president and secured a letter to authorize the release of his vehicle.

I am presently on the bank of the Blue Nile watching kites and the occasional tiny sailboat pass by. I can see a large, black and white, checkerboard patterned water tower across the river, upon which Jack says peregrines commonly perch. To my right is a steel arched bridge from which we watched a Barbary tiercel (*Falco pelegrinoides*) effortlessly fly out and kill a bat yesterday in the evening twilight. Behind me is the Catholic cathedral, around which Jack saw another Barbary flying this morning. None of the falcons are here now, as it is too warm in these exposed places; they are cooling off elsewhere in leafy solitude. There is a gentle wind. It is a beautiful day. In an hour or so we will go off to visit the only other falconer in Khartoum, Daoud Marrash.

We were successful in renting a little house, to which we now refer as *Bait es Sugúr*, home of the hawk, in a village, Burri el Mahas, on the outskirts of Khartoum. Jack bought some furniture and necessities, while we talked endlessly about falconry. To relax afterward we went to an open-air theater and saw *Shane*: the third time for me, and the first for Jack. I am presently trying to catch up on correspondence.

Mom sent me a letter. Among other things, she says the University of Colorado has sent an expedition to the Wadi Halfa area, on the Egypt–Sudan border, to do some rushed, last minute excavating of archaeological sites before the area is flooded by Lake Nasser. It's questionable that I can locate them. The upper Nile is a big river, and that is all I know about the area.

Oh yes, Chou en Lai, Premiere of the People's Republic of Chi-

132

na, arrived today from China to many welcoming posters and decorations. I doubt that he received a large reception. [He did not.]

29 January • Khartoum, Sudan

We discussed Jack's new book, tentatively entitled *A Falcon in the Field*. He wrote it while incarcerated aboard his ship in the Red Sea by a dock-men's strike at Port Sudan; it is to be a companion to his first book, *A Hawk for the Bush*.

Today we tried our hand at mist netting some birds for decoys. Mist nets are made of very fine strands of thread and erected to form invisible walls which then ensnare birds that try to fly through them. No luck, due to too much wind and poor locations. We got ourselves outfitted with a rental VW bug for £1.5 Sudanese per day for a minimum of two weeks rental. God knows when Jack's Land Rover, still impounded aboard ship at Port Sudan, will get here. All of his trapping equipment is in it. Meanwhile, we are mobile again! We bought a pigeon in the suk el Arab to use for bait tomorrow on our first trapping endeavor. We scouted out three falcons on a water tower in Khartoum this evening, probably all lanners but one possibly a Barbary. We also saw our tiercel Barbary on the bridge and a large, pale, haggard (adult) female peregrine with a broad malar patch was also there. We will have to look her over more closely. Meanwhile, Jack and I have been making a harness, barrak, Arab net, and dho gazza (various types of traps), to use tomorrow trapping. It is frustrating for Jack, since he brought all of these in his ship-bound Land Rover. We have to start from scratch making all of our equipment anew. We plan to leave for trapping at five in the morning. It is interesting and fun to learn how to actually tie a net from scratch. Jack is an excellent teacher.

I have seen lots of birds around Khartoum: white-vented bulbuls (*Pycnonotus barbatus*), blue-naped mouse birds (*Colius macrourus*), long-tailed nightjars (*Scotornis climacurus*), mourning doves (*Streptopelia decipiens*), laughing doves (*Stigmatopelia senegalensis*), and long-tailed doves (*Oena capensis*) are all common. There are some Egyptian vultures and yellow-billed kites, and I saw one hoopoe.

30 January • Khartoum, Sudan

We were up at 5:00 A.M. and drove east to a line of pylons, huge poles which support electric wires and on which raptors like to perch. Then we waited until it was light enough to see, about 6:00 A.M. We caught a "red" (first-year bird in immature plumage) tiercel Barbary in Jack's thirty-two inch × six-foot dho gazza, a net trap, using a young pigeon as bait. He knocked down the net on his first passes, seized the pigeon without becoming enmeshed, and remained atop his quarry, trying to dispatch it until we drove him off. He circled around while we re-set the net. We had him on his next pass, had the net packed up and were on our way within half an hour of first sighting him.

Next, we spotted a lanner which spooked and flew off. Then we found a haggard lanner, which was not in the least interested in our pigeon. We spotted a third lanner, red, which we decided to leave unbothered, as it was not on our list. We had made a list of birds we wanted to trap, which included those we would like to take back to England to hawk rooks, plus those requested by several of Jack's friends. We moved on to yet another lanner which we trapped easily between 7:30 A.M. and 8:00 A.M. It was a nice, brownish, spotted haggard female. She not only crashed into the net, but even ran back a yard dragging it along to kill the pigeon. There was much "rubbish," Jack's term for raptors useless for hawking, about, mostly Egyptian vultures, but none harassed the birds we were trying to trap. The weather was perfect and without wind.

We quit at 8:00 A.M., since it gets too warm here after that, and the falcons will normally not come in. Our trapping chances are good now because the falcons are queuing up for their trip north. Jack says Barbaries will leave in about a week. Sakers ought to be concentrated for the next two weeks. Then there will be a vacuum.

Jack has a little game he enjoys. As a personal challenge, occasionally he tries to start from scratch on a trapping day. That is, he first has to trap one or more bait birds; then he sets out to find a trappable falcon, preferably a saker, and finally, actually trap it. We have tried our luck a couple of times, but were successful only once at mist netting the required sparrows and getting out to catch our falcon. The main problem lies in securing the lure birds early enough to be able to trap a falcon before the heat of the oncoming day makes trapping impossible.

Most of our day was spent mist netting one sparrow; then we went shopping for provisions for Bait es Sugúr. Jack drove off in the VW and promptly destroyed a running board on a concrete abutment.

We began the taming process, "manning" our new falcons this

evening. Jack's lanner is a marvel. After her initial conniptions, seeming paralysis of legs, loss of balance, hissing, biting — the usual behavior of a newly caught bird — she quite calmed down, and after feeding bareheaded she allowed herself to be carried about nicely, without a bate (attempt to jump off the fist). Jack is very proud. He is looking at a revision of our "want list" for Tilshead to include a haggard lanner.

My tiercel Barbary, destined for Col. Meredith back in the U.S.A., was able to eat bareheaded, but subsequently went into a bating frenzy punctuated by panicked shrieks. I finally hooded him upside down. Jack awarded the lanner first place, the tiercel a distant second. It was no contest!

Daoud Marásh dropped by at 11:30 P.M. with a treasure box of hoods, leashes, gloves, swivels and other very useful items to substitute for those which are in the Land Rover. We now have a stock phrase, to be uttered when someone needs anything we do not have: "It's in the Land Rover." Daoud is a longtime friend of Jack; he lives here in Khartoum working as a printer. He is a falconer and prefers to fly lanners at small birds. Jack says it is a terrifying sight to see this six-foot-plus man thrashing a bush to death with a big stick, trying to evict some unfortunate dicky-bird for his circling lanner.

31 January • Khartoum, Sudan

9:00 A.M. Jack's lanner is really settling down. She hasn't bated yet, and she hoods and unhoods with only a token opening of her beak. She is even good out-of-doors in full sunlight. My tiercel has quieted down, too. After an initial monster bate upon being unhooded, he bated no more, and he reacted well to hooding and unhooding. He occasionally bites viciously at my fingers, scorning the fountain pen I proffer as a finger substitute; he knows well that biting it does not hurt me.

7:30 P.M. Jack and I have been carrying our birds about for an hour. Jack's lanner is very good. She sits quite composed, allowing Jack to stroke her and hood her nicely. She has not bated yet. The Barbary is progressing. He still stares at me, but he eats readily bareheaded. I gave him an acid test tonight. After two bates in the house, I took him, and Jack brought the lanner, outside to the village store next door. There, seated on a string bed, we were surrounded by children of various sizes, all of whom lacked any caution or self-control around the falcons. Both birds did well among the running, jumping, gesticulating urchins. They did not bate and fed well bareheaded.

A check of the bridge and water towers this evening revealed no birds on the bridge nor on the tower on the south side of the river. However, on the great rectangular water tower on the north side we observed a beautiful haggard Barbary, probably a female. Toward sunset three probable lanners, one for certain, came in; two of these retired to the latticework beneath the tower, disappearing into a stick nest (perhaps breeding?). The third bird usurped the Barbary's perch with a long, menacing stoop. The Barbary shifted to an inferior position.

1 February • Khartoum, Sudan

Jack and I worked the pylon line from 6:00 A.M. to 8:30 A.M., finding three lanners, four Barbaries and three sakers. One of the sakers was a real monster. We tried to trap the first saker with a dho gazza and a sparrow. She left the perch before we could get out of the way, flew over for a look and decided it was not worthwhile. We tried in vain for the next half hour to coax her down again. Since it was late, and since we had missed our saker, we trapped a little Barbary haggard tiercel for sport. He came in with a full gorge after a five-minute delay. What a greedy little bird but picture pretty! We photographed and released him.

On the way back we saw our third lanner, a tiercel which we needed for a barrak hawk, but as it was late, we did not try. A barrak or bundle hawk is a small, non-intimidating raptor used for trapping; it is released with a dead sparrow, which has been wrapped in a nylon noose-covered, leather device, attached to one of its feet. Larger raptors like sakers, seeking an easy meal, will frequently attempt to rob a lesser bird of its prey. The barrak hawk is loosed with some of its primary wing feathers tied together with thread, so it cannot fly strongly. Hopefully, a greedy saker will see it, attempt to rob it and become entangled in the nooses, thus trapped.

This evening, we took our birds outside for another interlude with the neighborhood children. My bird bated three times, Jack's not once. Jack again awarded his lanner first place. We fed them on two laughing doves and a gray hornbill (*Tockus nasutus*), which I had shot in an afternoon foray to a nearby wooded area.

2 February • Khartoum, Sudan

We mist netted three more sparrows on our veranda. Jack and I carried our birds an hour this morning to a carpenter's shop with lots of kids; there was banging, sawing, shouting and other distraction. We kept the falcons hooded until we reached the shop then unhooded them within. Both birds reacted well. Mine is still nervous and stares at me, but he had only one bate. Jack's lanner remains serene; she still has not bated once, due in no small part to Jack's judicious use of the hood. He has decided he would like to train this bird with no bates at all, a worthy and difficult challenge for the old master.

I have been making nylon nooses for a pigeon harness trap. The harness is a sort of vest made from a piece of leather that bristles with nylon monofilament nooses and is fitted onto a hapless bait pigeon. I also just finished making a barrak bundle, which rather resembles a tiny leather octopus covered with nooses.

We went to a forest near Gordon's tree. It was all fenced in, so we couldn't get close enough to see if sakers and lanners still roost there. Jack says they used to. Gordon's tree was named for English General Charles Gordon, a governor general of Sudan, who was killed in an uprising by a religious fanatic known as the Mahdi in 1875. Gordon was hacked to pieces and his head was affixed to the branches of the tree "where all who passed it could look in disdain, children could throw stones at it and the hawks of the desert could sweep and circle above." We did see a large flock of Maribou storks there, which perhaps ironically are scavengers.

3 February • Khartoum, Sudan

This morning was spent rounding up a refrigerator, but we had no luck getting it to work. There is no word yet on the Land Rover in Port Sudan. Jack is in a black mood with a bad cold. He has been rather disagreeable throughout the day. He is depressed, what with being ill, and nothing seems to be going right. We now have three stock phrases which we have had to repeatedly use to rationalize our poor run of luck and failure to accomplish many of our goals. We have assigned them numbers. Phrase one is "It's in the Land Rover." Phrase two, "It's Ramadan." Ramadan is a holy season, during which nothing gets done. And, phrase three, "You're joking, of course." Sometimes humor helps.

The only real run of good luck we have had has been where it most counts, with our falcons. Col. Meredith's little Barbary tiercel is getting quite friendly now. He hoods well and has almost made up his mind to jump to my fist for food. He sits bareheaded with his wings half open arched almost over his back, with tail spread, and seems quite interested in his surroundings. Jack's lanner is relaxed and unconcerned about anything. She is always gentle and exhibits a reserved dignity. Whereas my tiercel has an appetite, the lanner scarcely eats. We weighed them both tonight. The Barbary tiercel weighs 14½ ounces. The lanner is in excess of 26 ounces, bigger, Jack says, than the average female lanner. Our damned scales only weigh up to 24 ounces, so we have to estimate everything over that.

Jack and I visited the bridge to Omdurman, since falcons like to hang out there, and another pole line this evening. We found a big falcon and trapped her with Jack's infallible dho gazza in hope that she was a peregrine. No indeed! She turned out to be a quite large and beautiful haggard female Barbary. She came right in to a bait pigeon. She also weighs in excess of 26 ounces and seems heavier than the lanner. Jack says lannerets weigh about 17–21 ounces, and females weigh 23–28 ounces. Jack did once catch a 13-ounce lanneret. He gives Barbary tiercel weights between 14 and 15½ ounces, while females weigh in around 22½.

In our haste to trap a barrak hawk we set up a sparrow and dho gazza for a tiny bird we thought to be a kestrel on a pole. Jack was amazed that it did not come right in and said, "If they are coming at all, they usually start by now." It remained unmoved by our efforts. Close binocular scrutiny revealed the reason. It was an electric insulator. We both felt a bit foolish as we hauled in our trap.

At sunset a peregrine flew from the Omdurman water tower beside the Nile; it was hunting and returned with a house sparrow a few minutes later. There we also saw at least two kestrels (*Falco tinnunculus*), only the second time we have seen any here. Jack says they should be common; he can't understand why they are so scarce.

We returned to a tasty supper, including *ful Sudani*, a type of peanut soup prepared by our venerable cook, Mohamed Ziada, a turtle-like old gentleman that Jack has hired to prepare our evening meals. I played with the new and hooded Barbary falcon and found her quite steady. She bated only twice at the outset of first standing her on my fist. She hissed and puffed up but did not bite or bate. After a couple of half-hour sessions of carrying and stroking, she calmed down well. I put her on a rock in the mews, a spare room in which we house our falcons, for the night.

4 February • Khartoum, Sudan

Jack spent the morning running down information about his Land Rover. With his single shot .22 I killed some laughing doves in the woods by the river here by Burri el Mahas. Our falcons require fresh food, and these doves provide excellent nutrition. I finished making a pigeon harness for Jack, a real masterpiece with one hundred nooses. I want to snag a falcon or two to show Jack how it works.

Jerboas are little desert rodents with large jumping hind lags, big black eyes and long tufted tails. Raptors love to eat them. Hence, they make terrific bait for trapping. After dark it was time for jerboa hunting with Gasim Rizgala, a Sudanese friend of Jack who lives here in Khartoum. Gasim is my age. He has been to England with Jack and is very knowledgeable and clever with falcons as well as at helping us get any things done here that require an Arabic speaker who is familiar with the city. After a drive north out of Khartoum along a dirt track we cut into the desert across the sand, dodging bushes and occasional trees.

Our jerboa hunting consisted of driving through likely looking, barren desert with one of us perched upon the hood of the auto, net in hand, until any of us spotted a tiny, ghostly shape skittering in the periphery of the headlights. Then the chase was on, as the auto pursued the fleeing critter which zigged and zagged in a frantic, hopping gallop, until it finally stopped, its huge black eyes bulging, and crouched waiting to see what would happen next. The catcher then leaped from the hood of the car and approached quickly afoot with a long-handled butterfly-type net. If lucky he would plop the net over the cowering jerboa with no further incident. More often the jerboa regained its senses, although dazzled by the car lights, and fled again, this time pursued by both the car, which endeavored to keep it in the lights, and by the catcher, who beat the ground with great, swinging arcs of the net, usually a step behind the jerboa. We caught four and missed three. That is not a bad evening. No doubt we have established a benchmark for future jerboa hunters to emulate or surpass.

Our vehicle had a flat tire on the return trip home. That automatically canceled morning trapping.

5 February • Khartoum, Sudan

Jack's ship-bound Land Rover is on the way! It has left Port Sudan and should arrive any moment. And, Jack has won a telling victory over the *telaja* (refrigerator) salesman who held until now a strong position, having first secured Jack's £15 and then stalled four days on delivery of what looked like the first refrigerator ever brought to the Sudan. In any case Jack got his money back and has secured a working refrigerator for us.

With these two great pieces of information comes yet more ill fortune. Jack has injured his left knee; he now hops about with pain and difficulty. We seem to be getting our share of setbacks and bad luck. The surprising part is that our efforts with the falcons continue to go splendidly.

The male Barbary is feeding and standing well bareheaded on the fist in daylight out-of-doors. The lanner, as ever, is unruffled by everything including food. She eats perhaps one sparrow per day. The new female Barbary still exceeds the scale's capacity. She has settled down pretty well. Jack fed her bareheaded last night. Today he took her out-of-doors for a few minutes, unhooded and without incident. Then he set her back on her rock in the mews. She has a pretty, buffy-reddish head and nape. She is a very compact, short-tailed and stubby-winged, powerful bird. Jack and I are wondering if she will be the first Barbary to kill rooks on Salisbury Plain.

I shot three laughing doves and one turtledove (*Streptopelia turtur*) for the falcons this morning. It is currently siesta time. We are awaiting Ramadan breakfast, an evening meal taken after sunset, with an old associate of Jack. We will visit his home, and it should be a good feast. Ramadan breakfasts literally break fast which has been ongoing since sunrise. Since we are invited guests, our host will make sure that we have large quantities of excellent food. Tomorrow we go after sakers.

6 February • Khartoum, Sudan

We arrived at the pylons at 6:05 A.M., exactly on time, as it was just light enough to see. We found three lanners. Apparently the Barbaries have moved north, and we may not see them again. We trapped a 19-ounce haggard lanneret (male) on a sparrow-dho gazza net combination. We almost caught another lanner when we tested a new, low dho gazza in a stiff breeze. We set it upwind of the bird, which

140

was on a pylon, bait sparrow to the windward side. The net billowed out considerably toward the falcon. She would not come to the sparrow, so we substituted a jerboa which immediately got her attention. She came in low and flew up and over the net being suspicious of it. However, she then rolled and stooped from the bait side, plucking our jerboa deftly from behind the net and flying off to eat it. The jerboa, which had been tethered by a string around its neck to a peg, had been torn loose. All that remained was its head. Oops! Shortly thereafter we caught a red lanneret, which we will use as a barrak hawk.

One harrier, the only one I've seen since I got to Khartoum, flew by. We found and photographed the nest of a pair of tawny eagles (*Aquila rapax*). Both adults were present, one apparently incubating in the great stick nest about three-quarters up the pylon. There were two brown-necked ravens (*Corvus corax*), also incubating nests on the pylons. Small flocks of crested larks (*Galerida cristata*) and short-billed larks (*Calandrella brachydactyla*) flushed as we drove past. Egyptian vultures were common everywhere, as were the ubiquitous yellow-billed kites. I saw an osprey (*Pandion haliaetus*) improbably perched on the desert sand. Pied crows appeared in scattered pairs.

This afternoon we drove along the river in the acacia forest. I shot a long-tailed dove, an Abyssinian wood dove (*Turtur abyssinia*) and a gorgeous bird, a carmine bee-eater (*Merops nubians*). As usual, we saw a lot of laughing doves and blue-naped mouse birds.

Gasim fed up our new lanneret, now the designated barrak hawk, with the bird hooded this evening. Gasim seemed very proud of his accomplishment. Meredith's tiercel jumped three times to the fist over a yard's distance for food. The lanner female is still apathetic but reluctantly ate a jerboa. The Barbary female gobbled down a dove while hooded and cautiously nibbled while unhooded. She is still nervous and stares.

7 February • Khartoum, Sudan

Jack and I trapped along the pole line that runs about 35 miles to Jebel Auria this morning and found not a trace of a warrantable falcon. We did see six Egyptian vultures, a few yellow-billed kites, two more pairs of ravens and both crested and short-billed larks. This evening we returned to the pylons. We found one saker and set the net upwind, this time with the jerboa between the net and the saker. I wanted to try a downwind set up, as I do not think a falcon would have as easy an opportunity to throw up (fly straight up at the last second) over the net with the wind behind her. Jack was not yet ready to experiment. The saker was perched on a pylon together with vultures and a lanneret. The vultures shifted the lanneret to the next pylon; the saker stood her ground. We had pitched the dho gazza already, so now it lay between the saker and the lanneret. The lanneret stooped to the jerboa, and to our disgust it spotted the net, pitched up, then circled back and crashed into the net. After we had retrieved the lanneret and reset the net, the saker ignored our attempts. Jack walked in on her and discovered she had a tremendous crop of food. We left her for the night.

8 February • Khartoum, Sudan

Returning to the pylon line this morning, we had hoped to set up early on the saker; but she had left by the time we arrived. We continued on until we found another saker. I set the net as usual, and she came almost immediately, but she saw the net at the last second, threw up and circled back to the pylon. She would not come again and eventually flew off to the river. We carried on east and found yet another saker. This one came in after a good ten-minute's deliberation, but even with a pylon providing a disruptive background she saw the net, flew up and over, then sat down about 30 feet away on the ground. A passing truck displaced her; she would not be coaxed down again. Jack is of the opinion that sakers, unlike other falcons once they detect any trap, will not come into any other. This seems to be our experience. Possibly only the intelligent ones make it to the Sudan past the many falcon trappers in the Middle East.

On the way back I spotted what proved to be a red female peregrine on a pylon. Jack was astonished, as she was the first red peregrine he had seen here in 15 years. We trapped her easily with a pigeon and dho gazza, She was a very dark, sooty brown bird. Jack was extremely pleased.

We found one more saker, perhaps the same one we saw last night, at the west end of the pylons. She kept looking at something in the opposite direction and would not come to the bait. We drove home with our prize peregrine.

Jack's car arrived! It is "home" and unloaded. Stock phrase one, "Its in the Land Rover," is now obsolete. That makes two giant victories today, the peregrine and the Land Rover.

142

Since we now have a decent scale from the newly arrived Land Rover, we weighed the birds this evening. Their weights follow:

Peregrine female, red	35.5 oz
Lanner female, haggard	26.5 oz
Lanner male, haggard	18.0 oz
Lanner male, red	17.0 oz
Barbary female, haggard	28.0 oz
Barbary male, red	14.5 oz

The peregrine is a hurricane, even hooded, and will not yet eat. She is very jumpy, holds every feather erect and bates wildly. Her beak is badly scarred from an old injury; she is not a beautiful falcon. As of last night the lanner female is jumping to the fist. Gasim, Jack's Sudanese assistant, is dealing with the haggard lanneret, which by the way has been reprieved from bundle hawk duty, and has been resentenced to exile in the U.S.A. via Geoffrey Pollard, a British falconer friend of Jack. The new red lanneret has become the designated barrak hawk. The Barbary female is eating well hooded but not bareheaded. Jack is not rushing her. The tiercel Barbary is flying about four feet to my fist and has become very tame.

I observed the osprey along the pylons again today as well as most of the birds mentioned yesterday. In addition I saw small flocks of chestnut finch larks (*Eremopterix leucotis*).

This afternoon I shot four laughing doves and one turtledove in my acacia forest. I saw two Gabar goshawks (*Micronisus gabar*) flitting and gliding stealthily through the trees at dusk. There were also several gray hornbills.

9 February • Khartoum, Sudan

We left Bait es Sugúr at 5:45 A.M. for the pylons. We had a 30-ounce haggard sakret by 6:30 A.M. We spotted him on a pylon and decided to try our barrak hawk. Jack tossed out our bird, now named "Scruffy," with four primaries tied together on one wing and three on the other wing, replete with noosed sparrow barrak attached to his feet. Scruffy's hampered flight hopefully would make robbing him irresistible to a saker. We were 300 yards upwind of the saker, and Scruffy lumbered directly toward it. The saker sat tight until our barrak hawk had almost landed just beneath his pylon. Then he stooped beautifully and bound to the bundle in Scruffy's feet. Both birds fell to the ground flapping about in a cloud of dust and feathers. A tell-tale space between their feet indicated the saker had been snared. Overjoyed, we rushed in to secure both birds. One-and-a-half hours later our new bird sat quietly hooded on my fist with no bates, bites or conniptions. An hour later he bated when I picked him up, then settled down. Jack says he is atypically tame and should normally be throwing fits for 48 hours. He is a very nice falcon.

Our mews looks rather full now with seven assorted falcons. Gasim is to handle the three lanners, Jack the Barbary female and peregrine, and I the sakret and Meredith's Barbary tiercel.

We had another sortie to the pylons this evening, leaving at 4:30 P.M. and driving until sundown. We found a very tame Barbary falcon on a pylon; she allowed us to walk around the pylon beneath her. She was a lovely haggard bird.

We drove on to Baquier, the end of the stretch of poles along which Jack traps, and found one saker for which we tossed up our bundle hawk. The saker put in one half-hearted stoop as Scruffy landed in a bush. Jack chased him out, but the saker was through. We ended our outing with a twilight pursuit of little Scruffy over railroad tracks and through the desert until we finally got him back. Obviously, if we expect to retrieve a barrak hawk, we had best be in wide-open, uncluttered terrain.

Earlier, the new sakret went through a good half hour of bates and craziness until he was panting very hard. He just continued to leap blindly from anything on which he was standing, be it fist, perch, rock or even the floor. I finally eased him onto a rock perch. Tonight he hissed and puffed up and gave a good show but did finally settle down to eat half a laughing dove, hooded of course, ripping out great mouthfuls. Fortunately he gave out before finishing the dove, thus sparing my hand wounds and deformations from his powerful beak. No bates tonight.

Jack's peregrine ate hooded tonight after a good windmill bating session. She is still pretty nervous, but progressing.

10 February • Khartoum, Sudan

Jack and I made another pylon run this morning. The only bird we observed was last night's saker. We tossed out Scruffy the barrak hawk only to lure in a greedy tawny eagle. The saker was uninterested. Scruffy was retrieved unharmed.

144

Jack and I fed the peregrine and sakret bareheaded tonight. First we let them have a few bites hooded in a dimly lighted room; then we removed the hoods, continued feeding, hooded the birds again, gave them a few more bites and so on. The peregrine was initially hissy and bated then settled down nicely and fed. She rehooded without a bate. The sakret bated twice, fed calmly bareheaded and was rehooded without a bate. I am including details of our training and the birds' reactions for comparative purposes. I am curious about differences in the personalities of the different species and individuals.

Tonight, about two hours after feeding our birds we gave them more practice with hooding. The peregrine did not bate at all but stared at Jack continuously, a sign of distrust and fear. She took the hood without protest. The sakret bated initially but was fairly calm; he frequently roused, that is shook his feathers to realign them, kept his feathers relaxed, and chanced an occasional look around the room. A few times he bobbed his head in preparation for a bate, but I forestalled that by rotating in a circle to keep him from fixating on any choice prospective perch. He accepted the hood well, even though I had some trouble with feathers catching in the braces (leather strips that open and close the hood).

11 February • Khartoum, Sudan

I awoke to the beat of the "Phantom Drummer of Burri el Mahas" this morning. At dawn a daily ritual occurs. A villager whom we have not yet seen strolls through the village beating a drum, presumably to help us all recognize that day has once again begun.

We carried the peregrine and sakret briefly this morning, practicing hooding and unhooding. The sakret was surprisingly calm and rational. He did bate once out-of-doors, but for the most part was calm. The peregrine is still nervous and stares at us.

This morning Jack took me to the suk in Omdurman, a city on the west side of the Nile across from Khartoum. The bulk of the morning was spent purchasing a snakeskin and two lizard skins with which to make hoods. Jack also bought an immense python skin for June Woodford who will use it to make hoods and other falconry equipment.

This afternoon was chiefly devoted to repairing the Land Rover, which Jack says is suffering from "heat exhaustion." I shot five laughing doves for the birds. The sakret ate one as did the tiercel Barbary. Jack named his beautiful Barbary female "Saidna." She refuses to feed bareheaded because she is still too fearful. She is only one-and-one-half ounces lighter than the sakret, which dwarfs her in other dimensional measurements, so she possibly is extremely fat. The sakret, now named "Sindibad," feeds well bareheaded. I exposed him to the mob of neighborhood children, but that was still too much for him. He is such a reasonable bird. He seems quite intelligent.

12 February • Khartoum, Sudan

We returned to the pylon line this morning and found a saker before sunup. We pitched the Arab net trap near the base of the pylon adjacent to hers, hoping it would form a disruptive background. With poor light conditions, the camouflaged background and no wind, we had ideal trapping conditions. Using our champion jerboa, a veteran of limitless energy, as bait we induced the saker to come in with a hard, fast stoop. At the very last second she pitched up and flew plumb out of sight. Jack's wisdom proved true again.

Sakers only have to spot a trap once to be spoiled; then, once their suspicions have been aroused, they usually fly away and almost never come back. We found a Barbary, a probable haggard female, at the far end of the pylon line. It was a very pretty bird, unconcerned by our presence, and it watched us with interest. We did not try for her.

There is great trouble with the car now. It overheats for no seeming reason. Jack paid £15 to have it fixed and had to battle to get it out of the repair shop today. It still overheats just as badly as ever. This development may put a crimp in our trapping.

The sakret ate a few hesitant bites of dove this evening at sundown amid curious children in the village square in front of our house. He bated four times attempting to fly off to roost, but he was only mildly suspicious of the children. He had a good bout of hood scratching and head shaking, accompanied by jess biting, in his frustration. He somewhat resents the hood. Probably it is not a good fit. I must be careful.

Our Barbary tiercel is as tame as can be as long as he is hungry. Jack's Barbary female still will not eat bareheaded; she is evidently a very fat bird. Were she hungrier, she would be more interested in food and less in us. The peregrine reluctantly tore up a dove but flung most of it away without eating it. Jack is working these birds very carefully using very slow movements, only indoors and alone by himself, giving them kid-glove treatment.

Jack spotted a Barbary on a mosque in town.

13 February • Khartoum, Sudan

We searched the pylon line this morning. Very disappointing. We tossed out our bundle bird, Scruffy, on a venture in a nice, open stretch of desert near Baquier. He drew in a Barbary which made a couple of passes at him before Scruffy pitched on the ground. The Barbary flew away. Next, in came two ravens; we had an entertaining interlude as they stooped and harried Scruffy, trying in vain to get him to drop the bundle. No more warrantable falcons were to be seen.

We checked the Gordon's tree area this evening, tossing Scruffy up near the fenced area, where Jack used to trap sakers, in hope that one might come in. Nothing came in. I picked Scruffy up at the base of a tree by which he had landed. He is so tame that he rode bareheaded back from the field then ate readily on my fist. He looks like a big, puffed-up kestrel. We saw hundreds of Maribous which seem to have taken up residence in the forest where falcons roosted in bygone days. We saw six shovellers (*Anas clypeata*) and 20 black-winged stilts (*Himantopus himantopus*), plus numerous small waders on a little pond.

All birds got fed up this evening, except for the sakret who is fasting (stock phrase two, "It's Ramadan") until tomorrow. He is not fearful but is a bit difficult because he resents the hood, jesses, bells and their like. He kicks up quite a *haboob*, (Arabic for windstorm) with his tantrums. Since he does not take a big interest in food, it is time for a diet.

Col. Meredith's tiercel is still wolfing down all the food I give him. The lanner, christened *Jóhara* (Jewel), is steady and sweet. She is calm, dignified and unflappable. Pollard's haggard lanneret is still wild, bates a lot, and will not yet eat calmly bareheaded. The big Barbary, Saidna, stands as if carved of wood, every feather plastered tight down, always tense; she still refuses to eat bareheaded on the fist. The peregrine, Selema, remains nervous, still stares at us but is just beginning to eat happily bareheaded on the fist. She eats slowly, staring at Jack's face between mouthfuls, but she broke down tonight and took a good crop-full.

It is the end of Ramadan tonight! Gasim left for a three-day celebration in his village. Our cook, Mohamed Ziada, is taking a one-day holiday. Most businesses will be closed for three days of eating orgies after the month of fasting. Now stock phrase two, "It's Ramadan," so useful to explain frustrations, slights, bad service, lack of cooperation and general confusion, will pass into oblivion. We shan't miss it.

14 February • Khartoum, Sudan

Back at the pylons this morning we spotted a saker just inside "saker land" and decided to try Scruffy. He was under immediate attack as the saker stooped and seized the bundle in his feet. Both birds fell to the ground. After a breathtaking tug-of-war, while we waited to be certain the saker had been snared, she broke free, or rather let go. Then she repeatedly dashed at Scruffy, crest erect, hackles raised, wings spread in a most intimidating manner, as she snatched at the bundle. For perhaps two minutes she continued, then gave up and flew off. As I turned from following her with the glasses back to Scruffy, I saw another saker sitting on the ground about one yard from him. Scruffy flew, and the new saker beautifully stooped him repeatedly trying to force Scruffy to drop the bundle. When Scruffy pitched into a bush, she tired of the game. We tossed him up again, but the saker, though willing to stoop, refused to bind to the bundle.

Next we set up a paddam, or ring of nooses, around the bait for one of the sakers which had returned to the pylon. As we backed away it flew off, never to be seen again. Rather discouraged, we pulled up the paddam and our staked-out bait, Jimmy Jerboa, and reset them in view of the second saker which was now sharing a pylon with a vulture. Unfortunately, after we had set the trap, Jack noticed this "saker" was in fact actually another vulture: "Large rubbish," he called it. We pulled up the paddam and dashed on to the end of the line, just past Bequier, finding nothing. We decided to try to relocate one of the earlier sakers. We found one, tossed up Scruffy, who in the teeth of a sudden gale swept off downwind at a tremendous speed. The saker after some moments of hesitation chased and stooped but would not bind. We ended the morning with a super chase after Scruffy who by now had decided to seek a saker-free environment downwind. Jack and I are both gnashing our teeth now over this morning's events, having missed so many opportunities. And, Jack is working on a new barrak to supercede the one which failed today.

Only four trapping days are left, and social engagements are beginning to encroach on our time. Filling our list of requested birds appears to be a lost cause. However, we are game to try to the end. I saw a beautiful, "blue" haggard Barbary on the tower of the Catholic cathedral opposite the Sudan Club.

15 February • Khartoum, Sudan

We did not trap this morning due to strong winds and a late breakfast engagement with a trucker friend of Jack named Shibley. Shibley was in bed when we arrived, but unperturbed, he quickly arose, dashed outside and throttled a chicken. While we waited for the food to be prepared, Shibley played his mandolin and sang what I took to be local folk songs, while Jack took it all down on his tape recorder. Parenthetically, I should add that Sudanese people have a different concept of time than do Westerners. If you invite people for a meal and they agree to come, they may or may not ever arrive. If they do arrive, it may be hours late. This timelessness takes some getting used to.

I had a big day at the embassy. A giant packet of forwarded mail arrived courtesy of Steve Baer. Thank you, Steve!

We drove the pylon line in the evening. There was a large, dark saker just on the border of saker land. We sent up Scruffy to do his job, but the wise old saker was evidently the one that would not bind yesterday. It refused to leave the poles. Scruffy landed in the roadway, and in came the beautiful light-headed saker that had given us a show yesterday, snatching at the bundle on the ground. She went straight for Scruffy, and after a brief but breathtaking struggle was caught! As we ran in from the Rover to scoop up our prize, Scruffy was being dragged, upside down over the furrows of a plowed field. I was laughing joyfully as Jack and I secured both birds and congratulated each other. To me the bird appeared to be a small haggard, tiercel saker. We decided to drive a bit farther in hope of capturing a female. We found nothing and headed back to Khartoum.

Just outside the village of Soba the clutch went out, and the old Rover died in the desert. Jack and I locked up everything we could not carry and hitched a ride on an improbable passing truck. I was amazed to see a truck out here miles off road in the middle of the dessert. Jack carried Scruffy and I the new bird, now secured in a sock. [To prevent injury and keep a newly trapped bird quiet, it is usual to

149

slip it into a lady's nylon stocking, hooded and with feet taped. It can easily breathe and not overheat while so restrained.] As a matter of expedience we liberated Jimmy Jerboa with a hero's send-off.

Upon our return to Bait es Sugúr, the new bird was jessed and hooded. Amid the shrieks and frenzy produced by the new falcon Jack pointed to its tail. To my astonishment it was veritably a lanner and not a saker at all. We had so hoped for a saker that we had deceived ourselves until we got her to the mews. I felt foolish, but she did indeed, strongly resemble a saker more than she resembled Jóhara, our other female lanner. She was a 28¾-ounce tan bird, white headed with lightly marked breast. She was very violent and refused to stand on my hand.

Later, the sakret ate in the shop next door amid uncomprehending and unhelpful urchins and hags. Jack's peregrine, Selema, likewise behaved well in the same company. While we were in the shop, we received word that our landlord was highly concerned about what we were up to in his house; he might even wish to inspect the place. Jack and I brainstormed just how we might hide the birds from him in such a tiny and open place. Finally, we decided to remove all of their bells and hide them in the in the back yard among our laundry which was drying on lines. I was curious to see what would happen.

Jóhara jumped a leash-length for food. Even the Barbary, Saidna, ate on the fist, but only in our house alone with us and with no disturbances. Scruffy bears us no malice despite the indignations we have heaped upon him. He ate a full crop. He is ridiculously tame. I can pet him on his back and even scratch his head.

16 February • Khartoum, Sudan

I carried Sindibad for a half hour. He seemed quite tame even when exposed to the street urchins. I forestalled bates by judicious use of a tiring, a tough piece of food with very little meat with which to distract the bird. He preened on my fist indoors, a sure sign of tameness, while I chatted with Jack.

The new lanner finally sat on my hand and learned to come back up after a bate. I carried her for a half hour. She hissed and snapped and was quick to use her feet against being touched. Even hooded she was a very wild, but what a pretty bird!

We visited the Khartoum suk to hire a truck to haul in the Land Rover from its desert deathbed. Jack loosed a young, neighborhood mechanic (we hope) upon it. He dissected it literally with a hammer, extracting the offending clutch plate which had indeed burned up. The Rover rests tonight at our front doorstep, its viscera strewn in the street and tucked into its interior.

We laundered our sheets which did provide particularly good concealment and placed the birds on a cadge (a portable perch to which several hooded falcons can be tethered) among them. Jack decided to lock the mews door anyway, although it now appeared to be a perfectly ordinary, bird free room.

I began reading Jack's *A Falcon in the Field*, F.I.F. for short, this afternoon. I find it an interesting and very helpful book. I hope Jack does not take as long to publish this one as he did *A Hawk for the Bush*. Jack has written the book on pads of yellow, lined paper in longhand. He just wrote it straight through with hardly a correction or change. Amazing! What a mind for organization!

While I was in the midst of F.I.F. a horde of Sudanese youngsters laid siege to our gates and swarmed into the house, scattering throughout. They claimed they wanted to "water the flowers." Soon followed the landlord, who it seems is their father. He stormed in through the front door before I could stop him and proceeded to stalk through the house, complaining about his plants, which we have kept well watered, and poking his nose into every corner. Jack and I were seething. We quickly locked all of the remaining rooms. The chap even threatened to evict us. Jack told him he could take his bloody plants if he wanted them.

Eventually out came the real reason for the rude invasion. The landlord demanded to see what was in the mews. Jack refused him entrance which only irritated him further. Jack then verbally backed him into a corner and explained clearly just what he could and could not do in this house. The landlord still insisted Jack unlock the mews. Finally, Jack relented, and the man rushed in. He was visibly stunned to find nothing, not a sign of our birds. He was puzzled and confused and thoroughly outwitted. Our landlord left in a huff. Jack and I were both rather unsettled by this exceptionally ill-mannered and unsavory Sudanese invasion. However, we rejoiced in his vanquishing.

Later we carried and fed the birds. The sakret had withstood the brat barrage very well, with the aid of a tiring. Selema stepped eagerly to the hand and relaxed for the first time without her feathers temperamentally slicked down but now held comfortably loose.

Scruffy is in bad condition. He has assumed a horizontal position, tail held straight out. He has been doing this for several days now, but it has become more frequent and pronounced. He also has fits of a sort. He goes rigid, extends one wing out stiffly, with the other wing open but more limp. His head twists to the side and twitches and jerks convulsively. The attack is heralded by a few preliminary head twitches and lasts for 10–15 seconds. Then he is back to normal as if nothing had happened. His mutes or droppings are green and messy. His appetite is good. He has had one attack each day since we started using him for trapping and had two attacks today. [We subsequently suspected Scruffy may have been poisoned by pesticides in the highly sprayed Sudanese cotton fields.] We fed him up and released him, since the trapping season had come to an end.

We saw a Barbary later today on the palace building, presumably roosting for the night. Jack says they are not usually seen after February 15.

17 February • Khartoum, Sudan

The new lanner settled down and ate bareheaded tonight. She submits well to the hood, but she is still hissy and puffs up; she is very quick to bite. The sakret worked all day on his favorite pastimes, hood scratching and jess biting. He scratches the hood, then takes his rage out on the jesses, which he cannot seem to destroy, then scratches his hood again. It is a vicious circle.

The Land Rover is still strewn over the street. Its repair is evidently incomplete.

I walked to the Burri el Mahas water tower this evening. There were no falcons evident.

18 February • Khartoum, Sudan

The new lanner, named "Pearl" by Jack, had scarcely a bate today; she eats greedily, tearing out large bites of meat, and hoods well. She is quick and a real beauty, very light in color, with an almost-white head and a finely built body. The sakret is now fearless but strong-willed and restless in character. He spends the bulk of his time biting at his bell. He's coming one-and-a-half feet to the fist for food.

I had lunch with a gentleman named Jack Francis from the American Embassy. I also met Ed and Mrs. Claude, parents of Roger Claude, a 33-year-old biology teacher and Salt Lake falconer who wants us to send him a saker. He is on the list. [Poor "Rog" never did get a bird from our expedition.]

The Land Rover has been repaired. After taking it apart, the mechanic failed to return the following day. Jack sent Gasim to investigate, and the man was soon back on the job. Gasim explained with Sudanese logic that the man's infant daughter had died, so he had not come to work. Gasim reprimanded him severely and demanded he return immediately to finish the work. Loss of a daughter was no excuse. Of course, had it been a son, then that would have been perfectly understandable. This is clearly a different culture.

Tomorrow I head north. Jack will bring Gasim and the birds back to England soon. We will meet to use them to hawk rooks in March. It has been a wondrous sojourn here. We caught ten falcons, will ship two to the U.S.A., four to ourselves for use in England and turn the rest loose. I have enjoyed this stay very much. The Sudanese have been for the most part quite friendly. And, I learned a good bit about trapping from the old master, Jack.

19 February • Khartoum, Sudan

8:30 A.M. I am just pulling out of the Khartoum railway station. Jack and Gasim saw me off. I am riding second-class with three Sudanese chaps, medical students in Alexandria. We are passing through the desert: brown, sandy soil with barely green, scrubby, thin bushes stretching away to the horizon, very flat. I see occasional small children, frequently girls, tending goat herds. Sporadic camels browse along the way. As our train nears a village there are always a few donkeys. I cannot help but wonder what they find to eat. As the train brakes to a halt in front of a few mud buildings and a large water tower, the vendors, old men, women and children, invariably in grimy clothing, run up to the windows bearing little packets of lemons, bread, guavas, sugar cane, tomatoes and such. Then a small riot ensues as people debark to stock up on supplies before the train pulls out. People shout and struggle for a place to buy their goodies. There is a frantic scramble of passengers, when the train begins to move, to return to the comparative serenity of the train.

20 February • Abu Simbel, Egypt

11:00 A.M. After a cool night the desert is warming up. We have been crossing the Nubian Desert heading for Wadi Halfa through endless flat miles of mirage-bejeweled sand. Rock jebels or hills in the distance break the monotony. There is scarcely a shrub or for that matter any vegetation at all to be seen. There is less dust today. It almost asphyxiated me last night. It rolls into the car from every crack and opening. There is no escape.

The train arrived in Wadi Halfa at 2:30 P.M., six hours late, and I passed through customs with no difficulty. I caught another Nile steamer which departed at 4:00 P.M. Third class on this paddle wheeler relegated me to deck space. I found a good, sheltered area with two ladies, one Swiss and the other German. After a brief squabble with some other passengers to establish our territory, we have successfully defended it from new arrivals from villages along the river. Just about every square inch of deck has been claimed.

We had been eagerly anticipating a visit to Abu Simbel. It is a spectacular temple which will be flooded by the new Lake Nasser when the dam at Shellal has been completed. An heroic effort has been mounted to move the entire temple to the top of a cliff out of the flood's way. Since our boat was behind schedule, it only stopped for about five minutes, just long enough to exchange passengers. We arrived at night. The temple was illuminated purely by incidental light from a large crane which was unloading another barge. I scampered ashore and ran up to the temple. It did look stupendous in the shadows of artificial light, as it loomed above me. It was not possible to enter, our time being so brief and it being totally dark inside. Our heartfelt entreaties to the captain failed to extend the delay of the ship for even a few more minutes. I attempted to snap a photograph as we pulled away.

21 February • Shellal, Egypt

This morning, as I lay in my sleeping bag on the deck, I awoke suddenly to see right beside me an Arab kneeling on a goat and slashing its throat. While its blood gushed, I got up fast and removed myself and my sleeping bag from the gathering pool of crimson. That was not a good way to awaken. The goat was later cooked over a fire built directly upon the steel deck.

I've been talking with a New Yorker as we glide toward Shellal. He and his wife have traveled here across Asia from Japan. He reckons on traveling nine months, seven down and two to go, for $2,300 apiece. He strongly recommends Harian Books of New York for world travel information. The couple has spent two months in India and two in Japan. He says November through February is the best time to visit India.

The cruise to Shellal is pleasant. There are mud houses all along the bank. Occasionally we pass an old temple, but without a guide it is impossible to identify any of them. It feels weird to pass thousands of houses, each lifeless. Every village is deserted due to the program to resettle the former inhabitants somewhere above the floodwaters when the dam has been completed. The villages appear pleasant and inviting with their agreeable palm trees. There is green ribbon along the banks of the Nile. The land beyond is barren: brown desert with rocky outcrops, seemingly devoid of, and hostile to all life. I find it difficult to imagine how people could find a living here. Certainly the river is integral to their survival.

We arrived at Shellal at 4:00 P.M. Due to our tardiness we did not dock but have moved upriver about one mile to wait until morning. As a result there are many disgruntled people aboard.

22 February • Aswan, Egypt

8:45 P.M. I am camped on the lawn of the Culture Center, a modern building, plastered inside with photographs of the Aswan Dam, local handicrafts and smiling facsimiles of President G.A. Nasser. Opposite the Culture Center across the lawn stands the Fire Department, replete with a toilet, which incidentally rates so low I refuse to award it even one star, and a sink with water. The Nile is flowing past about 150 yards to the west, and the main street bounds us to the east. I am with the three women with whom I shared deck space: two from Germany and one from Switzerland. The two Germans have recently immigrated to the U.S.A. They are Elfrida and Anita from Germany and Blanch from Switzerland. They have brought me here from the boat, where we were third-class deck neighbors. They are exceedingly solicitous of me, and they have generously offered to take me to Edfu tomorrow to see the famous temple of Horus, after we complete a hasty Aswan sightseeing tour. Then they will go on to Cairo via the Red Sea, while I will head to Luxor. They are very sweet. I may return to Europe with Anita who is sailing on the same ship I plan to take.

I had a miserable morning. Our paddle wheeler pulled into the port at Shellal at 7:00 A.M. but did not unload until 10:00 A.M. There

155

ensued a series of disorderly queues and inevitable skirmishes with minor officials. I finally debarked at 11:15 A.M.

Anita and I drove to the police station in her VW bus. There the totally charming officer who was in charge allocated us a lorry with a driver who transported us in its rear to a small building filled with a model of the Sadd-el-Ali or high dam. A guide regurgitated facts in labored English about the dam and its benefits, then took us right out onto the construction site. In fact, we walked through the very tunnels that will conduct water to the turbines.

The entire Shellal region has become part of this monster construction project. For miles around the earth is torn up into great, rugged hills and valleys. There is noise and movement everywhere; bulldozers, cranes, shovels, earthmovers, railroads, ramps, all are going at a frantic pace. The air is filled with dust. What an immense project! It involves cutting a new diversion channel through solid rock, erecting the tremendous edifice which will house the turbines and laying the foundation for the new dam itself. There is building, moving, blasting, removing, all of it frantic. And, soon, in May, the new waters will begin to rise and inundate the very lands through which we have just passed, those now deserted lovely vistas of mud homes and graceful palm trees, the land of Nubia.

My ready cash reserves are low. I have £E 1.50. I am having a problem cashing a check for $100. The official exchange rate is £E 0.425=$1.00. If I had actual cash to exchange, I could get £E 0.60 per $1 on the black market. Thankfully, Anita has floated me a loan of $10 which will get me to Cairo!

I like Aswan. Although it sports a filthy suk and grimy people, I am pleasantly surprised to find the people are truly friendly, and I have not seen one hand extended for a donation. Aswan is a pretty green town on the Nile, small and with a nice flavor. Another pleasant surprise: there are pretty girls appearing in public in western dress. I haven't seen that in a while. For the past month the few women I have seen have been pretty much totally covered with more "modest" Arab clothing. [Note: the town of Shellal was inundated by the new lake and exists no more.]

23 February • Edfu, Egypt

On the road to Edfu, the narrow, fertile green ribbon along both sides of the Nile is abruptly bordered by rocky, sterile, arid hills on the east and sandy, rock-outcropped desert to the west. I have seen many crows that resemble pied crows but have gray instead of white patches. I am also seeing medium white egrets, larger than cattle egrets in the fields and of course, ubiquitous kites.

Whenever we stop, children gather to be photographed, but the women conceal themselves from the camera. I photographed a small girl driving a cow powering a water wheel at a well.

I have seen four kestrels, the first in days. We have just arrived at Edfu and have contracted an old dragoman (guide) with a cataract in both eyes to cross the Nile to the temple; his fee is £E 1 for our entire group.

The Temple of Edfu is magnificent, the best preserved temple in Egypt, and it serves as a wonderful example of how the less fortunate temples must have appeared before they were ruined. It was completed around 57 B.C., during the reign of Cleopatra, last of the Egyptian Pharaohs. Additionally, Edfu is the temple of Horus, the falcon god, and that seems appropriate on this trip.

The temple is bounded on its west side by two intimidating enormous stone pylons. East of the pylons is a large colonnaded courtyard, bounded on its east side by a hypostyle hall. Beside the entrance into the hall stands a three-meter-high statue of Horus as a falcon. Continuing east through the hypostyle hall, I found a second hypostyle hall, and beyond that some smaller chambers including a sanctuary where there would have been a statue of Horus, which would have been cared for by the priests. I loved exploring its dark corners, immersing myself in history and mystery. It was fun to try to visualize colorful rites and celebrations that were performed here so long ago.

After saying goodbye to the ladies as they parted for the Red Sea, I attempted to catch the 5:30 P.M. train to Luxor. An American couple Dick and Mary Abbot and a German, Klaus Gräfer, all colleagues from the steamship, were also heading north. We succeeded in boarding the 5:30 train at 7:30 P.M. It then pulled onto a sidetrack, where it remained until 10:00 P.M. We all were asked to debark and take the 10:30 P.M. express which left at 11:00 P.M. I am becoming accustomed to the vagaries of North African time.

Our train arrived in Luxor at 3:00 A.M. Finding some sleeping quarters became our all-consuming goal. Our merry band first inquired at the Station Hotel, which was closed; we rang the bell until we received a peeved response, "No beds!" Around the corner were two "Z" class hotels opposing one another on a grimy side street. First, we knocked at the Hotel Victoria. Then, we tried the other hotel. Mary and I simultaneously knocked on both hotels' doors. We tried beating on the doors. Mary even kicked hers vigorously. By now a cop had arrived plus some curious onlookers. Dick and Mary, especially, were becoming quite worked up. They could see a man on the floor just inside the door, but they couldn't rouse him. Dick had a police whistle which he began to blow, while Mary continued to assault the door with fist and foot.

The cop instructed us to go to the Luxor Hotel. Another member of our group, John, ordered the cop — actually shouted at him — to find us a room.

By now quite a few onlookers had assembled and crowded around. Mary had succeeded in raising the guardian of one hotel and been dismissed again with, "No beds!" She was screaming now, "What do you mean, no beds?" She upbraided him with an outpouring of the chronicle of our hardships. One of the Hotel Victoria residents called down in all apparent seriousness, "Do you want something?" As I was trying to persuade everyone to abandon hope and throw ourselves upon the mercy of the police, the door of the Victoria Hotel swung open. Klaus rushed in and quickly secured a three-bed room, while some Arab was endeavoring to force us back out, crying "No beds!" Mary was still raging, "What do you mean, no beds?" as we occupied Klaus's room and bedded down. The neighborhood slowly settled back to tranquility.

24 February • Luxor, Egypt

A hotel lackey awakened us at 8:00 A.M. with a request for passports. He just walked in, turned on the light and demanded passports. He got them but then returned moments later with a register for us to fill out. We groaned, explained we would do it later and told him to leave us alone. He kept thrusting it at me, saying, "Police. Police." Eventually, we gave in and complied. He returned yet again with yet another form, this time accompanied by another lackey. And, back he came with a fourth form. Then he returned with the first form. That did it. We threw him out. Mary threatened him bodily harm.

Half an hour later, when the door opened again, Klaus and I shouted at full volume, "Get out!" and we were not further disturbed.

158

That is except for the bed bugs, which had feasted freely on us at no extra charge.

I enjoyed a tasty shish kabob breakfast. Then we rented bikes for the day and rode off. We crossed the Nile in a dhow, the common Egyptian sailboat, to the temple of Deir el Bahari, the mortuary temple of Queen Hatshepsut. The queen was one of a handful of female Pharaohs, the most powerful of them at that. The temple was designed and implemented by a superb architect, Senemut, around 1458 B.C., near the entrance to the Valley of the Kings. The focal point was the Djeser-Djeseru or the Sublime of Sublimes, a splendid colonnaded structure of perfect proportion. It sat atop a series of terraces that were once adorned with gardens and was built into the cliff face that rose sharply above it. This temple and its adjoining buildings are considered to be among the great buildings of the ancient world.

We wandered over the hills exploring some of the abundant tombs of nobles. The best of these were protected by locked iron doors, but through cracks we could make out paintings and carvings on the walls inside.

While cycling to the Rameseum, the imposing funerary temple of Rameses II, it was necessary for us to plow through an army of children selling "genuine antiques, Monsieur." The structure itself, in keeping with the philosophy of Ramses II, intimidated me by its sheer magnitude. The temple was comprised of two stone pylons, or gateways, some 60 meters wide, one after the other, each leading into a courtyard. Beyond the second courtyard at the centre of the complex were the remains of a covered 48-column "hypostyle hall," a flat-ceilinged hall supported by columns, surrounding the inner sanctuary. I could imagine the awe that Ramses II must have inspired in his subjects thousands of years ago.

Klaus and I rode double on one bike on our return, while Dick took Klaus's bike which now sported a flat tire. We re-crossed the Nile on another dhow, then spent the evening wandering through shops in Luxor.

Here is a good place to mention that Luxor really includes three different areas, consisting of the City of Luxor itself on the east side of the Nile, the town of Karnak just north of Luxor and Thebes, which the ancient Egyptians called Waset, which is on the west side of the Nile across from Luxor.

25 February • Luxor, Egypt

Today Dick, Mary, Klaus, and I treated ourselves to a taxi ride for a visit to the Valley of the Kings, the Valley of the Queens, and Tombs of Nobles. The taxi dropped us off to stroll about as our interests dictated. It was hot and dry. I was able to wander off and be alone for part of the day. I felt the weight of the centuries slip away as I immersed myself into the history of this barren, yet beautiful place. I visited the tombs of Seti I, Rameses VI, Tut, and several other kings, as well as Nacht, in the Valley of the Queens and tomb #1 of the nobles. Descending into King Tut's tomb was especially exciting. I had read Howard Carter's description of his first entry into the tomb and recollected the amazement and chills it brought when he first beheld the magnificent treasures which were packed into this tiny space. Creeping into the ancient tombs and being able to observe first hand the wonderful artwork on their walls was eerie, almost dream-like. What wonders!

In the afternoon I visited Karnak, unfortunately without film (I ran out), trying to get a quick impression of it. Kestrels were nesting among the pylons and pillars. The temple complex was stupendous. I felt insignificant as I wandered through the immense columns. It was no wonder Egypt towered above other contemporary civilizations. It still does in some ways. I rode back in a commercial horse and buggy with an American translator from Genéve. Tonight I dined again on shish kabob.

26 February • Cairo, Egypt

Last night, I caught the 10:30 P.M. train, which left at midnight; I rode second-class in a compartment with five other people. It arrived in Cairo at 11:45 this morning. I was delighted to view Snofru's "bent" and "red" pyramids, Djoser's step pyramid, and finally the three great pyramids of the Giza complex as our train rolled past them.

First I secured a bed in the Garden City Youth Hostel. A good part of the day I spent trying to cash my check for $100. After considerable effort I finally received £E 42.68 for it. After successfully purchasing a ticket to Marseilles for £E 22.50, I celebrated, together with Dick and Mary who followed me here, with a tasty cheese-covered schnitzel supper at the Union Restaurant. I have really missed cheese.

27 February • Cairo, Egypt

I slept all morning, then visited the Cairo Antique Museum. It was wonderful! Here were the contents of King Tut's tomb spread through several grand rooms so we could appreciate their glory. Even the king himself was here along with his gorgeous golden sarcophagi! I was able to wander through thousands of years of Egyptian history in a few hours. Later, I took in a miserable film, *Counterfeit Traitor* starring William Holden. Dick, Mary and I filled up on beer and pizza, then made a five-minute taxi dash to sneak in just under the 11:00 P.M. curfew at the youth hostel.

28 February • Cairo, Egypt

It took two buses to get to Sakarra and Djoser's Step Pyramid, where I again met up with Dick and Mary. We visited some mastabas. Courtiers and families of the kings were buried in these low, rectangular, brick or stone structures. Like the pyramids they were built on the west side of the Nile, the west being a symbol of death, where the sun falls into the underworld. Mastabas were designed to ensure the well-being of the deceased in the afterlife. We ambled through more temples and admired the ancient architecture.

Djoser's Step Pyramid was a marvelous thing. (Djoser was a 3rd Dynasty Pharoh) We hiked all around it, admiring the ingenuity that had gone into its construction. It reputedly began as a normal mastaba but was subsequently enlarged by adding one mastaba on top of another until it consisted of six terraces about 60 meters high. The surface was originally veneered with polished white limestone, which must have looked resplendent in the sun. It is considered to be the first pyramid constructed in Egypt. The Step Pyramid was designed and constructed around 2360 B.C. by a man named Imhotep for King Djoser. Imhotep has been called an architect, astronomer, sage and high priest. The Greeks even worshipped him as Aesclepius, the god of healing. He was certainly a man of considerable talent and consequence.

At noon we moved on to Giza, to the three great tourist pyramids where we joined the crowds to explore. After beating off the ubiquitous dragomen and camel drivers who were hawking camel rides, we finally were able to enter the Great Pyramid. I felt a shiver of awe not unlike that I experienced probing some of the prehistoric caves in Europe. First, we ascended a narrow corridor which emptied us into the Great Gallery, a splendid, large passageway that ascended to the King's Chamber. The King's Chamber was an unremarkable rectangular room with a huge, red granite, open sarcophagus. It is unknown if the Pharaoh Khufu was ever placed within it.

Next we continued on to the Queen's Chamber. We were shown the "well," a hole thought perhaps to have been an escape channel for workmen and a couple of the original plug blocks which formerly sealed the Royal Gallery entrance way. This room was likely intended to house a statue of the king, but there is no sign of a statue now. Additionally, we saw the now screened-off entrance to the descending corridor which lead to the Subterranean Chamber, a room which lay at the very bottom of the pyramid.

Outside again, it would have been fun to climb the pyramid, but that was forbidden us. We strolled back to the pyramids of Khafre and Menkaure. Both of these had their entrances obstructed by iron gates and piles of stones. I climbed up Khafre's pyramid, hoping maybe I could bypass the gate, but I was foiled by a nasty camel jockey who rode over to shout at me. Interestingly, hardly a single tourist was to be found on this side of the Great Pyramid. All of the pyramids were dazzling in the afternoon sun, framed against the cloudy, blue-gray sky.

We wandered down to the Sphinx, which I thought to be actually rather ugly and badly proportioned from all but the frontal view. It certainly was still impressive. We enjoyed a cup of tea while waiting for the Sound and Light program to begin. The crepuscular illumination of the pyramids during this show was unforgettable. During the presentation the most beautiful and largest meteor I have seen swept across the northern sky. Shortly thereafter a satellite passed overhead. It seemed implausible to see two of man's greatest achievements here together, the pyramid and the satellite, separated by five thousand years of time.

3 March • Alexandria, Egypt

2:30 P.M. I await boarding the *Massalia*. Anita and I are in her VW "kombi" bus, while she is fixing lunch. I just finished a frantic morning of last minute shopping, writing a letter to Mom, and as usual, experiencing the pleasures of customs. I am trying to relax but still am pretty keyed up; this is at least partly due to a struggle with the dreaded Egyptian Crud, dysentery, which at present seems to be intensifying despite a dose of antibiotics I bummed from a fellow traveler at the youth hostel. Still, it is a beautiful day, warm and sunny. We continue to have to beat back the swarms of vendors and beggars, which seem to comprise an integral portion of the Egyptian experience. I fear I am becoming a little callous and curt lately. Politeness has its limits.

At American Express I picked up my mail. I learned that Les Busch went home in January. He intends to work a while, then go to Australia. He had, I discovered, a lovely red beard, which the Army forced him to remove before permitting him to board the troop ship. Les had been earning his living cooking chickens in a hotel in Sweden.

I spent the last couple of days drifting around Cairo, checking out the mosques of Mohammed Ali, Sultan Hassan and Ar-Rifai. They were all beautiful, but otherwise the time spent was boring. Perhaps the dysentery distracted me. I attended a movie, *Giant*, which had been on my list of films to see. It was a disappointment, again probably related to having intestinal turmoil. In a nice jewelry store I bought Mom an antiqued blue carved stone scarab set in gold plus a few other lesser scarabs for gifts. I am told that some enterprising Egyptians antique these modern-made artifacts by feeding them to goats. I think that is a marvelously ingenious idea.

Two days ago, as I was ambling down a Cairo street, I heard someone call my name. Astonished, I turned to see Les Stroud, the same chap with whom I roomed during my walkabout in London. He is on a tour in a Bedford van with ten Kiwis and Aussies. They are headed for Europe via Syria and Turkey after they cross North Africa.

I met a pleasant young chap, Wayne Kylie, who has hitched around the world from the U.S.A. via Mexico, Hawaii, Okinawa, Japan, Thailand, and on across to Egypt. He has visited over 50 countries. He now plans to hit Europe and the Soviet satellites. Wayne is quite remarkable and claims he has political aspirations. I will be interested to see if his name appears in the news over the next few years.

I also encountered two amazing girls, one of which was in a wheelchair, who have hitchhiked here from Thailand through Burma, India, Pakistan and Afghanistan by themselves. Just when I had been congratulating myself for completing a difficult journey, I happened upon these ladies who humbled me with their courage and achievements.

Dick and Mary Abbot arrived; we boarded the Messalia together. The ship is now taking on bales of cotton which are being unloaded from horse-drawn carts; it will undoubtedly be here a while longer.

I've been thinking about what I should do after rook season in England, that is, after May. There is still the possible Arctic trip in August–September to consider, and there is a biennial German falconry meet for which the American contingent plans to charter a plane. I might stay for that. But, I would definitely return stateside afterward. That would be November or December. Also, by traveling then I might get off-season travel rates. Anyway, I can defer these decisions until a bit later, when I find out more about the Arctic trip from Jack and Gustl.

4 March • Mediterranean Sea near Greece

We just passed Crete. The seas are calm. Hooray for dramamine! Last night we hit a few swells which turned everyone green, so I gulped dramamine until the water smoothed out. Anita and I are living in the VW, strapped to the deck. I seem to always be traveling on the deck. It is actually quite pleasant. I've had only one meal today, but we have been steadily snacking. My torn up bowels seem better today. The weather is sunny and cool.

5 March • Piraeus, Greece

Today was a good day, spent in Athens. We docked about 10:00 A.M. then took a train from Piraeus to the center of Athens. I walked through the narrow market streets, where I purchased an immense, old, woolen, Greek Army coat for $10; it will keep me from freezing. Then, I hiked up to the Acropolis to enjoy the magnificent view. I thought about picking up a pebble to keep as a memento but rejected the idea as symbolic vandalism. Later, I ran into Dick and Mary; we enjoyed some good shish kabob sandwiches for 12¢ per person at a little café in the train station. During our wanderings, we discovered a charming tiny Byzantine church, the Little Metropolis, in the old part of town. It was an artistic gem.

Since we were feeling cold and to pass time until supper, we saw the film *Freud, the Secret Passion*, starring Montgomery Clift. I feasted on octopus and the best salad I've had since last summer in Spain, this meal being accompanied by guitar music in a little taverna called The Brothers of Piraeus. We finished with a glass of retsina, a surprisingly pleasant local wine. Then, it was time to take the train back to the ship.

6 March • Mediterranean Sea near Greece

Our ship sailed about noon. We are winding our way through the islands of Greece. I feel somewhat bored but am reading to mark time until we reach Napoli, where Dick has promised us a fine pizza restaurant. Currently, Anita, Dick, Mary and I are intruding in the first class lounge. No one seems too upset by the presence of our lower class personas.

8 March • Napoli, Italy

We arrived in Napoli at 7:00 A.M. After breakfast, Dick, Mary, Anita and I hiked to the train station, the architecture of which Dick especially wanted to see. It was impressive with its high, glassed ceiling. We took a bus back to the market streets above the harbor to shop for provisions. Dick found us the little pizza place, where we shared pizzas and a quart of wine. At 2:00 P.M. we shipped out while the sun was just peeping through the clouds.

9 March • Ligurian Sea

It is rough, cloudy and chilly. I am glad for my new coat. We should make Genoa by 1:00 P.M.

10 March • Grenoble, France

We docked at Marseilles at 10:00 A.M. After some difficulties involving car insurance Anita and I headed north at 3:00 P.M. We passed through some beautiful countryside, a choice assortment of farms, hills, fields and forests. It was a crisp, sunny day with a few patches of snow still on the ground. We drove to just north of Grenoble, where we dined at 8:30 P.M., then sacked out in the bus at 9:30 P.M.

11 March • Zürich, Switzerland

Through rain, snow and eventually sun, we traveled to Zürich, via Genéve and Lausanne. First, we surprised Holly Baer at home, and next, her husband Steve in the sociological library of the Swiss Federal Institute of Technology (E.T.H.). We had a fine evening of beer drinking, discussing Africa and of course one of our favorite topics, Army life. Steve is collecting "junk" now, assorted gears, ball bearings and shiny objects, which he attributes to his drive to spend money. Holly is pregnant, expecting soon. Steve is bugged as usual by the academic system and in particular by having just been evicted from the office of the head of the math department at the institute. Steve had wanted to get a question answered, but he had been rudely dismissed. Steve is pretty tactless, and I wonder if he will manage to ever graduate? It was good that Holly cooked steak dinner tonight to calm him down.

12 March • Schwäbisch Hall, Germany

I am aboard a train to Schwäbisch Hall up from Stuttgart. It is 7:00 P.M. I just passed Gaildorf. It has been a long day.

Anita and I reluctantly left Zürich at 10:30 A.M., arriving at Stuttgart Hauptbahnhof at 3:15 P.M. En route we stopped at the Rheinfall, the largest waterfall in Europe, with its accompanying Castle Laufen, near the Swiss border. It was an impressive falls, and the castle was very picturesque. At the border I thanked Anita, bidding her goodbye and good luck. She was a sweet lady and was very kind to me. I am tired, fighting a cold, and I have much to do in Hall today and tomorrow. My self-imposed March 15 deadline to be in Tilshead with Jack is not going to happen.

At 7:00 P.M. I arrived in Hessental, the little village just outside of Schwäbisch Hall where my old army post, Dolan Barracks, is located. I walked up to the Cracker Box bar, to see if anyone was there. I found an old Army buddy, Bud Schultz, and later another, Bruce Dahle, dropped in; he was finishing his last day as a soldier and taking a European discharge. The proprietor, Günter Kelch, his wife and daughter, Gabi, greeted me warmly. They insisted on pouring me beers to celebrate my return. At 9:30 P.M. I hitched to the Kosts and found Pips was recovering from a throat infection. We talked long into the night about my African adventures and his recent trip to Ceylon. I slept on the living room floor, while Pips, who had been banished from his bed due to his coughing, slept on a neighboring couch. It felt good to be back.

13 March • Schwäbisch Hall, Germany

I headed to the post to see some old Army friends: Whitey, Kasper,

Charley Goodwin, York Butler, Selina, Armstrong and the ubiquitous lifers (career soldiers). We had a joyous reunion, but I found I did not miss playing my part on the N.A.T.O. (North American Treaty Organization) team anymore. I found my old flame, Margot, at Berger's Gasthaus in the evening and gave her some trinkets from Egypt. I was hoping for at least a little warmth, considering our long history. Surprise! Her new American boyfriend showed up. Margot made it clear who was now number one in her life. Although it was a shock to see her run off to him, I was relieved that she finally had her mind off me. Whitey and I rode in the back seat of Margot's familiar old Mercedes, while the boyfriend drove with Margot beside him. In German she explained that since I had declined to marry her, she had moved on to this chap; she was trying to get pregnant, thus entrapping him into marriage. I hoped she would not end up holding a baby by herself. Whitey and I sought diversion in another Gasthaus. At closing time a willing 19-year-old German divorcee took me home with her.

14 March • Southwestern Germany

I am aboard a train to Oostende at 9:00 P.M. by way of Heilbronn, traveling second class. I spent the day with Pips and my Kost family for rest and relaxation. I am not tired even after a long night with the German girl. I feel a twinge of sorrow for her; she was sweet and very lonely.

15 March • Folkstone, England

3:00 P.M. I am on a bus to Maidstone, Kent, to meet falconer friend Cyril Morley. It is rainy, cold and windy. It was a rough ferry crossing to Dover, but now I am too tired to get sick. I feel healthy except for a touch of the lingering cold, have a 34-inch waist, fat as ever, am shabbily attired and hungry. I am looking forward to some food and sleep. Tomorrow, I should make it to Tilshead.

BOOK THREE:
CULMINATION

16 March • Tilshead, Wiltshire, England

It was good to see Cyril and Jan again. They were good medicine. I hitchhiked to Tilshead, arriving at Jack Mavrogordato's home, South Manor, at 2:00 P.M. only one day behind schedule. Unbelievably, despite my being drenched in the rain, carrying my beat-up Spanish Army pack, enfolded by my Greek Army coat and garnished with my Rhodesian bush hat, a courageous lady picked me up! It is cold, but now a bit of sun is creeping out. Jack, Gasim, and Leonard Potter, one of the last of the professional falconers and an employee of Jack, are all here as are our new African falcons. Jack is off presently to a council meeting.

Evening now. This afternoon we flew the "old-timers," the four falcons Jack already had and which he has flown in previous years, to begin the process of getting them in shape. They flew just four to five stoops to the lure. Stooping to the lure is a training exercise in which the lure is swung in a circle on the end of a short line by the falconer. The falcon then makes repeated passes, trying to seize the lure in the air. The falconer almost permits the bird to catch the lure, thus encouraging it to fly harder. The lesson ends when the bird begins to tire, and it is given the lure with an attached bite of meat as a reward.

Our lineup of birds is as follows: Sakers: Shiva, a big, light-colored, eighth-year Pakistani haggard female that has not been flown for two seasons (due to being in a captive breeding experiment); Dhib (Arabic for wolf), a smaller, dark haggard female; Germany, the eyass tiercel, a gift from Gustl Eutermoser; and Sindibad, our new light-colored haggard tiercel from Sudan.

Peregrines: Venus, an intermewed (a bird kept through the molt) passage bird (bird trapped in its immature red plumage, usually while

168

migrating) from America and Selema, our new passage female from Sudan. Jack has an additional passage peregrine named "Texas" from America, but for some reason she is out of favor and he has chosen not to work with her this season. He is evasive about his reasons.

Lanners: Pearl, light-colored, haggard female, fiery in temper, and Jóhara, a calm, dark, haggard female, both new birds we caught in Sudan.

Additionally, Jack has Iceman, a haggard tiercel goshawk that is molting and will not be hunting until this autumn.

Germany's weight is 27 ounces, and Sindibad's, 29 ounces.

17 March • Tilshead, Wiltshire, England

The weather is cold with wind and snow; it's miserable. Jack has allocated the birds, two apiece, one old-timer and one new-hand, to each of us to handle. I have been apportioned Germany and Sindibad; Leonard gets Venus and Jóhara; Gasim has Dhib and Pearl; Jack will fly Shiva and Selema. I carried Sindibad for three-and-a-half hours today with a tiring. He is a lovely, gentle bird and is becoming fairly tame. I fed him a full crop of rabbit and one day-old chick.

Germany was very greedy, bating eagerly towards me; his manners on the fist are awful. I tried to exercise him, jumping him from his block perch to my high-held fist for bits of meat. I could hardly keep or get him off it. Selema had a plugged up nose today. She was very heavy and breathed noisily. Jack put a drop of eucalyptus oil in her nares and brought her indoors. Tonight she seemed OK.

18 March • Tilshead, Wiltshire, England

More snow, rain and cold. We can't put the birds out; the weather is not fit to fly them. No progress. Sindibad is indifferent to food after yesterday's full crop. I gave him one day-old chick. Germany was as greedy as ever and ate three chicks.

19 March • Tilshead, Wiltshire, England

More rain but clearing with sun in the late afternoon and warmer. We flew all of the old-timers. Germany stooped hard at the lure but raked off when he tired. I retrieved him after ten stoops; he was so tired he could hardly stand on the lure. The other falcons flew well. Venus has not figured out the lure stooping idea yet. Leonard introduced Jóhara to the lure. Gasim had Pearl jumping to his fist for tidbits. Sindibad at

28½ ounces was definitely not sharp (hungry). He jumped to the fist from his block but was a little wild. Definitely, too high.

I read a new book, *The Peregrine Falcon* by Robert Murphy, a fellow American. I think it an excellent book for young people.

Jack brought in three Japanese chicken sexers from the hatchery to South Manor to examine the two tiny young eagle owls he is raising in order to determine which is a female. These men daily examine the most private parts of newly-hatched chicks at the poultry farms to determine which are pullets and eventually will produce eggs, and which are cockerels, considered useless and killed. The Japanese qualifiedly pronounced both owls to be pullets. Jack plans to raise one female owl and sell the other.

20 March • Tilshead, Wiltshire, England
It is still wet, but at least the rain let up a bit. We weathered all nine birds on their blocks on the lawn. They made an impressive display. Later, we exercised all of our falcons.

21 March • Tilshead, Wiltshire, England
Tonight I introduced Sindibad to the lure, a dead rook that Jack trapped. He was hesitant about jumping down to it on the ground, much preferring to come to my hand or a hand-held lure. He allowed me to approach him on the rook. Germany stooped very hard to the lure today and touched it twice, which terrified Jack. It is Jack's opinion that if a falcon hits the lure, even one of his super-light-weight lures, it might be seriously injured. Much as I dislike keeping the lure so far ahead of the falcon that it never gets very near it and as a consequence will never fly all-out to get it, I will do so to placate Jack. Jack is the master here. A light breeze gave Venus an opportunity to stoop with and against the wind. She is doing well. Dhib wanted to fly, but Gasim was not ready to try her. Shiva flew with dash and shifty maneuverability that seemed incredible for a bird so large. Tomorrow we will try for our first rook.

So, why hunt rooks? Good question. Foremost, it is legal to hunt rooks. Unlike crows, which make every effort to take cover, hide and avoid aerial combat at any cost, rooks will try to outfly a falcon and frequently do so. Like crows, they are intelligent and good at improvising strategy to save their necks, so they provide an aerial challenge.

Sometimes rooks will ring up very high with the falcon, and those flights can go for miles. If a falcon is chasing a rook into the wind, the falcon is faster and an endurance race is on. Downwind both birds can go fast, and a rook has a better chance of securing cover in trees. Hence, falcons are slipped at upwind rooks, preferably at rooks that are at least 100 yards upwind and far from cover. Ideally, a falcon will steadily force the rooks into the wind, strive to climb well above them as she closes the gap, then begin to stoop them. She will try to keep them from turning downwind. Sometimes they will turn and the flight comes right back over the falconer. A long high contest is the goal, and a kill is an incidental bonus.

Rat hunts, hunts that degenerate into having to repeatedly evict the quarry from cover while the falcon makes low passes at it are not considered stylish (but can be fun).

22 March • Tilshead, Wiltshire, England

More rain as usual. I carried Sindibad some this morning. He is getting calmer. He is trusting, gentle and appears intelligent.

This afternoon, Roger and Jean Upton, falconers from Marlborough, together with Guy Grossman, another acquaintance of Jack, came by for an afternoon's hawking. Jack slipped Shiva first. She followed some rooks, not those intended by Jack, to the rookery. She did not really try. Leonard flew Venus next; she just circled and landed on a signpost, hoping for Leonard to produce the lure. Leonard walked off, and she took wing, passed him, and went into a flock of starlings. Leonard called her down.

I made a long stalk with Germany, then threw him off into the wind at some rooks that were way up the valley. Only then did I notice he was still wearing his hood. He flew in tight circles with his feet dangling down and head back. I blew my whistle to guide him down. What a way to impress the crowd! I felt very stupid.

Later, I flew Germany with Leonard at my side to direct me, since I had clearly demonstrated that I was a novice at this game. Germany put in a beautiful flight, which I only half observed, due to my fumbling with tangled binoculars and searching for my lure, which I had humiliatingly neglected to bring along. Leonard handed me his. I must have looked pretty silly, especially while loping across the field in my flapping Greek Army coat. Germany's flight continued out of sight, and I thought he must have killed. Then I saw Jack swinging his lure. Gasim followed suit. I tried to get out Leonard's lure, the line of which had snagged on my coat while I was running. Germany caught Jack unaware, coming in low and almost got the lure. Jack hid it, so Germany perched on his head. I tried to lure him off in compliance with Jack's pleas, but the sakret was having none of that. He flew to the ground and ran around Jack looking for that lure. I hurried in and picked him up, once again feeling foolish (and not for the last time). Later we learned that Germany had indeed killed his rook in a nearby barn, but a man had chased him off it and back out of the barn.

Gasim slipped Dhib at a lone rook which was in an excellent set up, far from cover up the valley. She refused, her weight being too high. Leonard and Jack flew Venus and Shiva again with both birds being less than enthusiastic about flying.

Sindibad readily jumped to the lure this evening. Selema is coming to hers too. Jóhara comes five feet. Pearl, still too fat, hasn't come yet.

Roger Upton informed us his passage falcon was killed last week while hunting near Marlborough. A passer-by clubbed her while she was standing on a rook. [The man who killed Roger's bird was subsequently fined £10 in court.] Roger also said he just lost Gypsy, a bird lent him by Geoffrey Pollard. Guy has just lost his lanner falcon. [In those times radio telemetry had not yet been incorporated into the sport, so it was much easier to lose a bird than it is today. If we lost sight of them, and they did not return, we often had to search for hours or even days to recapture them. We were not always successful.]

23 March • Tilshead, Wiltshire, England

We flew the old-timers at easy rooks this morning. The most notable flight was by Shiva. Jack found a slip for Shiva by the "piggeries," a nearby pig farm. She flew right past the first ones directly to a youngster, which she picked handily out of the air. She had it on the ground in one foot by the head and shoulders, holding it as easily as if it were a sparrow. First kill 1964! Congratulations all around; full crop for Shiva; brown ale tonight for us in celebration.

24 March • Tilshead, Wiltshire, England

Shopping for food in Salisbury this morning superseded hawking since it was raining. This afternoon I slipped Germany in a 14-mph breeze at the piggery. He had a lovely flight; his rook put in, and he followed it down, alighting on the ground, allowing the rook to escape. He followed it downwind in a flight that could have gone for miles, so I called him back.

Shiva flew next after a long stalk by Jack; she flew close to the ground at a crow, which initially took to the air but then gave up, dropping into the short grass. As Shiva arrived he leaped about a foot into the air, where she grabbed him. It was too easy, and we all had a good laugh. Jack picked her up chuckling, "Clever old girl. It's not her fault if the crow wouldn't fly." Indeed, it was not. Jack lauded this eight-year-old falcon, who had been sitting in the loft with no exercise for two years with, "Shiva, two, love."

I got a good slip for Germany. He made a very pretty flight at a flock of rooks, cutting one out and forcing it down and away from cover with a marvelous series of stoops until he finally nailed it about a yard above the ground. What a flier he is! It was my turn to buy the ale tonight. The rook's upper beak, together with those from Shiva's rooks, was summarily nailed to the door of the mews. [Useless information: it was Jack's tradition to commemorate the passing of each hawked rook and some incidental quarry by nailing up its beak. By the end of the season the door sported a column of beaks for each successful falcon. Of course I brought home the beak of a particularly good rook that Germany killed.]

25 March • Tilshead, Wiltshire, England

Cool and cloudy with occasional sun and lots of wind but no rain! I carried Sindibad a half hour today. Here is a progress report for the birds we brought from Sudan, to which I shall henceforth refer as the "new hands:" Sindibad comes 20 feet to the lure with no hesitation, but he always walks the last yard. His weight is still too high. Jóhara is coming well over short distances to the lure. Selema is doing likewise, and Jack is ready to put her on a long creance, or line. Pearl sometimes jumps a leash-length from her block to the lure.

In winds up to 20 mph we flew the seasoned falcons this afternoon. Germany refused two good slips. Shiva selected a wrong rook, ignoring those better positioned; it got up and away before she could get to it. Venus refused once and made a feeble effort on the next. Dhib, given a miserable slip, tried to head her rooks off but could not.

She then put in a good flight at two crows with, unfortunately, no kill. Gasim was justifiably proud.

Jack continues his battle with an Army major who is reluctant to recognize Jack's access pass for hunting in the military area, Imber Firing Range. I will bet on Jack in this disagreement. In confrontations he is formidable.

26 March • Tilshead, Wiltshire, England

It is a beautiful, cool, clear, sunny day with winds from 12–15 mph. We are cutting all of the new hands down in weight, as they are all a bit heavy. I photographed some of the more cooperative birds, including the young owl, Madam Butterfly, so-named in commemoration of the Japanese chicken sexers.

This afternoon every bird had two slips. Shiva chased the wrong rook into the trees, pursuing it like a goshawk. She missed. Venus was next and refused. Dhib and Germany flew in a "cast" or team at two crows. Germany went after Dhib, so I called him down. Dhib went on to put a crow into cover but missed. Shiva, given another good slip, checked at a rook a long way off to our right. She chased him into the trees; another miss. Venus, after a long stalk by Leonard, at least flew in the right direction, but she gave up within 200 yards. Jack said she came back faster to the lure than she flew in the attack. Dhib, after an excellent slip, checked at a rook way off to our left, putting him into a tree. Gasim and I repeatedly evicted him. After a long flight Dhib got him. Germany at the piggeries put a rook into deep cover, but missed. Gasim proudly bought the ale tonight.

27 March • Tilshead, Wiltshire, England

Another pretty day without wind. Sindibad received short rations this morning; one-quarter crop of washed meat had him ravenous this evening. I am putting him on a morning schedule, so I'll lure him tomorrow instead of tonight. His weight is 26½ ounces. Germany weighs just under 26 ounces.

Shiva made a long flight at some rooks once again through the trees. One of Jack's former falconers, Derek Moore, came along to beat the woods for her. Germany flew twice. First, he went way downwind and stooped out of sight. I retrieved him. His second slip was at a lone rook which proved to be sick, so he killed it easily. Venus was flown at an extremely easy rook, killing it with no trouble.

Dhib made a good effort, putting some rooks into cover. Then, she waited above patiently for us to flush them. No luck. Her second slip saw the rooks to cover before she could reach them. There was no wind to help us today.

This evening while I was carrying Sindibad with a tiring, he spotted Nimrod, the eagle owl, father of Madam Butterfly, in the owl cage. Sindibad began to scream at him. He did not like the owl and watched it intently, uttering a low, quacking squawk whenever Nimrod moved. All falcons instinctually dislike owls.

Mike and June Woodford, falconer friends from Evershot, dropped by this evening. We had a nice chat about the American falconry field meet (Thanksgiving 1963 in Centerville, North Dakota) and caught up on the latest gossip.

28 March • Tilshead, Wiltshire, England

All of the new hands are on morning schedule. All but Pearl are flying a good 50 feet to the lure on a creance. Sindibad is showing an excellent response.

This afternoon's hawking chilled us with a very cold wind which could have been a little stronger to make the flights more interesting. Shiva followed her rooks to the trees. She killed one in cover by crashing in after it. Venus started well for a change but gave up within 100 yards. Dhib got in a stoop at her rooks before they reached cover. On her second slip she turned downwind, and by the time she came back overhead, the rooks had long departed.

I loosed Germany from the rim of a valley, about a 100-yard slip. He went like a rocket, and he put on a spectacular attack, very long and hard, against one of two rooks. He would feint with his stoops, not actually dropping, but intimidating the rook to drop. I was certain he could not miss, but as he stooped again and again, the savvy old rook just managed to avoid him. In the last few yards just before cover Germany put in three very hard stoops; he missed and followed the rook into the trees. Leonard and I were standing speechless in front of a wire barrier, fearing that in the act off crossing we would miss part of this wonderful flight. Both of us pulled out lures to get him back. I rewarded the tiercel with three-quarters crop on the spot. His flying weight was 25 ounces.

Jack let Madam Butterfly out of her big cardboard box for a sortie around his living room tonight. She was delighted, exploring as far as her stubby young legs would take her until she inevitably collapsed; she rested a while and enjoyed some television, too.

It is one year ago tonight that I finished my life as a soldier. I am reminiscing a little about that evening. I had sat in Berger's bar back in Schwäbisch Hall, Germany with my soldier buddies then walked up to Lilly's and the Cracker Box, two other bars frequented by Americans, for a last beer with my buddies. Then Les and I played pool in the basement of Headquarters Battery of the Thirty-sixth Artillery until two in the morning. It does not seem like a full year ago. I shared an anniversary beer with Jack tonight. I wonder if Les Bush or Steve Baer is aware of today's significance for me? All day I have thought about that marvelous event I am commemorating. And, tonight, as the actual hour approaches, I think about how fast this past year has gone, and I wonder with some anxiety what the next year will bring.

29 March • Tilshead, Wiltshire, England
I have been reading Rachel Carson's book, *Silent Spring*. It is the most terrifying book I have ever read. I feel sick from reading it. Happy Easter, the fourth anniversary of my enlistment! Now I feel appropriately miserable in part due to that book.

This morning Sindibad came 40 feet to the lure on a creance. So did Selema. Roger Upton, John Woodford, and another young friend of John joined us for hawking. Shiva had a nice flight, killing her rook in a brushy, roadside hedge. Germany took a long flight downwind and missed. Dhib had a good slip but couldn't overtake her rooks. The weather was cold and damp with a chill northeast wind.

30 March • Tilshead, Wiltshire, England
Sindibad came well, 30 yards, to the lure. It was a cold, 35°–40°F, overcast day.

Derek Moore and two other young men accompanied us hawking today. Jack is very accommodating to friends who ask to come along. Shiva had two flights. She held back on the first flight until the rooks got to cover then had a rat hunt after them in the trees. Her second flight was at a crow and of good duration at the piggeries. Jack, his Clumber spaniel, Tessa, and I repeatedly forced the crow out of cover. Finally, Jack and Shiva teamed up, diving beneath a tin pig shelter, and Shiva triumphed. Dhib had a poor slip and couldn't overtake her rooks. Germany had a good slip and a nice long flight; his stoops were too short to be effective, and he kept too close to the rook. Missed.

The evening was spent as usual watching TV [Jack especially loved to watch *Dallas*] and reading with Madam Butterfly rampaging about the floor, flapping her stubby pinfeather wings, accompanied by hopping up and down and much beak snapping. She muted horrid, oily messes on the carpet and nibbled at any new object she discovered. She has grown very tame.

31 March • Tilshead, Wiltshire, England
It was a record afternoon with five slips and four kills. Germany flew first; in a lovely slip he overhauled his rook. It crashed into a fence, and he took it, terminating what had promised to be a fine flight.

Venus flew seriously for the first time this season. She put a rook down by a roadside fence. Leonard and I beat it out repeatedly; we had a good rat hunt which found the falcon and rook more than once narrowly avoiding oncoming traffic. She killed it with an assist from Leonard as he dove under a barbwire fence, then hopped, skipped, and jumped in to help her.

Dhib caught a fairly easy rook in a short flight after a poor slip. Shiva, who had missed earlier, tried again but spurned the targeted rooks. Instead, she chased one that was downwind, killing it in cover as usual, this time in a rookery. She is getting pretty clever at that now. Jack's cinematographer got a few shots for a film Jack wants made. [I never saw any of the footage and do not know what the ultimate outcome was of the project.]

Leonard and I had a good chat session about the "old days." He spoke of Kim Murre, a young falconer who was killed in World War II and his exploits, about how dashing and enthusiastic he was. Leonard spoke of Captain Glibert Blaine, the famous falconer for whom he initially worked here in Tislhead. He told of how wild Captain Blaine's hawks were and how he used to give them tirings on the blocks, an activity forbidden by Jack. He said Blaine would go into a trance-like state when he watched a falcon stoop. He spoke of differences between a peregrine's and saker's techniques in hunting rooks. Briefly, a saker will frequently follow a rook to cover, then crash in to catch it. A peregrine generally prefers an aerial contest; it will attempt to cut a rook off from cover and avoid crashing into

177

cover after it. Leonard instructed me how to know when a pheasant is ready to cook. After its corpse has hung from a nail by the legs for a period of weeks, its weight pulls its body free, and it falls to the floor leaving its legs suspended from the nail. He says the pheasants smell so terrible by then that his wife can't stand to be in the house with them. But, he assures me that when cooked, pheasant smells and tastes absolutely wonderful. I was enchanted listening to Leonard's reminiscences.

2 April • Tilshead, Wiltshire, England
Cold and windy with a mist bordering on drizzle; same as yesterday. We couldn't fly. I rate this weather miserable plus.

Jack introduced me to Jim Corbett's books. Mr. Corbett was a hunter who spent some years hunting man-eating cats in India and Africa. His books make for a terrific read. Fortunately for me, Jack has several of them.

5 April • Tilshead, Wiltshire, England
The sun came back! With it unfortunately came wind. The new birds were not flown. We did fly the old guard this afternoon in winds up to 18 mph. Shiva had two slips. The first was unremarkable resulting in a miss. The second flight was at a singleton which mounted very high above her and easily reached cover.

Venus killed a crow after a long stalk by Leonard and me. She went off with great flopping wing-beats, very slowly herding the rooks upwind. When she singled out a crow her style changed. She went directly at him gaining altitude, took a short stoop and had him. As we approached, Venus and the crow were having a terrific fight on the ground; at one point Venus was flat on her back holding the crow at legs' length as he tried to bite her from above. Leonard resolved the conflict in Venus' favor.

Germany in a nice slip went low along the ground, as was his custom, allowing the rooks to gain too much height, so they could sneak downwind while above him. He missed. As I called him down from a considerable height, two partridge got up. He put in a tremendous, long stoop; they dropped into cover, and he continued in to the lure. Leonard said he would have applauded if Germany had hit one of the partridge.

Dhib got hung up in the nylon, quick-release leash on her slip;

she flew off downwind, having missed any real chance. Germany took another 100-yard slip again going low, but this time he mastered his rooks. There was no cover for a good half-mile. A lone rook got up to the side; he checked at it, executed a series of short, fast stoops, and finally brought it down. Leonard assisted him while I panted in.

6 April • Tilshead, Wiltshire, England

It was a really beautiful, sunny spring day. We flew all of the new hands on a creance this morning. Tomorrow they will fly free. This afternoon, since Jack had to attend a committee meeting of the local Tilshead government, Leonard, Gasim and I went hawking. We picked up Derek Moore as a last-minute guest. Into a light, northwest wind Shiva went first, herding her rooks downwind into some trees where she could play goshawk; she missed.

Dhib, in a very nice slip, had a rook upwind and below her cut out from the flock; then, she changed her mind and went downwind, chasing one into the rookery. Another miss.

Leonard slipped Venus who cut one right out of the flock, then quit, just when she had dominated him.

I flew Germany last in the same slip situation that Dhib had just flown. He went off well and allowed a rook to get downwind before making two stoops; it escaped to the rookery. I whistled and lured, but he did not return. We scoured the countryside for a good half-mile, but he had vanished. That was at 4:00 P.M. We searched until 5:30 P.M. on foot, then until 6:45 in the car watching for disturbed rooks. Discouraged and dreading prospects of facing Jack and a dismal, early morning search tomorrow, we returned home. As I was exiting the car, Gasim, who had gone on ahead, ran back shouting, "Germany here!" I went with him and saw, back in the corner of the mews, the tiercel on his block. I could scarcely believe it.

Jack gave us the story later. He had just arrived home from his local council meeting when he received a call from a man who had seen a falcon on a rook and thought it might belong to Jack. Jack told him no, he had not lost any hawks, but perhaps it did belong to another falconer, so he would come right out. The man meanwhile, to prevent the falcon from flying off after eating the rook, took the rook away and hung it on the barbed wire fence; that puzzled Germany as to how to continue his meal. When Jack arrived two miles south of where we had slipped, there sat Germany, meditating upon the rook. Jack, having neglected to bring along a hood, let Germany feed up on the rook in the back of the car on the way home. Jack opined that in 40 years of hawking, this was the first time he had found a hawk before he knew he had lost it.

7 April • Tilshead, Wiltshire, England

It was a red-letter day: beautiful, sunny, weather with a light west wind! We flew some of the new birds free for the first time. All went smoothly, except for Sindibad, who was too high at 27½ ounces; he basically went wild. A hungry hawk is an obedient hawk and vice versa. He would not come down to the lure and bind. I tossed it on the ground, so he picked it up and carried it way off. I got him back when its line got caught. He was very nervous and almost unapproachable. My fault. Pearl came about 60 feet on the creance.

Dr. Gordon Jollie, the assistant secretary of the British Falconers' Club, accompanied us today. Shiva botched her chance and chased her rooks to cover. Then Venus refused her rook, checking at a pigeon.

Dhib went off on a good slip by Gasim. All but one rook had fled by the time Gasim got ready, and that rook gave us a spectacular show. Dhib drove it continually upwind, always dominating it, as they rang up and up together. She made repeated short, choppy stoops, each time ending downwind of her rook, always pressing it upwind. Finally, when near the rookery and very high up the rook made his bid and dove. Dhib hesitated a second, then stooped and missed. Both birds threw up. She had him on the next stoop. We all shouted, but the sound died in our throats as the birds parted after a ten-foot drop. Dhib put in one last, tremendous stoop, following him into the rookery, and missed. That rook definitely earned his freedom. Gasim was all smiles, and Jack reckoned that was the best flight he had ever seen.

Shiva was up next and checked twice at undesirable downwind rooks, chasing them to cover. Then Venus refused her next slip. Shiva again took a lovely slip and had a beautiful flight. She cut out and herded one rook crosswind. They both went up quite high. Unlike Dhib, Shiva did not stoop but pressed on for more altitude. Then came three fine stoops followed by one long, hard one as the rook made for a bush. By the time we arrived, Shiva had him in the open on the ground, a good hundred yards from the bush. Certainly that was the second best flight of the season.

Venus had one more try, pursuing a rook hard and getting in three short stoops before he got to cover. It really was a red-letter day.

8 April • Tilshead, Wiltshire, England

None of our birds flew well today. General O'Carol Scott, president of the British Falconers' Club, stopped by on his way to Caen, France for a conference on birds of prey. He dropped off his tiercel gos for Leonard to care for while he was away.

9 April • Tilshead, Wiltshire, England

Jack left for the Caen conference. We flew the new hands loose. Sindibad tried to carry, still high at 27 ounces. Pearl continued her training on a creance.

The afternoon was lovely with a 10–16 mph wind out of the west. We had nine slips.

Shiva flew first, refusing to chase. Dhib behaved in a like manner. Venus in a good slip went off like an owl again; she then turned downwind, flew directly at a rook and took it in the first stoop about 20 feet above the ground. Germany blew a good slip, hovering over my head while looking back at me over his shoulder for food. Leonard showed him a lure, and he landed on Leonard's head. Shiva started at a rook on passage but couldn't make up her mind; she finally stooped a flock of small birds. Dhib flew again but with clumsy handling by Gasim came off wrong. By the time she had righted herself all rooks were away upwind; she continued on, singled one out and in fine style put him into the trees. Germany next flew in a circle and landed on my fist. Shiva was indecisive then flew off in the wrong direction.

Dhib dueled a single rook, pushing it into the wind and driving it over a hill and out of sight. I picked her up in my glasses, as she gained altitude about 30 feet behind the rook. A mile away now, she fetched him and began making slow, shallow stoops. The rook, being very far from any hope of cover, decided to climb. She climbed with him. The flight drifted back over us now at several hundred feet, the rook evidently trying to gain some trees. Once over the trees the rook made several attempts to dive into them, but being hundreds of feet up it was too well controlled by Dhib, whose very steep and spectacular stoops cut him off until they had both drifted too far downwind for him to achieve cover in the trees. He tried even harder to out-climb the saker. Dhib finally made a mistake. She did not pitch up high enough after one stoop, thus allowing the rook to gain altitude superiority. She broke off in a long, shallow dive, from which Gasim called her back. It was absolutely the best ringing flight I have seen.

10 April • Tilshead, Wiltshire, England

Shiva had a fine flight at Heartbreak Bottom but missed. Venus killed a rook after a brief flight which had just begun when the rook bailed into a barbwire fence; there she got him. Dhib up next, refused to pursue her rook.

Germany at 27 ounces had a good slip, dropping from my fist, getting up a terrific speed skimming the ground as is his custom, so that two rooks did not see him until he had covered half the distance between them. He cut one out then put in some lovely stoops, until the rook finally got to cover.

Shiva drifted off downwind, and by the time she had turned around her rooks had too great a lead, so they escaped to cover. We tried Dhib and Germany in a cast, but Germany just circled back to my hand. Dhib continued but couldn't reach her rooks before they achieved cover.

11 April • Tilshead, Wiltshire, England

We attempted to get the new hands to stoop to the lure. They did not comprehend this new trick yet and refused to take the lure except when it was on the ground. It was Leonard's day off, so Jack decided we would not fly this afternoon.

Gasim and I went into Salisbury to see Disney's *The Sword in the Stone*. We both found it disappointing. I liked T.H. White's book *The Once and Future King*, from which it was taken, much better.

12 April • Tilshead, Wiltshire, England

Crisis! Lost hawk! Sindibad has been lost. While I was luring him this morning at Imber Firing Range, suddenly a group of Army tanks appeared just over a hill from us, terrifying him. He was already skittish about coming to the lure, and those snorting tanks finished it for him. Away he went. I chased him to where he had landed, trying in vain to get him back. Finally, as I was getting ready to wind him up with a creance, he took off in a gust of wind. He was last seen soaring over the artillery range in the distance. Since it was forbidden to enter the range during firing, we had no recourse but to wait where we were and to continue luring. Leonard rushed home to get Shiva to catch him, should we locate him. We put her up but to no avail. At 3:00 P.M. the firing flag came down, and we went onto the range, luring and observing the rooks for indications he might be around.

Later we flew Dhib and Shiva. Dhib had a nice slip at a rook but would not give chase. Shiva killed a rook in a pretty flight. She went into the wind, down one side of the valley and up the other, forcing her rook to the ground in the open. She killed him as he tried to jump out of the way. Dhib refused again, circled Gasim then went in to kill a straggler. Having discovered no sign of Sindibad, I was miserable.

It was time to retrieve Jack and General O'Carol Scott at Hurn Airport. Neither of them was on the plane. We returned to find German friends Gustl Eutermoser, Uwe Beyerbach and a surprise guest, Gustl's wife, Frau Eutermoser. We spent a very pleasant evening in conversation, catching up on news including that Gustl's prairie, Pawnee, one of three sent over by Webby, killed five crows before she was lost.

13 April • Tilshead, Wiltshire, England

Today was a day of ill omen. I had met Jack at the airport together with June and Mike Woodford, Roger and Jean Upton, General O'Carol Scott and Steven Frank, another excellent British falconer. There was no explanation of the one-day delay in their return. The trouble began when I broke the bad news about losing Sindibad to Jack. Jack was not happy.

We went out hawking this afternoon, a beautiful day with sun and a light breeze. Jack slipped Shiva above the Diper's farm, but all of the rooks reached cover. I slipped Germany at the bend above Diper's; he put in a very nice flight, forcing a rook into some bushes along a fence. After the rook had been repeatedly driven out by Leonard and me (rat hunting) it finally escaped to the trees. Germany vanished after it. We searched for one and a half hours with no luck. Another lost hawk for Larry!

Leonard flew Venus who simply flew directly up to a rook in the air and grabbed it. What a terrific footer! She certainly can catch rooks when she takes a mind. Dhib had one slip between Tilshead and White Barn; she started wrong, got in only one stoop and was unsuccessful.

However, our troubles were just beginning. At home Jack tried to put Nimrod the owl in for the night. "Nimmy" decided to have a go at a passing pigeon. He ended up in a giant tree behind the Browns' house next door, from which we spent the best part of the next two-and-a-half hours trying to lure him down. Meanwhile, Jack let a lure pigeon, which was tied to a string as an enticement for Nimmy, slip away. Half the neighborhood witnessed it. Very bad public relations! Leonard was able to retrieve it. But, Jack meanwhile had injured his knee by falling about nine feet out of the pigeon loft while he had been getting the pigeon in the first place. Then Leonard let a second stringed pigeon loose. Meanwhile, the owl was secured by means of a white mouse, which he could not resist. He flew down to catch the mouse and was quickly retrieved on the ground. Shortly thereafter a man called to inform Jack that Leonard's pigeon was hanging from a live wire and he should please come get it. While I held a ladder steady under Leonard, suddenly I was showered with blood as Leonard first tore the pigeon's head off in trying to free it and then tore the rest of the pigeon from the string, leaving one tell-tale leg hanging from the wire. It was a miserable show.

We had an interesting conversation this evening. In Germany Uwe has saved some 40–50 goshawks from gamekeepers each year at a cost of DM 10 apiece. Gamekeepers trap the goshawks in order to protect their game birds. The hawks would normally be killed. However, this small reward is enough to motivate at least some gamekeepers to commute the death sentence and hand over trapped birds to Uwe; he wants to send some to England for breeding and repopulation. We all think it a splendid idea. [The goshawk, which had been extirpated as a breeding bird in England by 1964, has now been reestablished as a result of this and other efforts made chiefly by the falconry community.]

14 April • Tilshead, Wiltshire, England

Today we had better luck than weather. It was too windy. We were afield prior to 6:00 A.M. and sunrise. We found Germany within an hour about three miles downwind of the slip. He had killed last night. Shortly afterwards, Leonard and I removed the incriminating pigeon leg from the entangled line on the wire; better public relations.

Madame Butterfly is getting quite large now, three pounds, ten ounces. She's very cute, nibbles on everything and still produces the most horrid messes. She eats about 12 ounces of food every day and should be airborne in another two weeks, according to Jack. Now she just practices revving up by flapping her wings and snapping her beak furiously.

Webby writes me that his new falconry book, *North American Falconry and Hunting Hawks*, is at the printer's and will appear "shortly."

15 April • Tilshead, Wiltshire, England
Jóhara and Selema are coming well to the lure but have not begun to stoop it yet. Pearl flew on a creance.

In poor weather despite rain and wind Geoffrey Pollard came along as a guest today. Shiva had two slips. Her initial flight was along Imber Road and involved many stoops; then she pursued her rook into the trees like a goshawk and missed. Her second slip was at a rook on passage. She got in one wonderful corkscrew stoop before it climbed above her. She followed it to the rookery, where with repeated stoops she tried unsuccessfully to bag it.

Venus took a crosswind slip and had barely time enough for one stoop before her rook had reached cover. No luck. Dhib, at the farm before the piggeries, circled the car and Gasim before she went. She followed a rook to the trees without success. Jack grounded Germany, ostensibly because of the weather. I suspected it was due to my losing Sindibad and Germany over the past couple of days.

We had an interesting conversation with Geoffrey Pollard. Geoffrey told us about Ronald Steven's, another famous falconer and writer, recent abortive trip to Pakistan. In Lahore, Ronald met a Mr. Anderson, who showed him three light-colored sakers in a hut, "more like gyrs than gyrs," according to Stevens. Anderson sent Ronald off to a northern plain on a wild falcon chase to obtain "better ones." Of course it was January, and the migration had ended in November, so Ronald got nothing. By the time he returned to Lahore, the original three sakers had been sold.

We heard that the lanneret Jack sent to Geoffrey from Sudan and thence to an American named McCollom is killing pigeons well.

185

16 April • Tilshead, Wiltshire, England

Pearl flew free this morning with no problems. The weather began with fog followed by sun at noon, then progressed to light wind, stronger wind and rain. Gustl and Uwe returned for afternoon hawking.

Dhib was up first and wouldn't pursue. Shiva was flown next at some crows in a bush; it was a very long, 500-yard slip. It was too far. She never got close to them. Venus, after a long stalk by Leonard and me, had a beautiful flight at a rook, which she cut out of a flock of 30. She put in very clever stoops, sometimes feinting, sometimes "double stooping" (a normal stoop after which the throw up is cut short by another sudden stoop). Sometimes after a miss she attacked on the throw up from beneath the rook. After a long, hard, lovely flight the rook escaped to cover.

Below White Barn, Germany attempted a rook that would not fly until we were practically upon him. Once in the air he proved a very good rook, indeed. The flight went low, along the road, weaving between cars and trucks and in and out of the parallel running barbwire fence, up to the valley where four large cannons were firing on the Imber firing range. A group of cars had stopped by the road to observe the cannons. The flight continued over and between the cars, down to the cannons and back to the road again. Germany continued throughout to stoop hard, always dominating his rook. I panted along, shouting to keep the rook up. Soon they turned downwind and flew past me again very low. I could see the rook's beak was open. He was tiring. They passed our cars, Germany stooping magnificently. The rook put into some bushes in a farmhouse yard. Uwe and Gasim beat it out before I could get there; the flight continued up and up. The rook had gained too much altitude by now, so I called Germany down. It was a very hard flight that lasted about eight minutes.

Dhib was given one more slip but wouldn't go; she ended up waiting on nicely above us until Gasim lured her down. Since it was now pouring rain, we went home.

This evening Gustl showed us his new German falconry film, after which we showed him some slides.

17 April • Tilshead, Wiltshire, England

There was trouble this morning when Jack insisted on flying Jóhara and Pearl together despite Gasim's protestations that Pearl was not ready. After a luring mix-up Jóhara refused to permit anyone to pick her up. Leonard brought Shiva and a pigeon for emergency backup. Eventually Jack and I wound her up after she had killed the pigeon. Winding up is a method to catch a falcon that is semi tame but unwilling to permit close approach while it is positioned on the ground. The falconer pegs down one end of a long string to the ground; then, holding the other end of the string, he circles the falcon at a distance the bird will tolerate, effectively winding the string round and round its legs. While pulling the string tight, the falconer or an assistant makes in to the bird and secures it. This was a close call.

The weather was cool and sunny with some clouds and a gentle breeze. We took to the field this afternoon with Gustl, Frau Eutermoser, Uwe and Nimrod, the owl. Jack placed Nimrod on a four-foot pole in a likely looking valley upwind of a rookery, where the rooks could see him as they flew past on passage. I thought it would have been better downwind of the rookery, so any rooks that came in would have to fly against the wind to get back to cover. Jack prevailed. He hid in a bush about 100 yards downwind of the owl, while we waited above in our cars. Rooks hate owls. They love to mob them. Eventually a rook came in. It was soon joined by several others. Jack cast off Shiva, but the rooks out-climbed her; since the slip was so short, they succeeded in escaping to the rookery, where Shiva proceeded to wreak great terror among the nesting birds.

Next, Gasim hid in the same bush, but we moved the owl 100 yards farther upwind. Dhib had a fine flight and got in many excellent stoops. At Jack's request I tried to toss Germany off to give Dhib some help, but his weight was too high, and he landed at my feet then leaped back to my fist. Dhib continued to follow her rook, stooping it all the way to the rookery. She did not catch it.

Leonard tried the bush, but no more rooks would come in. A sparrow hawk coming down the valley shot right through the bush, passing just above Leonard's knee as he sat there. It continued on, having apparently not noticed him. We packed up Nimmy and moved on.

Venus had a very fast flight along the road but selected an out-of-position rook and chased it downwind. She put in beautiful stoops, crisper and faster than those of the sakers. She missed.

Germany was given a slip at a lone rook, but he refused. I threw him at it. He just stooped at me until I brought the lure out. As I was picking him up, Jack threw Shiva over my head. She turned off, heading downwind. A flock of rooks got up beneath her, a lucky happenstance for us, and she killed one by means of several spectacular head-on stoops just before it was able to reach cover. We called it a day at 7:00 P.M.

After a supper of Irish stew, we adjourned for bottles of brown ale at the Black Horse Pub to properly drink to the death of Shiva's rook, a fitting finish to a lovely day.

18 April • Tilshead, Wiltshire, England

Another very nice day with good weather, a brisk breeze and some sun. Jack grounded all of the new birds this morning due to the Jóhara incident yesterday. Family Eutermoser and Uwe Beyerbach left this morning for London; this afternoon they were replaced by John Bennet, a photographer hired by Jack to film our rook hawking, and Cyril and Jan Morley.

We had trouble finding slips. It is becoming difficult now because the rooks are becoming wary of us. They are fast learners. We tried setting out the owl at Imber Range, but no rooks were on passage there. We were able to get Dhib a slip on Imber after abandoning use of the owl. She refused to start, circled around Gasim then flapped off after a straggler which the main rook flock had left behind. She increased her speed and killed it as it put into a group of bushes.

Venus had a flight at White Barn but ignored the best rooks and chased a different bird downwind. She came even with it just at the rookery, then flew up and grabbed it in a shallow stoop. It slipped away from her and escaped.

Germany was next on the Chitterne-Shrewton Road. He took a long slip of 300 yards, and he attacked immediately, low and fast. He cut out a tailless, mite-eaten rook, put in a very pretty vertical stoop from 50 feet above it then two more stoops as it flew along the road. I tried unsuccessfully to keep it out of a bush, but it dove in. Germany dove in after it. He had it by its neck, hanging beneath him; he had almost strangled it to death by the time I came up. Good flight, inelegant end.

It was 6:00 P.M., and since Jack's leg was still bad from his fall out of the pigeon loft last Monday, he decided not to fly Shiva. Three slips, two kills. Very nice!

There was again much conversation this evening accompanied by entertainment provided by Madam Butterfly as she explored, flapped, chased Tessa, and decorated the rugs with her oily mutes. Cyril plans to visit the U.S.A. next March. Col. Meredith is in a San Antonio hospital; his situation is not good. [He died shortly thereafter.]

19 April • Tilshead, Wiltshire, England
Today is gray and cloudy with light rain and a light breeze. Jóhara made what could almost be called a stoop at the lure. She performed far and away better than Selema and Pearl.

This afternoon with Cyril and Jan Morley unconvinced we'd achieve much in the way of rook hawking, our little party set out in the Land Rover followed by Cyril's red VW. Shiva had a slip on the Lark Hill Range near The Bustard pub. It was a poor slip, crosswind, and she turned immediately downwind. She missed her rook then beat up the rookery for several minutes, stooping, wheeling and zig-zagging through the trees.

We drove on; then Gasim slipped Dhib up through the top of the Land Rover. She intercepted a group of five rooks and herded them nicely into the wind. She peeled off at a single, driving down with three good stoops; then she tail chased him into the wind keeping about one foot behind, trying to reach out to seize him. Desperate, he dove for a bush; she followed, catching him as they flew through it. We all were delighted.

Germany took a slip near Prospect, a slip which nobody including me liked. But, Jack insisted. One hundred fifty yards across a plowed field were four rooks feeding just next to a barbwire fence, which ran crosswind 200 yards to some bushes and good cover. Reluctantly, I slipped Germany and was disgusted to see him refuse, turn and drop back swooshing past me looking for food. I slowly reached for the lure and was just ready to pull it out, when he decided to go. Jack shouted, "Lure! Lure!" I yelled back, "Let him fly," seeing no danger in his chasing them to cover, which now seemed to bother Jack. Germany fetched one, and it put in along the fence. The rook flew along the fence, using it for protection. Germany stooped and killed it. While the rain drenched us both, I fed him up on the spot.

Venus put in a long, hard, very fast flight and some beautiful, screamingly fast stoops which forced her rook into a patch of bushes across the valley near its rim. She went in after it. When we arrived, she was sitting about one-and-a-half feet from it. We drove him out, and she gave chase. When the flight degenerated into a rat hunt, Venus sat on a fence post. Once we authoritatively evicted the

189

rook, she again gave chase. One stoop, and it dropped again into the shrubs. She crashed in, seizing it by a wing, where it hung screaming beneath her in the bush. I left my falconer's bag and fragments of my pants and skin on a fence while getting in to help her. In the excitement of trying to dislocate it's neck from its skull, I tore its head off. Oops! There were more congratulations and smiling faces all around.

All birds except Shiva having killed, we located a nice slip for her. Of course she chose a poorly positioned rook, pursued it to the rookery and missed. We found her another slip. Jack and I had to walk quite a way around the rooks to get downwind of them. Before we had gone half way they all got up. After a moment's hesitation Jack threw Shiva off, although it was a crosswind slip. The rooks were all far and high already. She went without hesitation, overtook a small group then forced one down, where it took refuge beneath the rusting hulk of an ancient tank. Unfortunately, Jack and I could not see this, but our comrades rushed to the scene in the vehicles. I looked back to see Jack luring, so I pulled out my lure, too. She came in while our friends were shouting. They were ready to flush that rook. The rook flew about one quarter mile downwind to a bush. Jack put Shiva back up for a one-mile rat hunt through the range and over great tank ruts. Eventually she connected with it beneath another shrub. Four kills in six slips. John Bennet, the photographer, got some good footage. Making this film may not be as easy as Jack thinks. Staying close to the action is not readily accomplished, especially while wielding a camera.

We saw Cyril and Jan off. Jack gave them Shiva's rook beak as a trophy and memento. I hope to see them in the U.S.A. next year on their trip.

22 April • Tilshead, Wiltshire, England

We have had miserable weather the past two days. Sure enough the weather became worse yet. We tried going out at 11:00 A.M. and had two slips in a 24-mph wind. Below White Barn, Venus started at some out-of-position rooks and began a downwind chase. Leonard called her back. As she turned, two other rooks passed beneath her. She cut one out and chased it downwind, killing it with a very nice, crisp stoop.

Next Shiva also selected a badly positioned rook. This time, making a low, crosswind flight, she caught it anyway. Tessa, Jack's Clumber spaniel, ran in and bumped Shiva up into the air again; Shiva carried her rook away. We eventually retrieved her. For the rest of the day the weather was extraordinarily poor with gales of wind, rain, sun and more wind. All birds were grounded.

23 April • Tilshead, Wiltshire, England
Too much wind today, so there was no hunting.

24 April • Tilshead, Wiltshire, England
11:30 A.M. Today is sunny and warm. We are just back from training the Sudanese falcons. Leonard slipped Jóhara at some rooks, which she pursued, but she quit after 150 yards. Jack entered Selema on a crow. She still won't take the lure unless it is on the ground. Evidently she will not be required by Leonard to do the requisite 20 stoops before entering. She looks ill to me. I think Jack has a lemon, but he is determined and forges on. Jóhara was flown at a hampered rook and brought it down. Pearl actually attempted to catch the lure in the air, ultimately succeeding. Well done, Gasim!

Jack is presently on the lawn with Madam Butterfly who is maximizing her outing by attacking Tessa in mock battle.

10:30 P.M. Jack, John Bennet and I just enjoyed a round of Guinnesses in the Black Horse, to celebrate an excellent day.

Here follows a recounting of this afternoon's happenings.

At 1:30 P.M. we were afield. Dhib had a perfect slip in a perfect place by Tilshead Camp at a passage rook. There was no cover. She was 150 yards downwind of the rook and above it as it flew down the valley, but then she refused. After waiting almost a full minute, she spotted another downwind rook then chased and killed it in some bushes in the rookery. We all rated it a miserable flight with Gasim dissenting. Due to her lackluster performance Jack did not permit her to feed up.

After a long stalk I flew Germany just outside of Tilshead on a 300-yard slip. As usual, he went low until almost upon them. By then most or the rooks had climbed above him, but he singled one out and forced it upwind, while gaining altitude, until he mastered it. Then came a series of downwind stoops until it bailed into some bushes. He followed it in. Since I was too winded to run in to evict the rook, I called him back.

191

Venus had a flight at Gore Cross, showing us some fine stoops all the way to the rookery. She missed.

Shiva's turn at the piggery. There were rooks literally everywhere, but Jack waited patiently and had Leonard slip her at three on passage into the wind. She began all right, and hundreds of rooks got up and away. She pressed on, intent upon her three, gaining height. Then, when everything else was up and away and the three were at her mercy, she turned downwind in a long, shallow glide into the piggeries, where we only now discerned a lone crow which had remained on the ground. She chased it from pigpen to pigpen, in and out, over and through squealing pigs. Once she even stooped at a piglet but eventually bagged her crow. Her flight was good for a laugh, even if not for the poor style of the hunt.

Dhib flew next in an unfavorable slip above the piggeries. The wind had dropped, so her rooks were able to achieve sanctuary before she could close; she beat up the rookery but caught nothing.

Germany, below White Barn and after a long stalk by me, had a good slip. He went in low. He singled out one rook and locked onto it.

Let me digress here to explain that sometimes, when Germany is too high in weight, he refuses to pursue a rook. Usually he commits immediately, and once locked on, tenaciously flies his rook, until it is either killed or hopelessly lost in cover. He does not generally quit once committed.

Germany caught up with and turned this rook , putting in several good stoops to intimidate it, then took it over a rise just out of sight. Before I could get to him it slipped free. So, he gave chase again. The flight continued to a house, over and around it. Eventually the rook perched atop the chimney. Germany circled, then came in. The rook dropped from the chimney onto the roof then ducked behind the chimney; then he dodged to the side. Germany flipped neatly over the chimney and seized the rook; both of them tumbled down the roof to the ground. I fed him up while the occupants of the house, no strangers to Jack's hawks, looked on.

Venus took a turn near Orcheston Road, a fine slip down into a valley from the road. She went off with terrific speed, great, powerful wing beats, wings arching high over her back. She put in a magnificent stoop, canceleering as if tied to the rook, down, down, down. Then followed some of the most spectacular stooping I have seen, very fast and with violent, unexpected directional changes. The rook seemed absolutely finished. She even tried attacking from below and the side. However, Venus had chosen a most excellent rook. She edged him away from a fence that he wanted to use for cover and in the end tried her best to cut him off from the rookery. It was to no avail as he outmaneuvered her and got to cover. I thought it an excellent flight.

Dhib had one more chance on the Chitterne-Shrewton Road. It was a good slip, but Dhib, frequently a poor starter, could not make up her mind and kept switching to new rooks as they continued to get up. The result was that she had but one final stoop at the last rook just as he entered cover. She tried unsuccessfully to force him out. Gasim flushed the rook, but she did not notice it until it had a good, hundred-yard lead downwind. She chased it until we saw her go into a long glide, following just behind it as it entered a row of large trees. She had it about five yards beyond the far side of the trees. We quit for the day with four kills.

25 April • Tilshead, Wiltshire, England

Today was another big day. The weather was cloudy with a light breeze and occasional drizzle. There was no flying for the trainees this morning. Dr. Keith Macy, a fellow Yank and the editor of the *Journal of the North American Falconers' Association*, arrived at noon with a young chap named Stansfeld. We headed out to hawk.

Dhib flew first at the Chitterne-Shrewton rookery. She was given a very nice slip and ignored it. Instead, she rung up and headed a good mile downwind. Another rook flushed. Dhib made a shallow stoop, caught it high up, and rode it to the ground. It was a poor show.

I slipped Germany at a rook on passage. He had a slow start because he got hung up on the glove release. Then he ignored my intended rook and drifted toward a flock of five which was a hundred yards upwind. These he fetched and made a long, half-hearted stoop at one just as it entered some trees. He rung up, now under attack by a lapwing and a kestrel, with which he sparred for five minutes. Finally, he came to Gasim's lure. Miserable show.

Shiva, in a slip off the Chitterne Road near two water towers, gave us a wonderful romp. She forced an crow into a thorn tree and then hit it a terrible whack. Both birds fell to the ground. The crow, cawing loudly, escaped Shiva's grasp. A terrific rat hunt followed through bushes and grass, telephone wires and culverts with all of us taking part. Finally, the crow made an error, and Shiva, now panting hard, pinned him in the grass, just as John Bennet ran out of film.

In a perfect neighboring valley by two barns, Venus had a beautiful slip. She started poorly with big, floppy, owl wing beats, refused the proffered rook and turned downwind after another. Jack whistled, causing her to turn and to fly hard upwind at a jackdaw (*Corvus modedula*) which sported some very unusual and noticeable white, primary feathers in his wings. She made two very clever stoops, then seized him, landing within 30 feet of Jack.

Germany at 25½ ounces in a close slip again got caught up on the glove nearly falling to the ground. He righted himself, then streaked into the wind. He cut out a rook, driving it down and into the wind. He stooped very hard, made his point with a terrific throw up, rolled over and stooped hard again, catching his rook beside an unsympathetic cow. By the time I reached him, he had the crow by the neck, holding it in one foot. His other leg was entirely stretched out behind him, foot clenched, being held securely by the rook's foot, which was wrapped around his thigh. I resolved the stalemate. Four kills today!

26 April • Tilshead, Wiltshire, England

It was a lovely, warm, spring day with a light south wind. We worked the new hands this morning. Pearl stooped the lure fairly well.

This afternoon we were joined by two other British falconers, Brian Vincent and Steven Frank. They were friends of Jack and wanted a chance to participate in the afternoon's hunt. We started at the two barns area, slipping Germany at a passage rook. He pursued it nicely, into the wind; then when he had it dead to rights, he atypically quit, dropping off downwind over my head. I called him down.

Venus had a fine slip about a quarter mile farther up the road and flew right up to her rooks. One rook dropped out at her approach, and in one amazing, twisting stoop, she had it. Nice flight!

Dhib, on the Chitterne-Shrewton Road, south of Tilshead, chose one downwind rook and chased it to cover. We drove out the rook, but it had a big lead on her; she was unable to overtake it. We spent some time trying to locate and retrieve her downwind.

Shiva was up next on the range where she had killed her 12th rook. Upon her approach one rook dropped out of the flock; she put in two giant, sweeping stoops before it bailed into a hedge. She shepherded it along the hedge, beating her own bush so to speak, and succeeded in killing it.

Germany took a mediocre slip at a passage rook, going low and crosswind down into a valley. He executed some beautiful, crisp stoops and throw-ups at a pair of rooks before they got into some trees. We repeatedly beat them out for him, but he had lost interest. The temperature being hot, he went on a soar to cool off. After a rapid sprint in the VW Brian got him down a mile or more away.

Gasim flew Dhib at a rook on passage where we last retrieved Germany. She had it perfectly controlled; then she chucked it and drifted on a soar downwind, rapidly gaining altitude. A mile downwind she came over some rooks which had decided to get up. She did not stoop but continued to drift along above them. Finally, she launched a series of long, steep stoops all of which missed. We conducted a ten-minute search to get her back.

John Bennet returned to Salisbury. Some of his film footage should be excellent. Later Jack and I talked about hawks with Keith Macy and made a tape recorded message to mail to Webby.

27 April • Tilshead, Wiltshire, England

A warm spring day with a gentle breeze. We flew all the new hands this morning. Then we were evicted from the field by an insolent herd of tanks at the Imber range.

The afternoon began well with a good wind. Leonard slipped Venus at Elsie Kite's place at a passing rook which had no tail and some feather gaps in its wings, a real snap. She pushed it upwind, dealt it a terrific stoop and a resounding whack, but it kept flying. She continued stooping it for a good mile downwind, hitting it at least once more. It would not be caught and barely escaped to the rookery. It was a gorgeous flight but bad luck for Venus.

Germany chased some passing rooks in the same area directly into an 18–20-mph wind. He flew his normal, low approach into the wind and had them nicely lined up ahead of him. Suddenly he made a long, shallow stoop off to the left to a mound of rubbish. We found him in a bush with a rook dangling from his feet. The rook had a strange, overgrown, "crossbill" beak but otherwise seemed fat and healthy.

The wind being too strong, further flights were cancelled.

28 April • Tilshead, Wiltshire, England

Jack slipped Selema below White Barn this morning. She went straight away and had a good flight at a rook, which escaped to the rookery. Jóhara took a short, crosswind slip but really had no chance to catch up with her rook.

This afternoon provided wind and pelting rain interspersed with brief glimpses of the sun, not good hawking weather. Venus was slipped near Two Barns at a flock of rooks; she went directly into the wind and easily killed one.

On the Chitterne-Shrewton Road, Dhib did not mount fast enough and was out-climbed by her rook. She swept away downwind in gusts over 20 mph. A good half hour later she came in to Jack's lure one mile downwind of where we had last seen her. She had blood on her beak and feet, evidently having been driven off a kill. Too windy, so we quit.

I am feeling very lonely tonight. I wrote Gaile in Rhodesia. Keith Macy left to return to America. He is a pleasant chap but has some domestic troubles. Too bad. I wonder what he will write of this adventure in the NAFA Journal?

29 April • Tilshead, Wiltshire, England

Sunny and windy. We tried flying Jóhara and Pearl in a cast this morning. The rook was away before they realized what was happening. However, they flew well together and did not crab or exhibit aggressive behavior toward each other. They circled from Gasim to Leonard to Jack for lures that were successively swung then hidden, not only to exercise them, but to get them accustomed to coming to any of us with a lure.

Gasim and I went to Salisbury to see the film *Zulu*. Neither of us liked it, and Gasim summed up his feelings about the Zulu bravely allowing themselves to be slaughtered by rifle and machine gun fire by commenting, "Zulu very stupid!"

30 April • Tilshead, Wiltshire, England

Sunny and windy. Jack slipped Selema at Imber Road. She put a rook into a bush then made a tactical error by going in after it. Of course it left at exactly the wrong moment and escaped. She came reluctantly to the lure.

Jóhara and Pearl were again flown in a cast and behaved very well together; they actually fed together side-by-side, wings overlapping and even picked morsels from each other's beaks. They were beautiful together and showed no signs of crabbing.

1 May • Tilshead, Wiltshire, England

It is sunny and cool with somewhat less wind, just barely flyable. Jack flew Selema out by the two water towers. She herded her rooks into the wind but lacked the stamina and drive to fetch them, so she broke off and returned to the lure. Jóhara and Pearl were slipped at a small rook flock near Nimrod's trees. Jóhara went downwind right after one with Pearl lagging behind. Pearl quit and came back. But Jóhara pressed on and bound to one high in the air and brought it down. Pearl, upon noting this turn of events, put on an initial burst of speed toward Jo but stopped when the rook broke free. She returned to us while Jóhara disappeared downwind. Our by-now-well-deployed falconers moved out, leaving Pearl on the wing to serve as a beacon for Jo. We had Jo back in ten minutes; she was in a rather wild state from the excitement.

This afternoon Germany went for a rook on passage above White Barn. He overhauled it, but due to the high winds, couldn't get into a good position to stoop. He abandoned it to go on a soar. By very good luck, Gasim later heard his bell and located him in a bush on a kill three miles downwind.

Venus attacked a flock of rooks in a plowed field along the Chitterne-Shrewton Road. She herded a group of five into the wind. One split off to the left. She caught up with him, but he was slightly above her, so they both turned downwind together. Venus thrust a foot up as she rolled on her back, trying to snag him on the turn. She missed, but it terrified him, and he lost altitude while she gained. Then she played him slowly, staying just above and downwind of him by a few feet making nice, short stoops, very patiently. They played this game among onrushing cars until she nailed him, and they pin-wheeled to the ground, fortunately off of the road.

Dhib blew off a beautiful slip just out of Chitterne along the same road. She went away downwind, made a big circle and came back low, the result of which was of course, that all rooks were well away.

In Nimrod's Valley, Shiva overtook her flock but passed them by, heading for a distant group of four that were tightly bunched and

197

perfectly positioned upwind. These she overhauled and was at least 30 feet above them when they turned beneath her. Instead of dropping on them she continued on past toward a distant rook which was making for the trees. Clever old Shiva waited until it got to cover, then tried to beat it out. She caught nothing.

Jack tried Shiva once more at Kite's at a nice flock of rooks. She employed the same old trick, ignoring the correct rooks and putting in a few stoops at a singleton lurking among some parked Army trucks and thence into the trees. Another miss. We quit for the day.

2 May • Tilshead, Wiltshire, England

Overcast with a light, fresh breeze; poor weather for flying. There is great panic in Jack's household. Sir Khizar Hayat Khan Tiwana of Pakistan approaches from London — together with his wife, stepdaughter, stepson, bodyguard and two drivers — for a visit.

Leonard and Gasim flew the recruits and had a nice flight, I am told, while Jack and I went into Salisbury to procure emergency rations and to exchange some money. We prepared a gigantic fruit salad, added prefabricated chicken, some fish and rice and served our new guests.

Sir Khizar, a tall, 64-year-old gentleman, graying but active, was quite interested in seeing some English hawking. Sir Khizar was a former Premier of the Punjab and a man of considerable wealth and consequence. According to Jack, he was one of the last people to practice classic falconry in Pakistan.

We took only the female falcons hawking. Germany was grounded as unreliable by Jack, considered most likely to cause an incident. I did not agree with Jack's reasoning. Jeff and Audrey Fletcher, friends of Jack, tagged along bringing our caravan to one Land Rover, plus three cars. Jack slipped Shiva at Greenland's; she had a nice flight, which ended in the rookery as usual with nothing.

Venus took a bad slip in a wind, which was too strong on the Lark Hill Range. She tried to cut off her rook, which was on passage, from the trees, but she could not overtake it before it reached cover.

Dhib again on Lark Hill in the impact area could not catch her rook in the wind.

Shiva, along the Chitterne-Shrewton Road, went about 400 yards downwind to a passing rook, ignoring those at which she was slipped. She put it into a bush out of sight. I started the Land Rover in pursuit. As I arrived she came in to Gasim. We quit for the day. A cardinal rule of falconry is that the more important the guest, the worse the showing will be. That seemed to be the case today.

At tea we had an excellent conversation with Sir Khizar, who graciously invited me to be his guest this year in Pakistan. His body-guard even promised me a very good cherrug (saker). They were persistent in their entreaties and attempted to get Jack to promise to come. Sir Khizar told me that falconry is now back in full swing in Pakistan, albeit game keepers must be bribed and officials must be coerced in order to secure hawking rights. Hunting birds are taxed to keep down their numbers, especially the goshawk which is used for partridge, for which the shooters compete. Nonetheless falconry flourishes. Gosses are difficult to obtain, costing £40 to £50. Falcons cost less. Hawking is done from horseback or American jeep. The best flights are at the "grass owl" (*Tyto longimembris?*); these are ringing flights in which a good saker either kills or is lost. Only sakers are used as the peregrine is too fast to give a good, challenging flight. I was told that although kites are still flown, it is not a common flight. This is due chiefly to the fact that few sakers will take kites well; that is, few are courageous or persistent enough. Sir Khizar rates kites as the most difficult quarry for a falcon both in the training and in the flight. Few sakers are good at it, and once they have been tried and trained for kite, they are useless for anything else. One must go through a lot of sakers in order to get a good kite falcon. In short, it is impractical.

Sir Khizar also maintains that good, ringing flights can be had from plovers, and he recommends Houbara bustard hawking with sakers, of course. Houbara are the traditional quarry for sakers in the Middle East.

Sakers are trapped by means of a partially seeled barrak kite, the trappers following it on horseback. The kite's eyes are partially closed by means of a thread passed through the lower eyelids and tied atop the head, a common and relatively painless procedure used in the Middle East, which helps prevent the kite from avoiding a wild saker. The kite is released with a barrak bundle affixed to its feet, and with luck, a greedy saker will be caught in the barrak nooses. Hawks are tamed by two methods: by carrying and manning or by drugging, which is dangerous as it may kill the bird. Pakistanis prefer red sakers to haggards and claim they are easier to train. Falcon trapping begins in September and is best then and in October. Hawking continues through the winter.

I was sorry to see Sir Khizar leave as it was fascinating to hear him talk. I cursed myself for neglecting to take any photos. Maybe someday in Pakistan.

3 May • Tilshead, Wiltshire, England

Sunny with winds up to 26 mph. We flew the lanners in a cast downhill at a flock of rooks at the piggeries. They both went low and fast and were into the flock with almost no warning. Jo stooped, putting a rook down, and Pearl nailed it. Jo dropped down to aid in the tussle. Both birds were quite amicably holding it down when we arrived on the scene. The entire flight seemed to last about ten seconds and spanned less than 100 yards. The lanners behaved beautifully towards one another.

Despite redline winds Jack flew Shiva on prospect at Lark Hill. (Jack has a hand-held device which measures wind speed. Redline is 20 mph, Jack's cutoff point for flying a falcon. In winds higher than 20 mph it is too easy to lose a bird.) She separated a rook out of a flock, pursuing it over my head; she broke off and came to me, looking for a lure.

We tried to get Venus a slip but had no luck. We had to quit due to high winds.

Trees are turning green. Flowers are opening. House martins (*Delichon urbica*) have returned. Spring is definitely in the air. I feel restless, lonely and a bit apprehensive about what sort of life I will find back in the U.S.A. I feel that I have been running away from life and responsibilities long enough. To be truthful, the thought of quitting Europe, the travel and the freedom which I have known is very disquieting. I dread the rut of part-time work, odd jobs and general uselessness. A time for decisions approaches. I am not entirely tranquil about transitioning to a new way of life. I'll miss the road and the European circuit. Oh yes, I find myself wishing for a girl with whom to share life as a comrade and partner. Nesting instinct? My present financial resources total $301.80. Maybe it is time to go to work.

4 May • Tilshead, Wiltshire, England

Sun, clouds, rain, hail and wind. Leonard is feeling bad. Jack is off to

London to shop for a 1929 Rolls Royce. Perhaps he wants to project a more stately image of a country gentleman? He already has a beautiful old Rolls open sports tourer.

We tried the lanners in a couple of slips this morning, bad slips with no success. There was no flying this afternoon.

Derek Moore came by, and we had a nice chat about his former employment as a falconer by Jack. He must have been rather wild for Uncle Jack. I later heard one story about the irate father of a girl whom Derek had been "dating," who showed up at Jack's front door with a shotgun looking for Jack's falconer. Derek conveniently was not to be found. Derek and I concurred that Jack Mavrogordato is a man whom, no matter how well and long one knows him, one cannot ever really completely fathom. Jack is very private inside.

5 May • Tilshead, Wiltshire, England

In Salisbury this morning I bought a pair of suede shoes for $10. Since being in the Army, I refuse to buy shoes that have to be shined. When I returned to Tilshead we tried unsuccessfully to get a slip for the lanners.

After lunch about 3:00 P.M. we took out the old-timers. Leonard slipped Venus, along the road to Imber near the rookery, at a flock of rooks which were following a tractor. She did not go high enough at first, and they all got downwind, so she was able to get in one stoop only. She missed.

Germany, along the same road but on the side directly opposite the piggeries, was slipped at a rook on passage. He turned directly downwind at another, which he stooped. Ignoring my lure, he quit his rook and came back high over the piggeries. He put in a few hard stoops at another rook. He drifted a mile to the rookery then chased a rook into cover where he disappeared. A 15-minute search discovered him plucking an eyass rook on the ground. End of season for Germany! Once baby rooks start to fledge clever old falcons soon figure out that there are easy meals available in the rookeries. They will ignore slips and simply fly to the nearest rookery for fast food. The falconry community has a name for this undesirable behavior, "flying cunning." It is wise to ground a bird that has begun to fly cunning.

After a long stalk Gasim flew Dhib at a feeding rook flock. They reached cover before Dhib could overtake them.

Above White Barn Shiva put a rook on passage into some bushes after a good flight. It flew off and escaped when we arrived to help.

Today's weather was beautiful and sunny with a 12–15-mph wind. Leonard and his family are all ill. Perhaps they have the flu. I hope we are not next.

6 May • Tilshead, Wiltshire, England

The morning dawned sunny and warm with light winds, very pleasant. About 11:00 A.M. we took the new birds out. Selema had a slip above White Barn but gave up when the rooks easily out-climbed her. We looked hard for a suitable slip for the lanners. Finally, we found a slip for them at a flock of rooks feeding among some cows on the hill above Chitterne along the Chitterne-Shrewton Road. Jo went right at them. Gasim slipped Pearl after Jóhara had a 50-yard lead. Pearl attacked immediately. Jo quit when she saw Pearl and circled back. Pearl continued, putting a rook down among the cows. When she noticed no help was forthcoming from Jo, she gave up and returned to us.

We took the old hands out, sans Germany of course. Venus took a beautiful, long slip, wide open and without cover. She started well but suddenly veered off to the right at a crow which was passing low beneath her. She stooped twice, knocking it down. As she threw up a second crow attacked her, allowing the first to conceal himself in the grass. We chased off the attacker and flushed the original crow, but Venus was evidently hung up on the ground by a jess. By the time she had freed herself, the crow was about 150 yards upwind. She pursued it, putting him into a herd of cows. Fearing the cows, she refused to go in after him. I evicted him. He hopped into a little ditch where she caught him.

While we fed Venus up, another flock of rooks moved in near Dido's bush (another colloquial name used by Jack). Dhib was cast off. She rose slowly above us, making no forward progress into the wind, while the terrified rooks rowed upwind, gaining both altitude and distance. Dhib was in no hurry; she even circled once downwind to gain a bit of height. Then one rook, by now several hundred yards upwind of her, panicked and dropped into Dido's bush. Dhib flew past it to the next bushes, where the rest of the flock had now put in. She was stooping at them as we drove up. She nabbed one without our help.

After Dhib had fed up we voted the rook which was still cowering in Dido's bush an excellent candidate for Shiva. It flushed before we could circle downwind of it. Jack cast off Shiva anyway. As soon as the rook saw her, he returned to the bush. Shiva went in after him. We could see them hopping from branch to branch, bouncing in and out of the shrub. A great rat hunt was on! I was throwing chunks of mud and at one point a five-gallon can at the rook. Jack was firing his starter pistol and even climbed a tree. After five minutes of major chaos, Shiva killed it. Three kills in one and one half hours.

7 May • Tilshead, Wiltshire, England

Cool, overcast, light rain with redline winds. On the way back from picking up chicks at the hatchery to feed the falcons, Leonard spotted a young rook in a field with its flock. He wanted to capture it. Jack slipped Tessa the spaniel, who ran it down and retrieved it. All sakers are hereby grounded. Catching new-fledged rooks is not sporting.

At 2:30 P.M., Venus had a slip at Imber Valley, just off the C-T Road in a long, open valley, at a passage crow. She flew him well, putting in nine hard stoops and forcing him into a bush half a mile downwind. Leonard called her back. We spent hours getting a slip for the lanners, finally succeeding at Heartbreak Bottom. It was a good slip at a small flock feeding on the ground with no cover. Pearl went immediately, but Jo refused. When the chase got difficult Pearl broke off and returned.

We wasted another hour stalking imaginary magpies. As there was too much wind, Selema was grounded and fed up.

Jack stalked six rooks along a fence at Imber Valley. He slipped Venus. With one stoop and a dip, she had number 49 for the season. *Nimshe el bait tawále!* (Arabic for "Let's go home now!")

8 May • Tilshead, Wiltshire, England

Gale winds today but sunny and warm. Jack put Germany up for the molt, loose in the outside pen in anticipation of a breeding attempt. The wind dropped to redline, so we went out at 2:30 P.M.

Venus had a slip at Middle Barn, a jog in the C-T Road, a nice flight with some fine throw ups in which she would twist and try to grab the rook while coming up from below. She put it into upwind cover. It took us ten minutes of luring to get her back.

Selema was next in Imber Valley. She went right at her rook

very hard, very fast. As she closed he veered off and up to the left. I was astonished to see her continue in a straight line without so much as glancing at him out and down into the valley, never slackening her pace. Then a stoop — at a pigeon which had been hiding on the ground. One more stoop, a miss and back she came. Jack was disgusted. She had blown a very fine rook slip.

After a long drive over the countryside we ended up at the piggeries. Jo and Pearl were slipped in a redline wind a good 200 yards from a flock of rooks feeding on the ground. Pearl went right off, climbed, and overtook them, trying to attack from beneath and seize one on the downwind turn. She missed, and they all got above her. Gasim called her back. I looked to see where Jo was. She was hovering about 20 feet from Leonard, never having started, just waiting for the lure. We fed everybody up and headed home.

I spent the day packing and getting my affairs in order in preparation for my trip back to the U.S.A. Madam Butterfly has been banished from the cottage to a loft outside.

9 May • Tilshead, Wiltshire, England

Warm and sunny with too much wind to fly today. I continued to pack and wrote up some information on use of the noose harness in trapping for Jack's new book, *A falcon in the Field*, the book which he wrote in Port Sudan. I have not yet been able to secure proper booking for my trip home. Tentatively, I will leave May 19th for Iceland. Iceland Air has the cheapest flights to the U.S.A. Of course since it has been over a year since I separated from the Army, I have to get myself home without military help.

10 May • Tilshead, Wiltshire, England

It is an absolutely beautiful, spring day: warm, sunny with little wind. Jack and Gasim weeded the garden this morning. Jack vented venomous cries of "*Um débba!*" (an Arabic obscenity) hurled at offending clumps of weeds and accompanied by slashing attacks with a hoe. Jeff and Audrey Fletcher, friends of Jack, dropped by for hawking this afternoon. I remained home to organize for my trip and to watch the Monaco Grand Prix on the telly. Jack later related how the lanners had each simultaneously caught young rooks on the rise and how Selema had two unsuccessful flights.

13 May • Evershot, Dorset, England

I am at the Woodfords' home, Summer Lodge, in Evershot. The weather continues to be warm, sunny and lovely. It certainly was the experience of a lifetime to hawk with Jack, Leonard and Gasim. I will miss them and their kindnesses to me. But, with the end of rook season I could no longer justify staying. It was time to go. Jack called today to say the lanners, led by Pearl, killed a good rook today. Excellent! This brings our total to 50 worthy rooks.

We tried to fly June's Colorado passage prairie falcon today but were unsuccessful in finding a slip. This is miserable long-wing country with its brush, hedges and trees.

I spent two days accompanying Mike Woodford on his veterinary rounds. After watching him reach his arm full-length into the back end of a cow to push back a prolapsed uterus, stitch up a pig's everted anus, draw blood from the side of a horse and worm a flock of sheep, I decided that the romance of veterinary medicine is not for me. June helped me make a nice falconry glove. She is a very talented hood and glove maker.

One of the more fun aspects of my stay are evenings spent at the Tiger's Head Pub. Dave Woodford, Mike and June's son, and his friend Paul Bramley have been part of some rude and obscene sessions in the Tiger's Head Pub and even at home here. Their latest topic of discussion is a nasty disease, which goes by the name of Holevil or Brewer's Ass and allegedly results from drinking too much beer. So far, none of us has succumbed to the tragic malady.

I spent the day rummaging through Mike's library. Especially interesting were Phillot's notes on hawks and falconry in India, and the wartime *Journals of the Falconry Association of North America* with articles by Robert Stabler, R.L. Meredith, W. Spofford, Al Nye, M. Nelson and H. Webster [all patriarchs of American falconry].

I saw a nice tawny owl (*Strix aluco*) being mobbed by blackbirds last night. Also observed some house martins and cuckoos (*Culculus canorus*).

14 May • London, England

At 10:00 A.M. David Woodford gave me a ride to Sherborne, from whence a nice couple took me almost to London. A young caterer brought me the rest of the way by 2:00 P.M. It was a beautiful day, green and springy. I checked Philbeach Gardens, where I had stayed with Gaile and Gay, hoping to see a familiar face but had no luck. I met two Aussies, Phil and Murray, both nice chaps, working on their VW bus, the *Fahrt Wagen*. We shot the breeze all afternoon. Another fellow, Alex Stewart, arrived around 6:00 P.M. We rounded up a final chap named Pav and spent a nice evening reminiscing about mutual acquaintances over pints of bitter. Pav and his girl, Jean, plan to go to Australia this year. Alex has put me up in his room, since his roommate is currently absent. I feel secure now.

16 May • London, England

After a late-night bull session with Alex last night I slept in until 10:00 A.M. this morning. It was another lovely day. I called David Reid-Henry to make an appointment to see him tomorrow. David is perhaps the finest painter of raptors in the world. Then I rang up Geoffrey Pollard and went to visit him in Uxbridge. Geoffrey had five peregrines weathering on his lawn: The Pro (Pakistani passage female), Houbara (Persian Gulf passage female), Lady Sue (American haggard female), Tiger (new Persian Gulf passage female) and Elsa (origins unknown). I enjoyed a very pleasant day talking with Geoffrey and his wife. They graciously invited me for a delicious chicken supper. All of his birds, except Elsa, are lovely to see, very tame, and most jump readily to the fist even without food for an inducement. Houbara and Tiger are probably *F.p. calidus* sub species, very pale in color. Geoffrey feeds his birds on their blocks. He moves very slowly and methodically even when he is not around the birds. He is not enamored of fellow Brit falconers Philip Ware and Gordon Jollie.

17 May • London, England

I met David Reid-Henry in his home on the outskirts of London, a crowded little place with a small, fenced yard in the back. He was exceedingly friendly and to my joy dragged out masses of sketches, drawings, bird skins, etc. He explained how he works. He draws hundreds of sketches from life, works in pencil, stores everything, then lets it all incubate; he works up ideas from these resources which may or may not then evolve into finished paintings. His work-studies are sacred and are kept for reference to be used for future paintings. He also makes sketches of ideas for laying out paintings. These are not sacred, and he has left instructions in his will that these should all be burned upon his death. He wants only what he considers his warrantable work to survive him. From his work-studies and sketches he derives his actual paintings.

His tiny studio was crammed with boxes, skins, drawers, papers, drawings and an immense perch for his prized African crowned eagle (*Stephanoaetus coronatus*), Tiara. A little, white-faced Scop's owl sat among the litter of books, paintbrushes and sundries, which were scattered in profusion amidst liberal quantities of eagle mutes. He bowed politely when I noticed him.

An absolutely magnificent painting was in progress on David's easel. It depicted a wide panorama of an Arctic valley. A white gyrfalcon, perched on a rock in the valley, was looking intently over its back down the valley toward some ptarmigan which were flying in the foreground. The sun was just low enough to bathe the falcon in a rosy glow. It was a breathtaking masterpiece.

David had a photographic memory. He frequently painted scenes, which he would let sit sometimes for years then later fill them in with birds, mammals and other details. He roundly criticized Roger Tory Peterson, and Fen Lansdown, famous fellow bird artists, for carelessness. He showed me a copy of Peterson's *European Field Guide to the Birds* in which he had very carefully corrected every inaccuracy he could find. Scarcely a page was unmarked.

David's sole contact with nature was his postage stamp-sized yard which was filled to capacity by his eagle, one buteo and a loft of pigeons. A neighbor's family of cats occasionally tempted fate by wandering too close to Tiara the eagle.

David was trapped in this microcosm with an unsympathetic wife and two daughters who shared no love for their father's birds or painting. He works on, however, trying to finish up all of his many commitments so that he may eventually escape to Southern Rhodesia for a few months.

As is traditional when any two falconers get together David and I raked a few of our fraternity over the coals. He especially deplored Ronald Stevens and narrated at length those unpleasant encounters he had personally experienced. David had been formerly employed by Ronald to come to Ireland to paint some large canvasses with falcons. David's complaints against Stevens included being given very meager food, being treated as a servant and being sequestered far from Ronald's falconer guests. Other negative observations followed. Stevens, according to David, kicked a goshawk so hard "its

207

feathers flew," shook a falcon from his fist in a fit of rage, refused to take up a lost falcon, claimed deck feathers were on the underside of the tail (they are on the top), spent £300 on a horse race ticket, gave away gifts that he had previously bestowed on David, was squandering the family fortune, bought a new car every year, had a gay brother, had expended a succession of professional falconers, flew birds only when someone was there to run for him, had bizarre methods of feeding his falcons and so on. I was pretty sure that David never forgot a slight. Oh yes, on a positive note, Ronald's sister was the "only sensible one in the family."

David liked Uncle Jack and Alan Savory. He criticized Geoffrey Pollard for not being an ornithologist and for killing sick falcons and for not saving their skins. He did not like South African falconer Rudi De Witt.

While we perused his many sketches and studies, David noticed my poorly concealed zeal to have one of his works. Most generously, he sold me a lovely little African peregrine tiercel head study for the meager sum of £3. He also quoted me a price on another unfinished little portrait of Dora, a one-winged peregrine, which I will be able to buy once I return home. I was overjoyed!

David also insisted I hold Tiara, the crowned eagle. I was not at all keen to do so, having noted Tiara's raised hackles and crest when I neared her and of course her enormous feet. But, David was not one to be dissuaded easily. With profound reluctance I permitted Tiara to board my well-gloved forearm. She placed her beak about one inch from my nose, erected her crest and gazed deeply with her yellow orbs into my eyes; she clamped down on my arm so hard that it went numb. I was holding her jesses securely, as you might imagine, but with the loss of feeling in my hand and arm, I became concerned about whether I could restrain her if she decided to move up my arm to other body parts. Satisfied that I had sufficiently experienced the eagle, David relieved me of her. Only then did he tell me about how she had once killed a German shepherd dog, which some fool had released at her in a London park. And, he told me how she had been banned from the London underground (subway), on which he formerly had traveled with her around London. He told about how she had patiently waited on her block for the hated neighbor lady's cat to stalk within leash distance before she destroyed it. My heart was still racing from my own brief encounter with Tiara.

I got mixed up on the trains, returning on the underground at midnight and had to take a taxi for 10 shillings. Rats! Alex, thoroughly pissed from beer drinking, greeted me warmly, and we spent some quality time bemoaning the lack of females in our lives.

18 May • London, England

10:20 P.M. I just got back from visiting Cyril and Jan Morley in Kent. It was a pleasant and quiet day. They are good people. Cyril has canceled his proposed trip to America for want of money.

Tomorrow I will leave this life and land behind. It has been a wonderful experience. I almost wish it could continue indefinitely, but it is time to stop running from responsibility. Speaking of which, I have to knuckle down and write some letters, so good night.

19 May • Manchester, England

I am over Manchester at 18,000 feet, going 400 mph in a BEA (British European Airways) Vanguard. It is smooth. I like watching the clouds, and as always I wish I could float among them and drift through them and bounce in them. I can apperceive their buoyancy, and it is easy to imagine that it might somehow be possible to negate the law of gravity to play in them.

I have not been pleased about making this journey home. I am still apprehensive about returning to the States. I now tend to regard this side of the Atlantic as home. The U.S.A. with its high prices, responsibilities lurking in dark corners, decisions which will have to be made (such as how to earn a living) have me edgy. If I felt I were coming home to the way of life which I am leaving behind, I would be eager to see my old homeland and its people. But this flight marks the end to a life of as complete a freedom as I can imagine. I do not readily embrace beginning the life of responsibility.

With $58 total resources in my hand, I am coming into Glasgow now over the scrubby suburbs, leaving the open country and life behind.

20 May • Reykjavik, Iceland

11:00 P.M. I arrived here in the wee hours to find a several hour flight connection delay. It occurred to me that I might extend those few hours into a few days. A quick inquiry confirmed that I could stay for weeks before continuing on home. With a little diligence I lo-

209

cated the Hafnarbudir, a place for sailors by the docks, for temporary lodging.

I have a room with four Icelandic chaps at the Hafnarbudir; it is modern and clean but not cheap (Icelandic Kroner 105.50, or $2.45 American). My roommates speak no English. The watchman, Aree, is a friendly, one-legged chap who likes to converse and does speak English.

I spent the day exploring Reykjavik and met Dr. Finnar Gudmundson at the museum of natural history. The museum director, he was a giant of a man and very helpful. He was critical of falconry as a sport. I had a difficult time defending falconry against his arguments and came out feeling a bit of a failure at so doing. There are too many falconers, who to my way of thinking are rather wretched people who either can't or won't keep their birds properly. These folks are every bit as much falconers in the eyes of the uninitiated, as are those who really do practice the sport with skill and integrity. Of course, since each of us considers himself one of the latter category and many of the rest as the former, the non-falconer is faced with the whole spectrum of people called falconers. Thus, it was not easy to defend my sport.

I searched out the youth hostel which had moved and was closed. I met Helen, a chubby American girl from Ohio, who is an exchange student. I met some sailors, a Marine named Mike, two Israelis, Moshi and Ami, a German, Dieter, and an Englishman named Lynn. We discussed the merits of working on fishing boats or in factories. The pay runs from IK 35 (35 Icelandic Króna) on up. There is plenty of work for everybody. I think I will start work tomorrow and save up enough to see a bit of this island. I am down to $47.

Girls here are beautiful and plentiful and always seem to occur in groups. Good hawking!

I have taken a job as a hod carrier. I start at 1:00 P.M. tomorrow, and it pays IK 50 per hour. Since I get motion sick on a swing, I have decided against fishing for a living.

21 May • Reykjavik, Iceland

I am sporting a few blisters tonight, but it was really an easy afternoon's work. Because of a high incidence of earthquakes all construction here — and there appears to be a construction boom — is of concrete. We are plastering the inside of a house now. I know how

210

that works. As far as I can figure, I am the assistant of a 20-year-old chap named Maggi (pronounced Matyi). He is a nice young guy, and although we have positively no common ground on language, I have learned he has a wife, at least one kid and another kid on the way. He has also wrecked a Ford Thunderbird and likes Fats Domino. That's pretty damned good I think for my first day!

I scrapped the Hafnarbudir for a tiny but clean third-storey room, all to myself on the outskirts of town on Marahlid St. My landlord is friendly, and thank heavens he speaks English. I have made friends with the store owner on the corner and have even been noticed by a teenage girl next door. I rather like Iceland.

The surrounding countryside is very barren, just rocks and mosses, truly tundra-like. There are all sorts of interesting ducks, gulls and other birds around. I have to save up to buy another Mountfort and Peterson field guide, damn it. Lost the old one.

The chap who got me this job by the way not only lined it up for me but drove me out four or more miles to work and even gave me a pair of rubber boots. How's that for helpful?

The food is good, if you like fish, sausage, yoghurt, and sheep heads. At home I had a supper of cheese with some smoked fish topped off with a genuine, Iceland-grown banana. This evening as I looked out the window of this miniature room I thought, "I'm happy here." Probably that is related to my relief at not returning to the U.S.A. and of realizing a dream I have had for years, experiencing an Arctic summer.

30 May • Reykjavik, Iceland

After a week in Iceland I discovered it is impossible to achieve my arctic dream here; Iceland is sub-Arctic. Nevertheless, it is an interesting place. The weather is momentarily beautiful, sunny and warm.

I am still on my construction job and have run my assets to $90. I expect to work another week to bring that to $120, then head north to look for gyrfalcons. I have a bit of concern because from the map I see there is no town or village for many miles in the area where I want to go. But, there are two hotels in the area which may be open and may provide me temporary haven. Anyway, there are lots of farms about, so I'll be safe. I will be cut off from resources and aid and highly limited on transportation. If I can find shelter and

211

transport, I expect it will be dear, and money will not be my strong suit. But, I have to give it a try.

There is an American Fulbright student, Cal Roeder, living here on the same floor. He seems friendly but is a bit strange in some ways. I do not think him a good candidate for my associate. I also met an American girl, Pat, who comes by to chat with Cal. She is pleasant. Anyway, we are all off to the films tonight after a supper together. I shall be at my sparkling best tonight in jeans and a dirty shirt.

Last Friday, feeling lonely and tired and wishing frankly for a girl, I wandered into Reykjavik. I checked out a few cafes including the Café Tröd where I tried to enjoy a milkshake. The place was dead except for aggregates of teenagers, all dressed fit to kill. While walking down Fríkirkjuvegur, I was accosted by a friendly, drunken chap by the name of Sigurdur Jonson who assured me he liked Americans. He was 25, big, a little fat and quite jovial. I saw that he would be difficult to shake, and having absolutely nothing else to do, I went with him.

Siggy spun a tale of beautiful women, Iceland's finest, who assembled every Friday night at the Hotel Borg for dining and dancing. He assured me that, although they were difficult to befriend, they were well worth the effort.

At the Hotel Borg the doorman took one look at my white, wash pants, yellow jersey and blue, nylon zip jacket and explained that he was frightfully sorry, but there was no way we would be allowed to enter. Siggy was crushed but not ready to capitulate; he spoke to me of the wondrous girls at the Clubidur, Reykjavik's only nightclub, as best as I could gather. "The women are pretty but most have made mistakes," Siggy explained. "They ask you for no money, for sure. I promise you. They ask you to go home with them. They like your pretty face, nice and brown. But first, you got change clothes." No matter that I was unprepared with a change of clothes. He had clothes at his hideaway. I said no thank you. If I were not good enough this way, to hell with them.

We were next refused entry to the Naust and several other establishments because of Siggy's inebriated condition and my substandard clothing. We ended up taking a taxi to his little nest across the street from the American Embassy. There among empty whiskey bottles and grime lay a wrinkled blue suit and grubby shirt, replete with a large red, wine stain. Into these I climbed, leaving my own clothes behind. The marine guarding the American Embassy was induced to call us a taxi which whisked us away to the Clubidur, where despite my newly donned attire and careful attention to holding Siggy up, we still could not get past the doorman.

Another taxi took us back to the Hotel Borg. This time we made it inside. I bought the tickets since Siggy had paid for the cabs. I had a coke and danced to a fairly good band with teenage, gum-chewing girls, all extravagantly dressed. Finally, I couldn't take any more fun and walked home. The sun had just set. Here that meant it just dipped below the horizon for a brief interlude then rose to circle the skyline once again. It is light here all day. Night has no meaning.

The next day I had to work until 6:00 P.M. Then I walked to town to retrieve my clothes and to return Siggy's. No Siggy. I tried again on Sunday. Still no Siggy. I picked the lock, changed, relocked the door and have not had a night out in the week since.

A typical day consists mostly of work. I leave about 7:30 A.M., arriving at work at 8:00. We have a coffee break from 9:15 to 9:45 or 10:00, then lunch from 11:30 to 1:00 P.M. Lunch is wonderful, all the boiled fish and yoghurt I can eat. There is more coffee between 3:15 and 4:00 P.M. We quit work between 5:00 and 6:00. I am usually home around 6:00 P.M. Then it is straight to the bath, followed by honey and cheese for sandwiches, read a little *Njal's Saga* (an Icelandic Saga about a long-gone hero named Njal) and into bed. Occasional variation includes talking with housemate Cal.

I saw a couple of whooper swans (*Cygnus cygnus*) fly over Kópavogur today. On the lake in Reykjavik there were a few greater scaup (*Aythya marila*), many mallards and arctic terns (*Sterna paradisaea*). On the inlets between Reykjavik and Kópavogur, common eiders (*Somateria mollissima*) and Eurasian oystercatchers (*Haematopus ostralegus*) were abundant. I saw a few golden plovers (*Pluvialis apricaria*) and a whimbrel (*Numenius phaeopus*). Around midnight, redwings (*Turdus musicus*) could be seen singing from TV antennae throughout the suburbs.

31 May • Reykjavik, Iceland

Betty Davis played a terrific role in last night's film in Reykjavik, *What Ever Happened to Baby Jane?* Today, Sunday, is windy and overcast at 1:00 P.M. I feel restless, but there isn't much to do, so I will probably write a few letters. My total resources are now $72.

I took a walk down to the harbor this afternoon and watched black-headed gulls (*Larus ridibundus*) and arctic terns feeding in the breakers. There were a few black-backed gulls and herring gulls (*Larus argentatus*) and one ringed plover (*Charadrius hiaticula*).

4 June • Reykjavik, Iceland

I just picked up my mail from the embassy for the first time since I arrived here. My job prevents me from going during open hours, and I had to chat up a guard to get it out tonight. I had a letter from Steve Baer. Steve reported his new addition to the family is due momentarily. Also, he flunked school when he went to München instead of taking his final exams after a year of study at Zürich's Swiss Federal Institute of Technology. But, Steve isn't interested in degrees, only knowledge, which he is getting despite the school and its attempts to thwart his creativity and thinking. Anyway, he feels he's accomplishing his ends and has what he needs from the institute, and that is the important thing. I admire him.

I'm still no closer to deciding on a profession. I don't think being a lecturer will work since I'm still stage shy and always have been a bit tongue-tied. Perhaps I could write but probably not well enough for professional status. Oh well, I'll come up with something. Maybe I will be back to school but not for an M.D. I don't want to kill people with my mistakes.

6 June • Reykjavik, Iceland

I finished work yesterday. I now have $92 including American and Icelandic currency. And, I have round trip tickets to Akureyri and Myvatn off in northern Iceland on an expedition to find gyrfalcons. I am just about packed at 10:00 P.M. I received a letter from Jack Mavrogordato today and learned that Pearl caught rook #52, to finish the season. I also had a letter from Busch, who is working in Dayton, saying that I have to visit en route to Colorado. I guess I will. Gaile writes that the Africans in Rhodesia have cooled down with cooler weather. She, Gay and Tricia just returned from a week in Mozambique.

I have managed to stay friendly with my housemate Cal by being outgoing and interested in his work on medieval languages, his favorite subject. As long as I am willing to converse on his ground, all is well. I will stick with my earlier appraisal of Cal. He is a hypo-

214

chondriac and an inveterate door locker. Personally, I always leave the door to my room unlocked when I am home.

7 June • Lake Myvatn, Iceland

6:15 P.M., partly cloudy. Today was a big day. I said goodbye to Cal and walked to the airport. Our DC 3 rose into the air at 9:00 A.M. We flew rather low over some extremely barren country, glaciated mountains and valleys. I saw the great Langjókul and Hofsjókull, two very impressive glaciers which sprawl out for miles. Coming into Akureyri we dropped low down into the valley below the mountaintops, buffeted by some turbulence. I sweated profusely and felt pretty nervous watching rocks go past where clouds should have been. We dropped into Akureyri around 10:30 A.M. It was a small town situated at the head of Eyafjördur glacier with mountains rising gently all about it. A mixed flock of black backed gulls and arctic terns flushed from the runway as we landed. I saw some tufted ducks (*Aythya fuligula*), mallards and scaup in the area. I met two Swiss chaps, Willi Meyer and Kurt Koller, who work with Swissair out of Copenhagen and are on vacation. They rented a car to drive to Myvatn for the day and offered to take me along. I gladly went in the new Austin which reminded me of a little Land Rover.

It was a nice drive over some very wild volcanic and glacial landscape. I noticed power line poles, which might be good for attracting post breeding season gyrfalcons. Flocks of dozens of golden plovers were along the route. I saw one raven. By Lake Ljósavatn several redwings flitted across the road. We stopped to take photographs along the way, then had a couple of sandwiches in a little café at Einarsstadir. I noticed a whimbrel by Lake Másvatyn. Approaching Myvatn where the Laxá River flows into it, there were some mergansers and several Barrow's goldeneye (*Bucephala islandica*). All along the south side of the lake were hundreds of red-necked phalarope (*Phalaropus lobatus*) apparently feasting on swarms of tiny flies, which had fallen into the water. We passed mallards, gadwalls, scaup, and Slavonian grebes (*Podiceps auritis*) and arrived at the Hotel Reynihlid. I was issued an even tinier room than I had had in Reykjavik; it featured no heat, light, water, places to hang anything or places to take more than one step in any direction. It had two beds, one table and a mirror, all for IK 100 per day ($2.35). It suited me fine. Within minutes of arriving I had learned that there is a man here who collects duck eggs and is very bird wise; the local taxi driver knew all about bird life and told me there is a gyrfalcon nest within ten kilometers!

The settlement at Lake Myvatn is tiny. There are two competing hotels, the Reynihlid and the Reykjahlid plus a handful of other buildings. The hotels form the backbone of the place as pretty much everything social focuses at one or the other.

Willi, Kurt and I drove out to Námaskard, an impressive geothermal area, took a few photos and had a delicious swim in a cave located down in a crevasse with hot spring water. They dropped me off with good wishes at the hotel, then headed back to Akureyri, thence to Reykjavik and Copenhagen, where they will report for work at 8:30 A.M. tomorrow.

By the lake I met the egg collector, Willi Pálsson, a 70-year-old man who is a bit deaf, a bit inebriated but a lot friendly. He has a farm here which has been in the family for seven generations. He raises sheep. Seasonally, he has farmers collect duck eggs, which he sends all over the world. We talked over a beer downstairs at the Reynihlid. He told me about how he collects, candles and ships about 3000 eggs per year, always leaving at least four eggs of each clutch in nests. Apparently there are a lot of people who like ducks. Adjourning to his room, we talked a bit about falconry. I learned that both Philip Ware and Ronald Stevens have been here in bygone days to take gyrs home, and that Ronald Stevens' book, *Laggard*, includes a description of his trip here. It seems Stevens stayed across the street with Sveridur the taxi driver. It was a very bad year for gyrs, as there were few ptarmigan. Ptarmigan, like most species of endothermic vertebrates in the high latitudes, are cyclic, and that year was a ptarmigan low point. Gyrfalcons feed primarily on ptarmigan here, so with a lowered prey base, their numbers decreased too. Ronald had permits for eleven gyrs, ostensibly for wartime work to keep birds off airfields. Since no young were available here he trapped five haggards with a dho gazza net and pigeons, as far as I can figure, and Willi took five eyasses from Isafjördur for him, ten birds in all, which Ronald took to England. Philip Ware, according to Willi, took a handful of eggs plus two gyrs. Willi said there was an American falconer with him at the time, but could not recall his name.

Willi told me that 40–60 years ago when the climate was colder, both white and black gyrs nested here sometimes in the same nest and that he saw them. He says white gyrs do not often come here any-more and then only from Greenland in the winter. He says ptarmigan here are on an eight-year cycle. At ptarmigan nadir gyrs are forced to eat carrion fish which wash up on the shores. The Icelanders say that when the *Fálki* (gyrs) eat fish, they will produce no young.

There is a gyrfalcon nest a few kilometers south of us at Dim-muborgir, where a farmer, Helgi, will show anyone the nest for a small fee. There is supposed to have been a nest east of us, where the land is owned by our hotel people. They have not yet checked this year, but I will.

Sveridur, the taxi driver, was to come by and tell us about his brother's experience with a nesting merlin which evidently attacked him, drawing blood. However, I did not get the full story since Sveri-dur was on his way to a celebration and had only time to down a shot of "Bob's" brand gin before he was off.

Willi asked me if I knew an American falconer whose name was that of the dictionary. I inquired if that would be Harold Webster. Yes, indeed! Webby had asked him if he could get eggs or birds to Kefalavik where Webby's U.S. Air Force friends could take them to the U.S.A. Apparently the plan was never realized.

8 June • Lake Myvatn, Iceland

The weather is overcast and cool. I just met a Swede, an old man named Wallstrom, who is plucky and friendly. He is setting out for a 21-kilometer hike from the southwest corner of Myvatn along the south side of the lake to here. I will talk to him at supper.

Willi and Sveridur took me to Dimmuborgir and pointed me in the direction of the gyrfalcon nest. Along the way I found a merlin nest with four eggs in one of the rocks. Both adults were defend-ing the nest and looked very pretty. The male was especially beauti-ful. I walked through the tortuous mazes of black lava pinnacles and rocky cliffs. It was a weird world of naked, raw rock, dwarf willows, mosses and lichens. I was soon lost in the confusion of the rocks but eventually heard the low, angry sound of the old gyr's voice. I turned to see her circling about a quarter of a mile off. As I proceeded toward her, she became quite agitated and seemed to be defending a particular cliff which I supposed housed her eyrie. Soon I heard a higher pitched voice and saw the male coming in from the north. He flew up to her, and they came together with much screaming and whee-chucking, apparently transferring some recently slain morsel. Then the female flew off, vanishing behind the cliff. The male now quiet, circled up.

The eyrie was an old raven's nest, liberally garnished with mutes and feathers. As I climbed to it the female reappeared and circled noisily for as long as I remained, stooping frequently within 60 feet of me. The tiercel remained silent, circling so high that I lost sight of him. The eyrie was no more than 20 feet up, an easy climb, almost a walk in. It contained three well-grown young, each with about one inch of its tail feathers down. All had full crops. Two appeared to be females and one a male, judging by foot size, since there was no appreciable difference in body size. All of them remained quiet until confronted by my hand, at which they hissed but refused to strike with feet or beaks. I photographed and left them.

I can scarcely contain my feelings upon seeing a gyrfalcon wild and free come screaming out over her rocky eyrie in this remote and rugged land. Seldom have I seen anything that stirs my emotions so powerfully. This is her domain, not mine. It is a harsh land in which I am the stranger, the trespasser. She is a part of the landscape, and it is just not the same when she is gone from it. I have seen gyrfalcons in America and in Europe, but something of the nobility, of the wild majesty of these falcons is lost when they are transported to the modern world.

The flight of a wild gyr, about which much has been written, seems more saker-like than like a peregrine; its wings, especially those of the female, are wide and rounded, definitely different from those long, pointy wings of the peregrine. Gyrs appear to be very powerful.

I met Mr. Wallstrom on the way back. I gave him the directions to the eyrie, then walked back, noticing redwings, golden plovers, redshanks (*Tringa tetanus*), snipe (*Gallinago gallinago*), tufted ducks, red breasted mergansers (*Mergus serrator*), scaup and meadow pipits (*Anthus pratensis*). I stopped to appreciate some Icelandic ponies in a stone corral.

Upon returning to the Reykjahlid, I discovered a shiny new tourist store. Two Aussie girls who hitched up here, Barbara and Mary, were drinking Cokes. I joined them, and shortly thereafter Mr. Wallstrom joined us. He spoke of the birds he had seen including the gyrs at Dimmuborgir. This evening an American birder showed up, and tomorrow we will all go to see the gyrfalcons. I dislike bothering them again, but these people want to see them, and I shall help them even as I was helped.

9 June • Lake Myvatn, Iceland

Last night around 11:00 P.M. a mob of teenagers swept in. They took over Hotel Reynihlid. They spent last night dashing through the halls, warring and shouting. No one got any sleep. I think they are about to pack up and move out (I hope, I hope, I hope). I learned to my dismay that the hotel is charging the two Aussie girls IK 30 per night for a room like mine, youth hostel rates. I have been charged 100. I will see what my own youth hostel card can get me later.

I took Mary, Barbara, Mr. Wallstrom and an American birding lady from Wisconsin to Dimmuborgir to see the falcons. The merlins were quiet, and we saw only the male briefly flitting among the rocks. We quickly left them to find the gyrfalcons. From afar we observed the female flying around. One of the urchins from last night's wilding showed up and climbed to the eyrie. The old female did not scream, but rang up quite high. There was no sign of the adult tiercel. As we left, we saw two more people coming out to the nest. God knows how they found it.

In the afternoon I went to Dalfjall to see if gyrfalcons were still there. I found the nest a good mile from the road in a beautiful place, a cliff on a high hill overlooking miles of rolling land, a magnificent setting. I had a good climb over some very crumbly rock and discovered my nerves were a bit shaky. I did not attempt to enter the nest, although I got within eight feet of the young birds.

The old girl, a light-colored, very pretty falcon, flew overhead screaming but never came within 80 feet of me. There were five young; I believe at least one was a female, as she seemed much larger than the others. All were well grown with about two inches of their primaries and tail feathers down. They screamed nervously at me. I took two photos, then climbed down, since I was precariously balanced and still somewhat shaky. This nest was exactly as I have imagined a gyr nest: lofty, windblown with wild crags, rising hundreds of feet above the sweeping plains. The old falcon, hanging high in the wind overhead, completed the picture. The tiercel never did appear.

I saw pieces and feathers of many ptarmigan (*Lagopus mutus*) around the eyrie. I also saw a live ptarmigan as I was coming back to the road. Redwings and meadow pipits abounded. I was told by Sveridur that this is an excellent year for Ptarmigan. They shot over 1000 this year with rifles. He thinks the young gyrs are early by about three weeks due to the mild winter. The large number of young gyrs seemingly correlates with plentiful ptarmigan. I also saw a ringed plover (*Charadrius hiaticula*) by Námaskard.

11:45 P.M. I just finished a bull session with a Dutch chap who is camping nearby. Jan was full of information about the geology and the birds of Myvatn. Jan said he had visited a third gyrfalcon nest just north of here. They had three young. I will try to check it tomorrow or Thursday.

I had a nice walk this evening to a unique place just south of here. It was a tremendous basalt crevasse which ran several hundred meters from north to south; very spectacular. It was full of nooks and crannies and even had warm spring pools in the sheltered caves formed at the bottom. I would like to try a swim there. [In retrospect I wonder if this was part of the mid-Atlantic ridge that runs through Iceland.] I ambled through a dwarf birch forest amid lava outcrops and stalked a ptarmigan to within six feet before it flew off, croaking with annoyance.

10 June • Lake Myvatn, Iceland

I have just seen something that literally took away my breath. I had a walk north, up over the rolling heather and willow covered hills and valleys in a cold wind with dust clouds and occasional drops of rain, to an area called Sly. This was the place where Jan said he found the gyr nest with a raven nest nearby. I was at the north end of Sly, a spot called Seljadalur, and I was mystified as to the falcon's nest location. I saw lots of pipits, golden plovers and several ptarmigan. There was a fabulous panorama of the lake and craters in the distance and the crossing of an historical lava flow, which oozed down the valley to the lake in the 1700s. I passed high above a little lake and was mobbed by some black-headed gulls, which came in from a quarter mile away. I continued north until I came to a beautiful, flat-bottomed valley bounded by a high cliff on the north side. Two ravens immediately appeared to scold me. As I approached the cliff they became quite agitated. Jan had told me that falcons and ravens nested somewhere here, so I was expecting to see the old falcon at any minute. I wondered how these wonderful, huge ravens would fare in a contest with the falcons.

By the time I arrived at the cliff no falcon had appeared, so I walked back down the valley and climbed a hill to see if there could be another place they might be nesting. I could find no really promising alternative sites, so I sat down and pulled the coat over my ears to keep out the wind. I waited to see if anything would show up. After five minutes the ravens, which had quietly returned to their cliff, began to croak in alarm. They drifted down the valley, downwind toward me, then swung over the rocky-sloped side of the valley to the west. I stood up when a gyrfalcon stooped at tremendous speed at one of the ravens. It threw up in the wind which was by now a gale. There followed half a dozen beautiful stoops which drove both ravens down into some bushes on the valley slope. Every time a raven would attempt to leave its bush, the falcon would turn, sometimes right over on her back and roar down. Once the ravens decided finally to stay down, she flew east across the valley about 300 meters. The ravens took to the air, each heading in a different direction. In a flash the gyr was back, and she came down with such a stoop I thought she must kill a raven. But, she never struck it, no matter how close she came. She herded both of them back down into that same bush.

This time they stayed down. She drifted downwind over me. I expected her to start screaming at me, but I was wrong. She paused above me, turned into the wind for perhaps three seconds, then flipped downwind, vanishing down the valley in the most incredible burst of speed I have ever seen a falcon make. Within seven seconds of being directly over my head she diminished to a speck and was gone. I actually counted the seconds. I stood there stupefied with my mouth open and said out loud, "My god!" I cannot believe any bird can match the gyrfalcon in flight.

I went out with Mr. Wallstrom and Hal, a young American chap, this morning to the Laxá River via the northwest route. We passed a tall mountain called Vindbelgjarfjall, where Sveridur says there are gyrs. We stopped along the way to watch ten whooper swans and various ducks, including scaup, tufted, widgeon, teal, red-breasted mergansers, mallards, common scoters (*Melanitta nigra*) and Barrow's goldeneye. We continued on to the Laxá, where in the stream's rapids we observed six pair of harlequin ducks (*Histrionicus histrionicus*). A little farther we saw three greylag geese (*Anser anser*), three more swans, a half dozen whimbrels, assorted redshanks, golden plovers, black-headed gulls and a few snipe. There were masses of red-necked phalarope, spinning around at the water's edge. We were attacked by some arctic terns, so close that one even tweaked my hair. Leaving my acquaintances, I hitched on back to the hotel for lunch.

11 June • Lake Myvatn, Iceland

It's a miserable morning — wind, wet and heavily overcast at 10:00 A.M. I shall write letters. Willi, the egg collector, told me there were and still may be gyrfalcon eyries at Fálkaklettur and Kraeduborgir.

It is 4:00 P.M., and I just took a walk to the lakeside, where I sat and watched ducks for an hour. I saw about 30 Barrow's goldeneye asleep or dozing, six red breasted mergansers, several scaup, tufted, old squaw (*Clangula hyemalis*) and common scoter. Of course the ubiquitous arctic terns and black-headed gulls attacked me. I saw a couple of redshanks and white wagtails (*Motacilla alba*). The weather is still horrid.

12 June • Akureyri, Iceland

I took an hour to stroll to the big crevasse just south of here. I disturbed a wheatear (*Oenanthe oenanthe*) and a winter wren (*Troglodytes troglodytes*), in addition to the usual birds. I settled up my bill at the hotel. Time to go home.

I am now in the Akureyri airport, having cashed in my unused bus ticket after hitchhiking here from Myvatn. I just splurged on polish sausage, potatoes, skyr and a beer. The weather is partly cloudy to overcast. I shall be flying out in less than an hour. I am gorged, hot and tired. I will mail a post card to my Mom saying I'm heading off on another adventure. I think it will be fun to surprise her when I get home.

13 June • Nearing New York City, New York

9:30 A.M. I am approaching New York on a DC-6 after a 12-hour flight. I flew into Reykjavik at 11:00 P.M. last night. Since it was warm and I preferred to travel light, I abandoned my Greek Army coat in the Reykjavik airport. I trust someone can use it. This plane left about 2:00 A.M. and tarried in Goose Bay, Labrador for 45 minutes. I have $67 and IK 7 to my name. I'm tired. Who can sleep on this goddamned plane? There is a bulky, fidgety Icelander who has been elbowing me for the entire trip. It is only three quarters of an hour until touchdown. I feel let down in a way but am eager to get home finally. It is tempting to speed straight through to Colorado, but that is unlikely. I want to check out my old New Jersey homestead and visit awhile with Les Busch.

10:30 A.M., New York. Entry through customs was easy. I took a bus from Kennedy Airport to the subway, then the subway to the bus terminal. The Somerset bus took me to Union, New Jersey by 12:30 P.M. I walked down to my old homestead and met the Shapiros, current owners of the former Crowley house, who were extremely hospitable. I enjoyed seeing my old home and the changes since we lived there. I was sorry to miss old Swen Westdahl, my former next-door neighbor; he was in Sweden at the moment.

16 June • Bedford, Pennsylvania

I spent the past couple of days looking for old friends from my high school days. Wes Lammerding, a former neighbor, drove me to Newark's Pennsylvania Station, where I caught a Greyhound bus to Baltimore at 10:05 A.M., arriving at 1:35 P.M. It took me an hour and a half to get out of Baltimore. I caught several lifts along highway 40 and ended up at 10:00 P.M. at the Bedford entrance to the Pennsylvania Turnpike, where I slept out on the ground for the night.

17 June • Dayton, Ohio

I was on the road at 6:30 A.M. and an hour and a half later got a lift. I caught four lifts to Dayton, arriving at 3:30 P.M., and found friend Les working at Metropolitan Clothing. It was really good to see him. We had lots to talk about, and we ended up dancing at The Apartment, a local club. We lined up tentative dates for tomorrow with a couple of girls we met there. I am feeling pretty mellow on whiskey sours. Total assets are now $48.77.

18 June • Dayton, Ohio

Tonight was a fiasco. Busch and I tried chatting up some girls at local, hot, nightspots, but struck out. We are not in Europe anymore.

21 June • Dayton, Ohio

Midnight. We had a terrific Father's Day. Les's mother, Mom Mc-Dermott, fixed a monumental turkey dinner complete with lemon pie, and the clan assembled. Les and I are now writing Gaile and Gay in Africa, having mutually agreed that these Dayton girls are not worth our time. Les has also just completed a great sign for me to use hitchhiking home: "Africa to Colorado." And, he decorated the cover of my journal. Time has really shot by. I don't feel like writing any more. To hell with it! Les and I are sipping the dregs of some scotch. Bedtime.

22 June • Marysville, Kansas
It was 2:30 A.M. before I got to sleep, not exactly an early evening. Les and I had a big breakfast after a difficult wake up at 5:30 A.M. I was on the road by 7:30 with Les's good wishes and his promise to migrate to Colorado this autumn. We had a good time in Dayton, even if we washed out on girls. People did not exactly compete for hitchhikers in Ohio, but as I moved west I found rides more easily. I was in Indianapolis at noon, Decatur at 4:00 P.M., Springfield at 6:00 P.M. Then I caught a ride with a Nebraska graduate forestry student, Scott, who took me in his VW to Marysville, Kansas. I enjoyed conversing with him on the long haul. I tossed out my sleeping bag at 2:30 A.M., and there by the roadside on a bed of rocky sand I went out like a light.

23 June • Somewhere in Kansas
I was up at 5:30 A.M. A Kansan, Howard Smith, picked me up at 7:15 in an Olds with the works. He is a drapery salesman and travels a lot. He knows a chap in Pueblo, Colorado, Farnsworth by name, who is a falconer. Surprise! Howard is making a business call, and I am in the car enjoying the cool breeze and warm sun. Howard will take me to Denver. Our estimated time of arrival is 3:00 P.M. He even has air conditioning! Talk about the luck of the Irish!

2:15 P.M. We are approaching Strasburg, Colorado. The mountains look terrific out to the west. Our gas tank reads empty, and we are hoping to make it to Strasburg for gas. It is a hot, sunny day but cool as the proverbial cucumber here, inside the car. I have just gone hoarse; my voice is shot. That's a great way to come home. I will try a Coors beer for therapy.

3:40 P.M. I am sitting in a Boulder–Denver bus in the Denver terminal. I am very tired, and my head is throbbing. Damn, I left my bush hat in Howard's car! Maybe that is symbolic in some way? We depart at 4:00 P.M. A blonde cutie sporting light blue jeans is about to board. If I were shaved and bathed, I might make a play. I do not feel at home here at all.

6:30 P.M. What a fine how-do-you-do! I am home in Boulder at last, and no one is here. Mom's apartment is deserted. I got myself showered and cleaned up but still feel pretty run-down. This place is packed full of my sister's family's stuff, so they must be visiting. I had best not unpack, since there is little room for my accumulated treasures.

I have to admit it does feel good to be back, and I guess this is as good a place as any to end this journal. I still feel apprehensive about my future. I have reached a point where I can no longer justify traveling as a worthy educational pastime. I feel deeply that it is time for me to give something back. I know that sounds vague, but I think I need to contribute something to this world, not continue to float along aimlessly. Maybe this is just another pause in my journey. I wonder if I can stop now?

POSTSCRIPT:
LOOSE ENDS

Perhaps a brief follow-up on some of the people who inhabit these pages is in order. My Army buddy Les Busch did come to Colorado for a while, and we did reconnect. He moved to California, joined the Merchant Marines and traveled the world, working his way up the chain of command to become a captain of enormous oil tankers. He is retired now, happily married and playing golf in Texas. Unfortunately, Les's journal of our trip has been lost in the interim.

My kind and generous friend Jack Mavrogordato, after a long and distinguished life, died in 1985 of a horrible and debilitating disease of the nervous system. His books, *A Hawk for the Bush* and *A Falcon in the Field*, both richly illustrated, are considered classics and have been reprinted. Since Jack was such an important part of my life and this book, I have jotted down some impressions that come to mind when I think of him. What first struck me were his eyes, deep brown and fiery. Jack's eyes glittered with a keen intelligence. They missed nothing. Those eyes, the most intense eyes into which I have ever looked, could see right through me. They could be warm and friendly or hot and dangerous.

Jack was unimposing in height and build, but he had the presence of a giant. He commanded enormous respect. His intellect and determination were formidable, as those who chose to be his enemies soon found out. I recall a TV interview that Jack had rehearsed with the reporter. When the show went live, the interviewer threw in a question that had not been included with those rehearsed. He asked how a small, mild-mannered person like Jack could take such pleasure in killing helpless animals with his falcons. Those eyes burned through the reporter for perhaps a full minute of very uncomfortable silence. Then Jack said quite matter-of-factly, "If you were a rat…would you rather be killed by a wild hawk or a tame one?" I interpreted this to mean Jack was not too subtly inferring that the interviewer was indeed being a rat, and that the killing of animals by predators was quite natural whether done with or without human participation. The reporter lost his composure and the interview concluded quickly.

Jack was quiet and reserved, but he loved to talk about falconry and travel. He spoke clearly and forcefully. His facility with the English language was superb. He was very private. It was hard to know what was going on inside of his mind. On those few occasions when he was in a bad mood, he would hum to himself. That was a signal to me to avoid anything that might provoke him and leave him alone. He liked the company of many men, but had few women he called his friends. June Woodford was one of them. Once you were Jack's friend, you were his friend for life. He was inordinately kind and generous. Some people took advantage of his kindness and generosity. Several rare and valuable books were stolen from his library by guests and visitors over the years. That pained him, yet, he seldom said a bad word about anybody, unless that person had chosen to be his enemy. A man really had to be deliberately unpleasant to him to merit the status of enemy, but once that switch had been closed, said person could be assured of incurring his wrath. Jack would go to great extremes to right a slight.

Jack enjoyed sharing his brilliant legal mind. He was active on the local council in his tiny village of Tilshead and was an officer in the British Falconers' Club for years. He committed a good part of his life to keeping falconry legal and protecting birds of prey.

Jack loved to cook and was especially proud of his curry dishes, which he made with Sudanese curry available only at his home. He liked to garden. But, most of all he loved falconry and dedicated his life to its pursuit and preservation as a sport. He was a true gentleman.

Leonard Potter is gone. My dear friend Dr. Wolfgang "Pips" Kost died of a stroke at age 70. I have maintained contact with his family who now live in Germany, Mexico and the U.S.A. Kindly and hospitable Gustl Eutermoser eventually moved to Spain where he raised horses, another of his passions, until his death. Lorant D'Bastyai wrote two falconry books, never made it to Africa and died many years ago.

Steve Baer ended up in Albuquerque. He became famous for designing and building "zomes," very space-efficient buildings based on warping Buckminster Fuller type domes. He is a successful businessman and has his own company, which among other things designs passive energy products. He is still a bit of a wild man. He never did graduate.

The girls of my story have all been lost to me. I did meet Gaile again in 1967 in London, and we corresponded for a few years after that. I have not been able to relocate her since. Margot, who made my Army days so much more pleasant, has disappeared. I sometimes wonder if she did marry and raise a family. It is nice to think so.

A good friend asked me why I have included scientific names of so many of the birds I encountered. Birds were important to me. I was excited to see so many birds new to me; therefore, I listed them. Common names vary from place to place and are often confusing. Scientific names, at least in theory, are unchanging and more reliable. I thought that if any reader were ornithologically inclined, he or she might more conveniently identify the birds I observed.

It may be of interest to the curious reader to know what I carried and wore while hitchhiking through Europe and Africa. I had an ancient Spanish Army backpack and a hand-carried beach bag in which to carry gear. To the best of my recollection, this luggage contained: one sleeping bag, one towel, one two-man tent, two pairs washable pants, one sweat shirt, one long-sleeved shirt, three T-shirts, three under shorts, three pair socks, one light jacket, one Rhodesian bush hat, one poncho, one mess kit with knife, one fork and spoon, one journal, writing paper, pen, envelopes, maps, toilet paper, soap, matches, one camera and film, a passport and my wallet. There may have been a few more items from time to time, but these were the basics.

In those days campgrounds were to be found in almost every town likely to be frequented by tourists. Some campsites had showers; some had little stores. Most of the campers, many of whom were young hitchhikers, slept in tents that were small by today's standards. RVs and trailers were not yet in vogue. It was very easy to meet people and form new friendships.

After living this adventure and having had over 40 years to let it incubate, I now possess the benefit of hindsight. I am astonished how much I missed of what was going on around me. Jack Mavro and Leonard Potter had names for the various places we flew our birds, names that undoubtedly had significance and were steeped in history. To my regret, I never thought to inquire about that history. I was focused on day-to-day survival, birds, raptors in particular, and absorbing as much experience as I could. In the background lurked the unsettling question of what I was going to do with the rest of my life. My odyssey was a rare and special opportunity, which I still feel uncommonly fortunate to have been able to experience.

The caves I explored have mostly been closed to the public now, primarily because the tremendous number of tourists entering them was contributing to the actual deterioration of the art which made them so special.

There were dramatic political events yet to be played out. The Sudan is more unsettled today than when I was there. Wars between the Arab North and the poorer, non-Muslim South have continued and worsened. The Congo has had an ongoing violent, unstable history. During his rule, Idi Amin caused an enormous number of deaths and untold suffering from which Uganda has yet to recover completely. The Rhodesias became independent. Zambia is still a restless and unsettling place. Zimbabwe has gone from one of the most prosperous and promising countries in Africa to a terrifying and ruined place that has seen a quarter of its people abandon it, and a terrible dictator is still wreaking havoc on the land and its people. Egypt has had turmoil and war and is now swept up in the Muslim resistance against the West.

Europe has merged into the European Union. The Soviet Union has been dissolved and the Iron Curtain torn down. The reputation of the United States and the value of a dollar have plummeted. Travel today in many of the places I visited is a much more unsafe venture than it was then. People I encountered while traveling were mostly young, adventurous, carefree risk takers. I think people today are more wary and suspicious. HIV has made the liberal sexual scene much more chancy than it used to be. I think that even with its warts the world was a kinder, gentler place in the early sixties.

I found myself at loose ends when I returned to Colorado in 1964. I took a minimum wage job in a grocery store and went back to school to obtain a teaching certificate. I taught science to junior high and high school students for the next 29 years, was married for twenty of those years, raised two wonderful children, divorced and was later retired. Falconry has continued to be an integral part of my life. I derive both enjoyment and remuneration performing as a semi-professional magician. Life is good.

THE WALKABOUT

GERMANY

• Köln

• Heidelberg
Heilbronn • • Schwäbisch Hall
• Stuttgart

Dachau •
Stamberg • • München
• Rosenheim
• Berchtesgaden

AUSTRIA

- Salzburg
- Innsbruk
- Feldkirch
LIECHENSTEIN
- Landeck
- Hochosterwitz

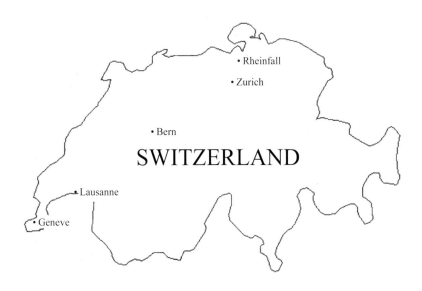

• Rheinfall

• Zurich

• Bern

SWITZERLAND

• Lausanne

• Geneve

ITALY

Como
Milano

Pegli Genoa

Viareggio
Pisa
Firenze

Roma
Rome Lido
Anzio
Terracina
Napoli
Pompeii
Capri Sorrento

FRANCE

• Grenoble

St. Jean Cap Ferrat

Monaco
Cannes   • Nice

• Montpelier

Marseilles
• Mas d'Azil • Beziers   St. Tropez
Montesquieu-Avantes •   Toulon
          • Moulis   Narbonne

• Perpignan

SPAIN

Santillana del Mar •
Novales •
• Santander
• Puente Viesgo
• Pamplona

• Barcelona

• Madrid

• Valencia

• Cordoba

• Alicante

• Granada
• Malaga

Cadiz
Gibraltar
Algeciras

BELGIUM

Oostende

SCOTLAND

• Glasgow

Liverpool

ENGLAND

• Newport

Sevenoaks • • London

Tilshead •
• Stonehenge   Dover
Clovelly •   Folkstone
• Evershot •   • Salisbury

Tintagel •

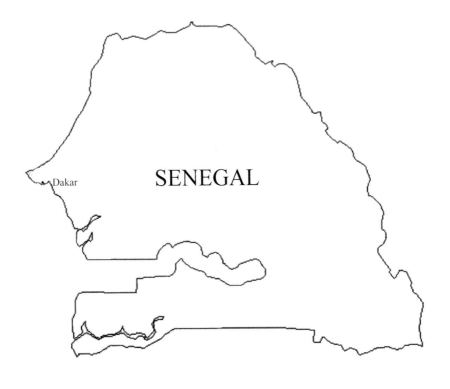

SENEGAL

Dakar

SOUTH AFRICA

- Louis Trichardt
- Pietersburg
- Potgietersrus
- Warmbad
- Pretoria
- Johannesburg

Orange Free State

- Bloemfontein
- Middleburg

- Craddock
- Cookhouse
- Grahamstown
- Cape Town
- Port Elizabeth
- Mossel Bay
- *Humansdorp*

SOUTH RHODESIA
(Zimbabwe)

• Salisbury

• Gwelo

• Bulawayo

• Mashaba
• Ft. Victoria

Tunduma

• Mpika

• Serenje

Northern Rhodesia
(Zambia)

• Kapiri Mposhi
• Broken Hill

• Lusaka

• Kalomo

Livingstone
Victoria Falls

Serengeti Park

Olduvai •
• Ngorongoro Crater • Kilimanjaro
Lake Manyara •   • Arusha   • Moshi

TANGANYIKA
(TANZANIA)

• Dodoma

• Zanzibar

• Iringa

• Mbeya   • Makumbako

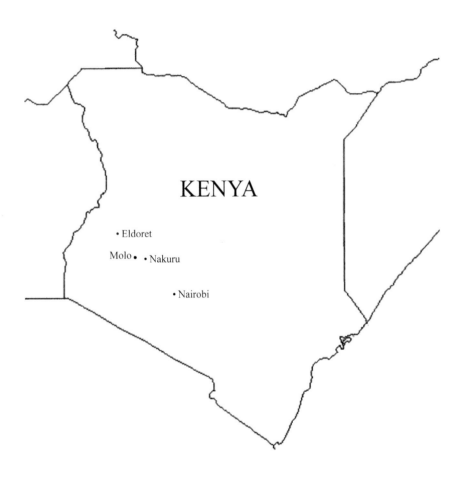

KENYA

• Eldoret

Molo • • Nakuru

• Nairobi

UGANDA

• Gulu

• Tororo

• Kampala • Jinja

SUDAN

• Wadi Halfa

Port Sudan •

Omdurman • • Khartoum

Kosti • • Rabak

• Malakal

• Juba

EGYPT

Alexandria

• Cairo

• Luxor
• Edfu

• Aswan

• Abu Simbel

GREECE

Athens
Piraeus

CRETE

Akureyri • Myvatn

ICELAND

Reykjavik
Keflavik

FALCONRY GLOSSARY

barrak   A noose-covered, leather device that is wrapped around a dead sparrow or bundle of feathers and attached to one foot of a decoy bird such as a kite. Large raptors are lured in and caught in the nooses while trying to rob the decoy bird of the supposed food in its foot.

bate   The act of a restrained falcon jumping off a fist or perch in an attempt to go elsewhere.

block   A perch on which a falcon is kept and to which it is tied.

brancher   A young hawk that has left the nest and is learning to fly or climb from one tree branch to another. Loosely, any recently fledged raptor.

Bruch   A German word for a commemorative trophy, such as a foot or beak or feather, taken from killed game and frequently worn on the hunter's hat.

cadge   A portable perch to which several hooded falcons can be tethered.

canceleer   To suddenly change direction or spiral in a stoop.

carry   A training strategy for a wild-caught hawk in which it is kept on the fist for some duration to help it become tamer. Also, the act of a falcon flying off with its quarry or the lure, usually because it fears being robbed.

cast	Two falcons flown together as a team. Also, the act of a raptor vomiting up the indigestible feathers, bones and fur in a compact pellet. Also, to throw a falcon into the air.
check	To break off from chasing the intended quarry and pursue something else.
crab	To fight with another raptor, for example over quarry or a territorial dispute.
creance	A line to which a falcon is attached when it is being trained and which prevents it from flying away.
dho gazza	A trap made of a small net supported between two rods and baited with a small bird or mammal pegged down next to it.
enter	The process of introducing a quarry that is new to a falcon, such as entering it on rooks.
falcon	A hunting bird of the genus *Falco*, characterized by fast flight, long, pointed wings, brown eyes, a "toothed" upper beak and a small tubercle in its nares. Also, female of any species of *Falco*, but especially the peregrine.
footing	The act of a hawk seizing quarry or sometimes the falconer with its foot.
fly cunning	Behavior of a falcon which has learned to fly to a rookery and eat easy young rooks either in or just out of the nest.
full gorge	State of being satiated with all a falcon can eat, characterized by a fully stuffed crop.
haggard	A raptor trapped as an adult.

harness   A falcon trapping device consisting of a leather vest covered with nooses and worn by a tethered bait bird such as a pigeon.

hood   A leather device worn over a falcon's head to blindfold it and keep it calm. Also, the act of putting the hood on a falcon.

hawk   A generic term for any diurnal raptor. A specific term for birds of the genus *Accipiter*, which have yellow or red eyes, short, round wings, long tails and are exceedingly agile hunters.

high   On the heavy side weight-wise, as opposed to low.

intermew   To keep a trained bird through the molt.

jesses   The leather thongs attached to a raptor's legs by which it is secured.

long-wing   Generic term for any falcon; it refers to their long pointy wings.

low   Light in weight, as opposed to high.

lure   A device, usually of leather, to which a piece of meat is attached and which is used to call back a falcon. Also, the act of calling back the falcon with the lure.

make in   To cautiously approach a falcon that is perched on the ground, usually while it is on the lure or quarry.

man   To tame a wild falcon or hawk.

mews   The building or chamber in which falcons are kept.

mist net   A large, fine-meshed net used to trap small birds.

musket	Male sparrowhawk.
mute	A falcon's excrement. Also, the act of defecation by a falcon.
nares	Nostrils.
paddam	A falcon trap that consists of a ring of connected, upstanding, large nooses placed around a central bait bird or mammal.
passage	A falcon trapped in its juvenile plumage, usually on migration. Synonymous with red hawk. Also, used to describe a quarry bird which is flying past the falconer and at which the falcon is subsequently released.
pitch	To cease flying and land on a perch or the ground. Also, can refer to the altitude at which a falcon waits on.
pitch up	Act of bounding back up after a stoop. Synonymous with throw up.
put in	To land in cover.
rake off	To break off from chasing the intended quarry and fly off in a different direction.
rat hunt	A hunt that degenerates into having to repeatedly evict the quarry from cover while the falcon makes low passes at it. It is not considered stylish.
red hawk	A falcon trapped in its juvenile plumage, usually on migration. Synonymous with passage hawk.
ring up	To circle up high into the sky.
rook	*Corvus frugilegus*, a type of crow. Unlike other

crows, it will usually try to outfly a falcon rather than immediately seek cover.

rookery   A place where rooks congregate to breed.

rouse   To puff up its feathers and shake them vigorously, thereby realigning them properly.

seel   To close the eyes of a raptor, temporarily blinding it, by means of a thread passed through its eyelids and tied atop its head. It is a relatively painless method of quieting a bird usually used in the initial stages of manning primarily in the Middle East.

sharp set   Hungry and eager to hunt. Synonymous with sharp.

short-wing   Generic term for any accipiter; it refers to their short, round wings.

slip   To release a falcon at quarry. Also used to describe the physical attributes of the location, terrain and situation of the intended quarry.

spar   Female sparrowhawk.

stoop   To dive at quarry from a superior height at a high rate of speed. Also used to denote the dive itself.

throw up   Act of bounding back up after a stoop. Synonymous with pitch up.

tiercel   Male raptor, especially of the genus *Falco*.

tiring   A tough piece of food with little meat, such as a wing, with which to distract a bird from anything of which it is afraid, usually used in the manning process.

traces   Leather straps that secure the hood. Also called braces.

wait on
To circle high above the falconer in expectation of being served quarry flushed by the falconer.

washed meat
Meat that has been soaked in cold water to remove much of its nutrition. It is used to help make a hawk sharp without lowering its weight.

weather
To place falcons on their blocks on the lawn out-of-doors.

wind up
A method to regain a skittish trained hawk that is sitting on the ground, in which a long string or creance is attached to a fixed peg in the ground; the falconer then walks the other end of the string several times around the bird, encircling the bird's legs with the string. By pulling the string tight, the bird may be prevented from flying off until it has been secured.

INDEX

A

B

bed bugs, 159
Bennet, John, 188, 190, 191, 194–195
Berchtesgaden, Germany, 13–15, 97 (illus), 232 (map)
Bern, Sweitz, 18, 23, 48, 234 (map)
Beyerbach, Uwe, 49–52, 183–184, 186–188

birds

bee-eater, carmine *(Merops nubians)*, 37, 141
bishop bird,
    red *(Euplectes orix)*, 66
    yellow *(Euplectes capensis)*, 83
blackbird, common *(Turdus merula)*, 57, 205
bulbul, white-vented *(Pycnonotus barbatus)*, 133
bustard, Houbara *(Chlamydotis undulata)*, 199
bustard Kori *(Ardeotis kori)*, 83–84
buzzard,
    augur *(Buteo rufofuscus)*, 68
    jackal *(Buteo rufofuscus)*, 68, 81–82, 84–85, 87, 91, 131
    steppe *(Buteo buteo)*, 68
chat, anteater *(Myrmecocichla aethiops)*, 83–84
crane, crested *(Balearica regulorum)*, 83
crow,
    black *(Corvus apensis)*, 63, 83
    pied *(Corvus albus)*, 65, 77, 141,157
cuckoo *(Culculus canorus)*, 205
darter *(Anhinga rufus)*, 94, 96
dove,
    Abyssinian wood *(Turtur abyssinia)*, 141
    cape turtledove *(Streptopelia capicola)*, 64
    laughing *(Streptopelia senegalensis)*, 63, 133, 136, 139–141, 143–145
    long-tailed *(Oena capensis)*, 133, 141
    mourning *(Streptopelia decipiens)*, 133
    turtledove *(Streptopelia turtur)*, 140, 143
drongo, fork-tailed *(Dicrurus adsimilis)*, 64
duck,
    Barrow's goldeneye *(Bucephala islandica)*, 215, 221–222
    common eider *(Somateria mollissima)*, 213
    common scoters *(Melanitta nigra)*, 221–222
    greater scaup *(Aythya marila)*, 213, 215, 218, 221–222

gull,
    black-backed *(Larus fuscus)*, 214
    black-headed *(Larus ridibundus)*, 214, 220, 222
    herring *(Larus argentatus)*, 214
harrier, 78, 83, 85, 141
hawk,
    African goshawk *(Accipiter tachiro)*, 67
    black sparrow hawk *(Accipiter melanoleucus)*, 62, 67
    chanting goshawk, pale *(Melierax poliopterus)*, 81
    chanting goshawk, dark *(Melierax metabates)*, 84, 131
    European sparrow hawk *(Accipiter nisus)*, 49–50, 52, 72, 187
    Gabar goshawks *(Micronisus gabar)*, 143
    goshawk *(Accipiter gentilis)*, 10–11, 49, 55, 67, 169, 174, 179, 184–
        185, 199, 207
    little sparrow hawk *(Accipiter minullus)*, 67, 72
    Ovampo sparrow hawk *(Accipiter ovampensis)*, 67
    red-breasted sparrow hawk *(Accipiter rufiventris)*, 67, 102–103 (illus)
    shikra *(Accipiter badius)*, 67
hawk eagle,
    African *(Aquila spilogaster)*, 67
    Ayres' *(Hieraaetus dubius)*, 67
heron,
    black-headed *(Ardea melanocephala)*, 96
    Goliath *(Ardea goliath)*, 95–96
    Squacco *(Ardeola ralliodes)*, 96
hoopoe, African *(Upupa africana)*, 64, 84, 133
hornbill, 71, 91
    gray *(Tockus nasutus)*, 136, 143
    southern ground *(Bucorvus leadbetteri)*, 91
    trumpeter *(Ceratogymna bucinator)*, 71
ibis, sacred *(Threskiornis aethiopicus)*, 71
kite, 131, 157, 199
    black-shouldered *(Elanus axillaries)*, 63, 65, 72, 83
    yellow-billed *(Milvus migrans)*, 63, 66, 68, 72, 77, 81, 83, 87, 91, 96,
        133, 141
lark,
    chestnut finch *(Eremopterix leucotis)*, 143
    crested *(Galerida cristata)*, 141
    short-billed *(Calandrella brachydactyla)*, 141

martin, house *(Delichon urbica)*, 200, 205

mouse bird, blue-naped *(Colius macrourus)*, 133, 141

nightjar, long-tailed *(Scotornis climacurus)*, 133

osprey *(Pandion haliaetus)*, 141, 143

owl,

    barn *(Tyto alba)*, 46

    eagle *(Bubo bubo)*, 14, 127 (illus), 170, 175

    grass *(Tyto longimembris)*, 199

    little *(Athene noctua)*, 38

    tawny *(Strix aluco)*, 205

    white-faced Scops *(Otus leucotis)*, 207

oystercatcher, Eurasian *(Haematopus ostralegus)*, 213

partridge, 10, 178, 199

    Frankolin *(Francolinus* sp.*)*, 69, 81,83

    yellownecked *(Francolinus leucoscepus)*, 85

pelican,

    gray *(Pelecanus rufescens)*, 96

    white *(Pelecanus onocrotalus)*, 95

phalarope, red-necked *(Phalaropus lobatus)*, 215, 222

pipit, meadow *(Anthus pratensis)*, 218, 220

plover,

    blacksmith *(Vanellus armatus)*, 83

    crowned *(Vanellus coronatus)*, 64, 85

    golden *(Pluvialis apricaria)*, 213, 215, 218, 220, 222

    ringed *(Charadrius hiaticula)*, 214, 220

    white-shouldered *(Hemiparra crassirostris)*, 96

ptarmigan, rock *(Lagopus mutus)*, 207, 216–217, 219–220

raven,

    brown-necked *(Corvus corax)*, 141, 147, 215, 218, 220–221

    cape *(Corvus albicollis)*, 64, 77, 83

redshank *(Tringa tetanus)*, 218, 222

redwing *(Turdus musicus)*, 213, 215, 218, 220

roller, 78, 82

    Abyssinian *(Coracias abyssinica)*, 131

    European *(Coracias garrulous)*, 131

    Lilac-breasted *(Coracias caudate)*, 84

secretary bird *(Sagittarius serpentarius)*, 69–70, 83

shrike, 87

    bokmakierie *(Telophorus zeylonus)*, 64

D

D'Bastyai, Lorant, 55, 58, 81–82, 100 (illus), 227
Dachau, Germany, 9, 232 (map)
Dakar, Senegal, 61, 240 (map)
Dalfjall, Iceland, 219
Dayton, Ohio, 214, 223–224
De Witt, Rudi, 64, 102 (illus), 208
Deir el Bahari, 115 (illus), 159
Dhib (falcon), 123 (illus), 125 (illus), 168–170, 172–183, 185–189, 191–198, 201–203
dho gazza, 67, 133–134, 136, 138, 140, 142, 216
Dimmuborgir, Iceland, 128 (illus), 217–219
Djoser, 118 (illus), 160–161
DuPree, Champion Jack, 19–20
Durban, South Africa, 64

E

Edfu, Egypt, 115 (illus), 155–157, 247 (map)
El Cordobés, 35–36
eland, 83
Eldoret, Kenya, 87, 245 (map)
Einarsstadir, Iceland, 215
elephant, 41–42, 83
Empress of England, 56, 61
equator, 87, 108 (illus)
Eutermoser, August, 11–13, 49–54, 60, 99 (illus), 164, 168, 183, 186–188, 227
Evershot England, 58, 175, 205, 239 (map)
Eyafjördur glacier, 215

F

Falconry Club of America, 54
Festival of San Fermín, 44
Firenze, Italy, 20–22, 235 (map)
flamenco, 38
Frank, Steven, 183, 194
Frederick II, 13
Ft. Victoria, Southern Rhodesia (Zimbabwe), 68, 242 (map)

G

H

Omdurman, Sudan, 138, 145, 247 (map)
Oostende, Belgium, 55, 167, 238 (map)
Osterreichischer Falknerbund, 54
ostrich, 63, 70, 82, 83

P

paddam, 148
Pálsson, Willi, 216–217, 222
Pamplona, Spain, 43–44, 237 (map)
Parcell, Charlie, 79–80, 82, 84–86
Pearl (falcon), 124 (illus), 152, 169, 172–173, 175, 180–181, 185–186,
    189, 191, 194, 196–197, 200, 202–203, 205, 214
Peebles, Gavin, 79–85
Philbeach Gardens, 55, 205
Piazza di Spagna, 23
Pietersburg, South Africa, 68, 241 (map)
Pips, *see* Kost, Wolfgang
Piraeus, Greece, 164–165, 249 (map)
Poles, Eustace, Major, 69
Pollard, Geoffrey, 143, 172, 185, 206, 208
Pompeii, Italy, 25–26, 235 (map)
Port Sudan, Sudan, 59, 131, 132, 133, 137, 140, 204, 247 (map)
Potgietersrus, South Africa, 68, 241 (map)
Potter, Leonard, 121–122 (illus), 168–169, 171, 172, 174–175, 177–179,
    181, 183–184, 186–187, 190–192, 195–196, 198, 200–205, 227–228
Prado Museum, 39
Puente Viesgo, Spain, 40–41, 237 (map)
pyramid, 119 (illus), 160–162

R

Rabak, Sudan, 110 (illus), 130, 247 (map)
rainy season, 74
Ramadan, 137, 140, 147–148
Rameses II, 159
Rameseum, 159
Reid-Henry, David, 206–208
Reykjahlid Hotel, 216, 218
Reykjavik, Iceland, 209–214, 215, 222, 250 (map)
Reynihlid Hotel, 215–216, 219

W

Z